BEHIND
THE SCREENS

The Structure of British Broadcasting in the 1990s

edited by
Stuart Hood

LAWRENCE & WISHART
LONDON

Lawrence & Wishart Limited
144a Old South Lambeth Road
London SW8 1XX

First published 1994 by Lawrence & Wishart
Collection © Lawrence & Wishart, 1994
Each essay © the author(s), 1994

ISBN 0 85315 774 X

Photoset in Garamond by
Derek Doyle & Associates, Mold, Clwyd.
Printed and bound in Great Britain by
Cambridge University Press.

Contents

CONTENTS

Introduction

Stuart Hood

Television in Britain is being reshaped by two forces: post-Thatcherite economic policies and new developments in technology. While it was inevitable that technology should bring changes in the form of the potential for many more channels – terrestrial, satellite or cable – there was no such inevitability about the application to the production of cultural goods of criteria applicable to other manufacturing processes. The confluence of these two forces in the 1980s and 1990s has led to a situation where the concept of 'public service' – a concept common so far to both the BBC and the ITV companies – is being questioned by the ideologues of the market. The result is a paradox. It is this: since the 1960s students of the medium and certain (not many it must be conceded) practitioners have developed a critique of various aspects of public service broadcasting and in particular of the BBC as its first institutional incarnation. That critique has been directed at the corporation's relationship to government and to the Establishment as manifested in the Board of Governors, which now contains identifiable Tory placemen. It is directed too at the corporation's élitism; its tardiness in recognising that we now live in a multi-ethnic society; its devotion to the monarchy (fanfares on royal birthdays); its supine acceptance of censorship, as in the farcical dubbing over of Sinn Fein voices. It is a criticism which Brian Winston deploys in his discussion of the role of 'Public Service in the "New Broadcasting Age" '. However, he also examines the difficulties facing the BBC, confronted as it now is by a government ideologically hostile to the brand of liberalism that inspired the concept of public service, 'virulently opposed to public enterprises' and 'apparently uncaring about the culture of freedom'. As the date for the renewal of the BBC's charter (1996) approaches, critics have increasingly found themselves defending the concept of public service which rests on the view that access to the electromagnetic spectrum – that scarce public utility – is a privilege that brings with it certain social obligations: the Reithean trinity of information, education, entertainment. In politics, as in other spheres of life, circumstances alter cases. Brian Winston argues that we need to reassess the BBC's weaknesses and strengths and above all address the problem of how it can be protected from the attempts of authority to subborn it.

What has happened as a result of Thatcherite or post-Thatcherite ideology is (as Graham Murdock points out in this volume) that 'broadcasting', defined as the devotion of institutional resources primarily to the making of programmes inspired by some sense of social responsibility, has been replaced by 'television' in which the priority is the accumulation of financial power in order to play a part in a world market. Here the main activity is the buying and selling of programmes of interest to that market, acquiring film libraries, seeking cheap material to fill the new channels and the increased airtime. It is a process which was officially blest when the ITV franchises were awarded as the result of a poker game in which money and cunning were decisive and the 'quality programmes' promised to the public was a secondary consideration, and in some cases window-dressing. The subsequent relaxation of the rules governing take-over bids by the ITV companies is leading to a concentration of financial power – an example of that tendency to monopoly and (ironically) decreasing competition within a capitalist market economy. The Department of Trade and Industry is reportedly interested in 'television' which it sees as an industry able to contribute to reducing our overseas trade deficit. It is a development which will enrich the already rich men who run these great companies and their share-holders who are seeing the value of their investment shoot up; what positive results it will have for the viewers is another matter.

Television programmes, as Colin Sparks reminds us, are produced by workers in a cultural industry. Today they find themselves, like workers in many other areas, under severe pressure. Their trade union rights have been eroded. Their wages are depressed. Moreover their industry has been atomized, as exemplified by the BBC's slogan of 'producer choice', its work force split up into production companies of varying sizes, often too small to be easily unionized, and with the staff which has no tradition of or understanding of trade unionism. So it is not surprising that there are no longer agreed and negotiated conditions of pay and employment. People work for what they can get.

What can a left-wing radical working as a producer in the industry do in these circumstances? This is a particular version of the more general question which runs: How do socialists/left-wing radicals live and work inside a capitalist system of which they disapprove or with which they are not in sympathy. The answer is sometimes by attempting to square the circle. As Don Coutts, an independent producer and director, puts it 'You end up by nibbling at both ends. Taking on a trainee and dropping the rates.' Rates is what much trade union activity was about in the palmy days of the 1960s and 1970s, when there was a tacit agreement between the television technicians' union and the ITV company managements to come to financial arrangements beneficial to both. Higher wages on the one hand, smaller profits to declare to the Broadcasting Authority on the other. Stuart Cosgrove reflects that they might have done better to make their demands in terms of demands about crèches and training education.

But is the changed structure of television entirely negative? Jane Arthurs argues that it gives certain advantages to women who have more opportunities. Women are still not adequately represented at managerial levels – a point which is also made by Phillippa Giles who, as a successful producer, is conscious of the 'glass ceiling' which cuts of advancement to the upper echelons of power. The argument for having more women there – apart from the basic one about equal opportunities – is that they could have an important effect on policy, and in particular on the representation of women on the screen; as in feature films, women in television programmes have traditionally been the objects of what Laura Mulvey in a celebrated formulation called 'the male gaze'.

'Quality programming' is a crucial term which has recurred in the debate over the future of the BBC, over the allocation in the debate over the future of the BBC, over the allocation of the ITV franchises and the role of Channel 4. It is, as the authors of the chapter on 'Culture, Quality and Choice' point out, open to a variety of interpretations. Frequently it is applied to programmes whose 'quality' is secondhand in that they are derivative, based on literary originals, marked by stylish sets – nostalgic period pieces. Others may qualify because of their display of professional and craft skills; others again because of their success in enlightening the audience on important social or political issues. Programme-makers in the commercial companies point to the BBC as the flagship of 'quality' whose continued existence provides an example and challenge. The television companies themselves employed the term for their own ends when competing for the franchises in the hope of clearing the 'quality' hurdle erected by the Independent Television Commission (ITC) – the aim being to prevent the size of the applicants' cheques from being the only determining factors as had been Mrs Thatcher's wish. As a term, the authors point out, it is full of ambiguities that require to be teased out.

In that debate, there is in some people's minds a polarity between 'quality programming' and 'popular television'. Mike Wayne looks at the debate about 'popular television' from a historical perspective, beginning with the contribution of the Frankfurt School to the subject and its appraisal of the nature and effects of popular culture in general. Fundamental to the conclusions of thinkers in this tradition is a deep pessimism. It leads those who subscribe to their views to despair of finding ways to make interventions in a culture industry like television. The testimony of John McGrath and Ken Loach shows that such deep pessimism is not always justified. The institutions of the television industry are not monolithic; there are cracks in the structures. Interventions are possible and necessary, not that the situation is likely to improve in the foreseeable future. Mike Wayne envisages that television in the 1990s will have to operate in economic and political conditions which will powerfully determine popular culture and its audiences. What is required, he argues, is a theory of popular culture which is consumer-led and which challenges these powerful forces, the key question being how to engage critically with popular television in a way that does not dismiss it or its audience as trivial or without cultural values.

If the BBC is the flagship of 'quality', Channel 4 has performed the same role in commercial broadcasting. Set up as the first broadcasting organization in Britain to be a publisher of programmes and not a producer of them, it has encouraged new talents and employed the skills of independent production companies; in doing so it has opened up areas of programming where the BBC had been slow to venture – notably those concerned with sexuality and race. It has also made an important contribution to British film-making. As a means of encouraging talent from outside the metropolis it has supported regional workshops, one of whose aims has been to bring the production process closer to the communities in which the workshops are situated. It is a development which is now seen as being in some disarray. Nadine Marsh-Edwardes was involved from the earliest days in the black collective *Sankofa*, which has produced important work for television and film. Her contribution touches on the experience of moving beyond the workshop sector, as well as the questions of how the black community has been represented on our screens. It is a theme taken up again by Thérèse Daniels, who raises the question in a historical review of changing programme policies and changing communities of to reflect accurately the lives on an increasingly diverse population of black and Asian people.

Originally funded by the ITV companies, who in return received the channel's advertising revenue, Channel 4 offered no economic competition to the commercial channel. It demonstrated at the same time that audiences small in market terms were worth targetting, provided they were well-heeled. In this sense Channel 4 has been a pioneer in 'niche' television, and attractive to advertisers who find the mass audience for ITV too undifferentiated and insufficiently wealthy. But the channel is now funded by its own advertising revenue with the promise of a safety net to be provided by the ITV companies in a case of emergency; it is thus competing with the ITV companies – and with satellite and cable companies – for a share of the television advertising revenue. This is a cake, which is not likely to expand greatly in the present economic climate. The question posed by Sylvia Harvey is, to what extent the channel will come under internal and external pressures to alter its policy so as to provide the kinds of programmes the advertisers believe will deliver the audiences they require.

In the case of commercial channels, audience size determines the slice of the advertising cake available to them. But as Brian Winston points out, audience size is also important for the BBC which has traditionally supported its arguments in favour of being funded by the licence fee on the grounds of its audience – around 50 per cent between BBC1 and BBC2. As a regressive tax, the licence fee has been criticised from both right and left; but it is perhaps the least unsatisfactory method of funding a public service organization. It will, however, be politically difficult to justify if, as seems likely, the BBC's audience share falls to, say, 30 per cent because of the proliferation of competing channels.

One topic Winston points out that has not been sufficiently debated is the governance of the BBC. The Board of Governors has became a quango. It has been composed traditionally of members of the establishment who have 'sensible' views on political and social matters, on taste, decency etc. It has been interesting to discover that one member in recent times had been an employee of MI6. The Board is drawn from 'the great and the good' and is therefore thoroughly unrepresentative. Its members have no identifiable constituencies. Their interests are undeclared. During the General Strike of 1926, Baldwin took the view that there was no need to commandeer the BBC because it would know what was expected of it. Today's government can be equally easy in its mind about the Board of Governors. The governance of the BBC is a political matter which deserves to be the subject of serious political debate.

The aim of this collection of papers is to stimulate debate of that and of other questions of broadcasting at a time when decisions are about to be taken which will determine what we see on our screens in the new century.

Acknowledgements

The idea for this book emerged from two events which took place in 1991-92. The first was a meeting entitled *Broadcasting and the Left*, organized by Bob Barker, Peter Keighron and Mike Wayne at the University of North London in February 1991, where Ken Loach, Colin Sparks and the Labour MP Robin Corbett debated the issue of broadcasting policy in the 1990s. The second event was a one day conference for academics and media practitioners held at University of Westminster in February 1992. Speakers at this event included Tariq Ali, Nic Garnham, Tony Lennon, Ann Pointon, Jean Seaton and John Woodward. Finally, I would like to thank Vicky Grut for all her hard work and thoughtful editing.

Stuart Hood, April 1994

Culture, Quality and Choice: The Re-Regulation of TV 1989-91

John Corner, Sylvia Harvey and Karen Lury

In this essay we want to look at the way in which questions of quality have figured in recent arguments about television policy. The emergence of 'quality' as a key term for contestation and debate in broadcasting[1] is directly linked to actual and proposed changes in the structure of the national television system. The 1991 re-allocation of regional franchises for Independent Television is the principal event here, one which we shall explore in some detail below. But a question mark has now been firmly placed over the funding and specific cultural remit of the BBC, whose charter comes up for review in 1996. This circumstance has provided focus for further debate about 'quality', a debate which is likely to intensify in the run-up to the decision on the BBC's future.

Arguments about what 'quality television' means, and about whether or not it is under threat and needs defending, have a specificity which is related to the nature of broadcasting as an industry, the socio-cultural centrality of television and the particular aesthetic-discursive character of the medium. However, they also have a generality which follows from their being, in part, articulations of a much broader, long-running debate about the condition of modern culture (so that the perceived 'quality' of television is in a direct and interactive relationship with the

1

perceived 'quality' of the society in which it is produced and watched). This debate is one which has given close attention to the causes, nature and consequences of a division between two broad categories of institutions, artefacts, tastes and social groups. On the one hand, there is a category variously described as 'élite', 'high', or 'official'; on the other, one variously described as 'mass', 'low' or 'popular'. Bourdieu's discussion of the 'high' and the 'popular' aesthetic in contemporary France[2] is perhaps the most sustained sociological treatment of this division. We shall return to these themes later.

There are considerable national variations in the way in which television has been positioned in relation to this division. Internationally dominant as a vehicle of popular entertainment (and therefore, from certain perspectives, an agency of the 'mass' and the 'low'), in some countries it has also been a considerable patron and mediator of the more traditional and 'serious' arts (and therefore, categorizable in parts as 'élite', 'high' and 'official'). The particular history of British television is perhaps distinctive in the degree of awkwardness and ambivalence surrounding the medium's cultural identity or role.[3] Developing around a state-funded BBC with a defined public information role and a cultural policy strongly informed by broader currents in national intellectual life and in the traditional arts, it has also developed a very wide range of entertainments in dynamic competition and co-operation with other spheres of the leisure industry (for instance, in sport, popular music and popular fiction). Debates about 'television culture' in Britain are thus particularly prone to conflicts (and confusions) arising from selective typification. For instance, a typification of TV based on soap opera (a typification deployed as imagined cultural disaster in the frequent use of the phrase 'Wall-to-Wall *Dallas*' to describe the likely consequences of deregulation) will give a different reading from a typification based on classic serial adaptations of serious fiction or on current affairs and documentary output. It is worth noting, too, that despite the extensive generic range of television in most countries, typifications of 'essential television' have played, and continue to play, a large part in debate about the medium's status and proper position in national cultural life. Such socially-constructed typifications allow the medium to be discussed in relation to simplifed, core ideas about what it really *is* (positively or negatively evaluated) and what it *might* be or *should* be. The cultural positioning of television shows considerable national variation; the United States being in most respects a contrasting case to that of Britain, for instance. Before turning to our specific analysis, however, we want to make some observations about the present state of the larger debate about cultural division and about how the idea of 'quality' has been used within it.

Culture, Quality and Inequality

First of all, it is important to note how the question of cultural quality relates to that of cultural *in*equality, though this relationship is rarely recognized and made explicit in cultural commentary. To argue for certain criteria of 'goodness' in cultural artefacts and practices is to imply a value system by which artefacts and practices may also be judged inferior or unequal. This value system carries broader implications for how the pattern of cultural consumption in a society is viewed. A conservative-elitist view might involve assumptions about a 'natural' hierarchy of taste and the innate inferiority of certain classes of people. A more radical and socially analytic assessment might point to fundamental inequalities in the distribution of cultural and educational opportunities and resources. Of course, in order to argue that sections of the population are culturally disadvantaged and deprived it is necessary to have some standards by which the 'goodness' they are not getting enough of might be identified. It is also necessary to have some argument both as to *why* they are missing out (e.g. differentials of availability and pricing or – more trickily – differentials in the disposition and competence required to appreciate 'goodness') and as to why such missing out is 'bad' *for them*.

These difficulties have been at the centre of what, in Britain, is at least a 150 year old argument about the relationship between the arts and the 'improvement' of national life (whether connected to a broader project of democratization or not). Raymond Williams'

3

Culture and Society[4] remains the classic historical study of the main contributions to this argument. The difficulty in fact consists of two problems, one essentially aesthetic, one essentially psycho-social in character.

The aesthetic problem is that of finding firm enough ground (aesthetic but also possibly ethical) upon which to base a qualitative assessment of artefacts – a value system – of a kind which can escape the subjectivity of 'taste'. The problem has intensified as a result of the strongly relativistic tendencies, and the emphasis on contingency, of postmodern theory. Whilst these tendencies and emphases have by no means been universally accepted, their influence has been enormous, and not only within academia.

The psycho-social problem is that of grounding an account of why differences in artistic/recreational involvement matter at the level of 'quality of life' (in something like the way that differences of material provision clearly do). It is on this point that accounts from the left have become particularly nervous in recent years. For in many societies, cultural difference has increasingly become naturalized and legitimated as consumer choice, and in this context the charge of 'élitism' is an easy and often effective one to make against *any* suggestion that some cultural products are 'better' than others (as we have observed above, a precondition of any cogent argument claiming the existence of an inequality which needs redress).

Grasping the troublesome nature of this relation between 'quality' and 'inequality' at the level of theory has, if anything, been blocked rather than aided by the standard usage of the term 'culture' within 'cultural studies'. This usage is founded on a presumption about the linkage between artefacts and lived experience so generalized as to inhibit specific interrogation of its conditions and processes. Mostly, however, the strains of the linkage show through, accounting in part for the uneasy and ambivalent tones of much work in this tradition.

The unease and ambivalence are there right at the start. For instance, in Williams' early essay 'Culture is Ordinary',[5] he notes a 'false equation' which would have it that 'the observable badness of so much widely distributed popular culture is a true guide to the

4

state of mind and feeling, the essential *quality* of living (our italics) of its consumers'. Williams' way of breaking down this equation is simultaneously to affirm both the existence of cultural standards against which 'badness' in the popular might be judged ('Very well, I read different things, watch different entertainments, and I am quite sure why they are better') and *also* to affirm 'the natural fineness of feeling, quick discrimination ... clear grasp of ideas' of those people he knows personally who are part of the audiences and readerships for 'distributed popular culture'. Whilst (with typical Williams' honesty) he confesses that he does not 'altogether understand this', thereby half-registering a contradictory element in his account, what he fails to do is to see how this contradictoriness works to undercut his own main argument that popular cultural provision (including television) is in need of reform. For if people do not seem to be adversely affected by their cultural choices, what grounds are there for perceiving the existing arrangements as constituting an 'inequality'? This question still provides a challenge to arguments for cultural change, though at the end of our paper we shall try at least to clarify the terms upon which a cogent answer might be offered.

We have noted some of the ways in which the 'TV quality' argument needs to be set in the context of a much broader debate about cultural division. We have also recognized how questions of aesthetics are related to questions of social relations and how the idea of 'quality' itself implies ideas of 'inequality'.[6] Let us now turn to discussing the particular shifts in the circumstances of broadcasting which caused 'TV quality' to become such a public issue.

Television and the New Legislation

In 1988, two years after the Peacock Report had explored some of the options for the de-regulation of British television, the government published its White Paper: *Broadcasting in the '90s: Competition, Choice and Quality*. Many observers detected in this document a tension between the thinking of the more traditional, and perhaps more culturally conservative, Home Office, and the more radical, deregulatory and free market-oriented philosophy of the Department of Trade and Industry. This tension between preserving standards, removing regulatory restrictions and creating new markets was to characterize much of the ensuing public debate. The White Paper itself argued that:

> ... a more open and competitive broadcasting market can be attained without detriment to programme standards and quality.[7]

The BBC was supported as the provider of 'high quality programming across the full range of public tastes and interests', and further recognised as the 'cornerstone' of British broadcasting; but the emphasis of the White Paper was on the new legislative framework for commercial or 'independent' broadcasting.

It is important, before sketching the basic contours of the 'quality debate' of 1988-90, to be aware of the particular significance of the BBC. The Corporation, ostensibly absent from the legislative agenda, because of the timing of Charter renewal, remained in practice a kind of 'structuring absence' for much of the debate. For it was widely believed, at least by broadcasting professionals, that two key factors were responsible for the maintenance of high standards: wealth and tough public regulation in the commercial sector, combined with the high cultural standards set by a BBC not subject to the normal imperatives of profitability. Such a combination was believed to ensure diversity and real programme choice across the system as a whole. This view, a kind of ecological approach to competition and standards, was confirmed by George Russell, Chairman of the Independent Broadcasting Authority (and subsequently Chairman of the Independent Television Commission,) the body charged with regulating commercial television. He noted:

> ... if you've not got high standards coming from the BBC that's when things will just tumble down like snowflakes.[8]

It was only towards the end of 1992 that serious public debate began on the subject of the role and future of the BBC.

The legislation, proposed in 1988 and finally passed in 1990, put private or commercial broadcasting at the top of its agenda for change. It was this sector that the then Prime Minister, Margaret Thatcher, had referred to as the 'last bastion of restrictive practices'. Interestingly, it was also from within this sector that what was to become one of the most effective lobbying organizations was born: the Campaign for Quality Television, started by staff at Granada in the autumn of 1988.

The single most controversial element in the White Paper was probably the proposal to put the commercial television licences out to tender, with the licence to be awarded to the highest bidder. However (and as it turned out, crucially) a modest, pre-tender, 'quality threshold' was outlined too. The idea of a 'threshold' – a hurdle or boundary – was a departure from the more tentative programming 'suggestions' or guidelines indicated in previous government reports and implied a more rigorous and 'businesslike' attitude towards the *products* of television. The 'threshold' consisted of three key requirements for the Channel 3 licensees: to provide regional programmes; to show 'high quality news and current affairs … in main viewing periods', and 'to provide a diverse programme service calculated to appeal to a variety of tastes and interests'.[9] The tender system itself (referred to as an 'auction' by its critics), was defended by the White Paper on two grounds: it would ensure a proper return to the public purse for the use of a scare resource (the airwaves), and it would provide a more 'objective method of licence allocation', removing from the ITC any subjective exercise of judgement in final decision-making.

The atmosphere of considerable alarm and anxiety concerning the effects of the 'highest bidder wins' system, was reflected in a House of Lords debate in December 1988, shortly after the publication of the White Paper. One peer suggested:

> It is the person who can tell the tallest story and who has the longest purse who will win a franchise.

While Lord Annan asked:

> Why compel the ITC to accept the highest bid even if it knows, and the informed public also knows, that the highest bidder is

either a crook or shark who will do his best to evade every control and peddle trash?[10]

Broadcasting professionals shared this fear and anger about the prospects for 'peddling trash' in an increasingly market-driven system, one in which high-bidding winners might cut costs by severely pruning production budgets and increasing the amount of imported, secondary market material.

These issues and concerns were pushed out to a wider public during the summer of 1989, when the Campaign for Quality Television placed a series of advertisements in the press, beneath the headline: 'Will Quality Television Survive?' Fielding an impressively diverse team of 'big names' (including Rowan Atkinson, David Attenborough, John Cleese, Anna Ford and Ludovic Kennedy) the Campaign argued bluntly:

> We will be able to make fewer high quality programmes, you are likely to get more junk television, and the only beneficiary will be the Treasury.

The Campaign concentrated their fire on two issues: the need to raise the quality threshold by specifying a wider range of programme requirements, and the need to grant the ITC wider powers and an element of discretion in decision-making, by adding to the proposed legislation an 'exceptional circumstances' clause. This clause would allow the ITC, in exceptional circumstances, to pay greater attention to the quality of programming proposed by a bidder and, as a result of this scrutiny, award a licence to a lower bidder. In addition to the deployment of arguments in public debate, the Campaign also pursued an extremely successful private lobbying strategy, persuading the Minister responsible, David Mellor, of the need to make at least some changes to the proposed new rules.

Thus it was that when the Bill was published (subsequently becoming law as the Broadcasting Act in November 1990) it included some enhanced programming obligations (adding children's and religious programming) and also the famous 'exceptional circumstances' provision. The wider political context, as well as specialist lobbying, clearly played a part in bringing about these changes. During its many months of hotly debated passage through both Houses of Parliament, the Bill was subject to over 800 amendments; it had, as one journalist remarked, 'caught the tide of ebbing Thatcherism'.[11] And the public and parliamentary debate made it increasingly clear to potential licence bidders that their programming proposals would be subjected to close and critical scrutiny.

The tender or auction system for awarding the licences seemed to remain intact as the market principle central to the ushering in of the 'new order'. Yet when the fifteen regional ITV licences were finally awarded in October 1991, only seven of them went to the highest bidder. How did this come about?

After two years of vigorous and sometimes ferocious debate, it was left to the ITC to implement the key provisions of the 1990 Act. They published their formal guidelines, the *Invitation to Apply for a Channel 3 Licence*, in February 1991. The document included a significant amount of detail on programming standards, not included in the Act, and was justified on the grounds that the latter had indicated an obligation on the part of bidders to: 'appeal to a wide variety of tastes and interests', and to devote a 'sufficient amount of time' to programmes of 'high quality'. This obligation the ITC guidelines elaborated upon.

The 'variety of tastes and interests' requirement was interpreted by the ITC to include ten categories of programmes: News, Factual, Regional, Religious, Children's Drama, Entertainment, Sport, Education and Arts. The statutory requirements only included the first five of these categories. But the ITC admonished: 'Applicants should note that a service with a more limited range than is indicated here is unlikely to pass the quality threshold'. The amount of weekly programming proposed in these ten separate categories had to be specified in the application. In addition, though relegated to the confidential part of the application and therefore not accessible to the public, detailed information on programme costings was required.

By these means, the ITC was able to subject the licence

applications to fairly stringent tests relating both to programme plans and to costings and, crucially, to the relationship between the two. By judicious use of those safeguards that were present in the Broadcasting Act, the ITC ruled that fourteen of the thirty-seven applicants were in effect ineligible, having failed to cross the imaginary line of the 'quality threshold', either in respect of programme plans, or business plans. This was an interesting move by the ITC. It removed the necessity of having to justify the merits of individual programmes by concentrating instead on the dynamic equation between programming provision and related costs on the one hand, and the cost of the franchise bid and estimated advertising revenue on the other; effectively removing the appearance of any aesthetically-based choices and implying a straightforward *business* decision. Of those who remained in the race, licences were awarded in each case to the highest bidder. And the stiff process of ruling on eligibility meant that the famous and much fought-over 'exceptional circumstances' clause was never used.

It is the view of many commentators that the ITV network has been seriously destabilised as a result of the 1991 franchise round, as high-bidding winners face the prospect of savage cost-cutting. Nonetheless, the result of a high profile campaign about quality and standards in broadcasting, together with a set of detailed programming requirements specified by the ITC, meant that the managers of commercial television had to continue to balance questions of quality and diversity against those of cost-effectiveness and profitability. The last word, in this section of our article, should be left with the ITC, who made their own attempt at defining quality in television:

> The ITC considers that the categorization of programmes as of high quality is a matter which cannot be reduced to a single formula. They may be programmes which have a special one-off character or programmes of marked creative originality, or programmes, from any category, of exceptionally high production standards, or any combination of these factors. Programmes of high quality may not be regarded as mainly or exclusively of minority appeal, and it is important that programmes of wide audience appeal should also be of high quality. High quality

cannot be guaranteed by any particular combination of talent and resources, although both are normally crucial elements. Moreover, those who seek to achieve high quality in one of the ways mentioned above may not always succeed even in their own terms. It would be wrong to penalize them for making the attempt.[12]

Versions of Quality

Like most contributions to the debate, the ITC definition focuses on 'quality' in individual programmes, though as a body it was also concerned about the overall quality of company output, mainly judged in terms of diversity of programme kinds. Its comments, constituting more a synthesis of definitions than a definition itself, also suggest the awkward multi-faceted character of the notion, only containable by developing it (as here) into something fast approaching a theological level of mysteriousness. What is particularly interesting about this definition is that the ITC allow themselves to develop an aesthetic perspective on quality television, and therefore in a sense to step outside their government directed brief. This can be detected in their guarded references to notions of 'originality' or 'creativity'. They are, nevertheless, still obliged to construct such an inclusive agenda that popularity and a high level of technical skill are also positively referenced, whilst none of the attributes are seen by themselves to *guarantee* quality. It is this multi-facetedness we want to examine here and, in order to do so, a basic typology might be useful. Often, of course, varying and conflicting definitions were only *implicit* in what was said and argued.

First of all, there was a notion of quality framed within the terms of a literary aesthetic. In practice, this meant the privileging of programmes which originated in conventionally valued literary texts, such as the heavily-cited Granada adaptations of *Brideshead Revisited* and *Jewel in the Crown*. Although these were also popular programmes, the terms of approval were linked to questions of 'educated taste' (including a perceived prejudice against mere 'entertainment') which often proved controversial, playing into charges of 'élitism'.

Secondly, there was a definition centred on television's public information role. Here, questions of quality were related directly to the responsibilities of mass media within a democratic order. Not surprisingly, the scale and independence of news and current affairs output were the focus for argument here and 'quality' was seen primarily as an attribute of a service rather than of particular programmes.

Within the broadcasting industry, a third definition was more strictly concerned with production values, defining quality in 'craft' terms as the creative use of technology. This definition was the one closest to the use of 'quality' in manufacturing industry (e.g. in the idea of 'quality control'), though it took account of the distinctive, cultural character of the industry.

Lastly, quality was also construed more or less directly in terms of what was popular. There were two possible interpretations here. First, that popularity itself was good enough, and that public choice and approval were the only real quality test. Quality television could be understood simply as that which was 'widely popular'.[13] Secondly, a more differentiated view of the audience was often put forward, in which it was argued that television viewers no longer functioned as a mass, but as a diverse range of different target audiences, delighting in programmes tailored specifically for their tastes and interests. In this more sophisticated socio-demographic context, series like *Hill Street Blues* were seen as significant examples, attracting a small but profitable audience (highly-educated and high-incomed) and therefore allowing criteria for programming to be grounded in discerning, non-mass, consumer choice.

These different ways of thinking about, and exemplifying, quality television were activated within a debate largely determined by the much more general, framing conflict between 'public service' and 'free market' ideas about how television should be funded and regulated. Some further discussion of this outer framework, familiar in outline and not peculiar to Britain, is necessary to understand the particular configuration of the 1991 debates.

The public service tradition is, of course, the one most closely associated with the history of British broadcasting. That broadcasting must 'inform, educate and entertain', is often quoted as the founding motto of the public service principle, and its ordering of the three functions has been seen to indicate their relative importance.

As indicated above, this view is closely associated with the belief that broadcasting should act as a force for national cultural cohesion, underpinning (and in part constituting) national identity. Such a belief is clearly articulated in the Annan Report on broadcasting, 1977:

> At a time when people worry that society is fragmenting, broadcasting wields it together. It links people, gives the mass audience topics of conversation, makes them realise that, in experiencing similar emotions, they all belong to the same nation.[14]

The upholding of this national role for broadcasting is necessarily linked to an insistence on a publicly regulated, securely funded base for a 'national' television industry. The television system, though not an institution of state, is nevertheless perceived of as a national institution, with almost constitutional responsibilities.

As a direct challenge to this, during the late 1980s, vigorously 'free market' approaches were prompted from a variety of sources including economists (Sir Alan Peacock, Samuel Brittan), businessmen (Rupert Murdoch) and politicians (Norman Tebbit). In their most radical form, these approaches proposed comprehensive deregulation and the introduction of a system of broadcasting based, not on perceptions of national cultural requirements or of political function, but on the individual choices of consumers from within an extended range of provision. This paragraph from the Peacock report (1989) states the case with utmost confidence and clarity:

> British broadcasting should move towards a sophisticated market system based on consumer sovereignty. That is a system which recognizes that viewers and listeners are the best ultimate judges of their own interest which they can best satisfy if they have the option of purchasing the broadcasting services they require from as many alternative sources of supply as possible.[15]

13

In this scenario, the generation of quality television would not so much be initiated from the 'top down' but would be the result of demand from the 'bottom up'. The emphasis on creative innovation by producers is shifted to an emphasis on a 'businesslike' sensitivity to consumers.

In accordance with this general principle, the most radical proponents of the free market approach found themselves able to deny that any other definition of quality provided an acceptable aspiration for a broadcasting system. It was from this position that debate itself could be held open to scorn:

> There is no need to enter into a metaphysical debate as to whether the consumer is the best judge of which programmes will benefit him, or his capacity for citizenship. The point is that no one person or group, or committee, or 'establishment' can be trusted to make a superior choice.[16]

Obviously, such a perspective was in line with dominant tendencies in the broader political culture of Britain at the time. Mrs Thatcher and her government were concerned to promote both a 'reconstructed' British economy and a 'reconstructed' national value system. In the latter, individual enterprise and consumer choice were key principles, displacing earlier emphases on public responsibilities and social welfare. The Prime Minister's much-quoted comment, in a speech, that 'there is no such thing as society' was only the most notable of many statements indicating the fundamental shift in principle from community to individual. The debate about television 'quality' was therefore often a directly political debate, even if not explicitly so. This sometimes had the effect of further complicating the patterns of alliance and enmity.

Certainly, the widespread antagonism felt within broadcasting and intellectual circles towards high profile 'marketeers' (primarily Rupert Murdoch, whose speech at the Edinburgh International Television Festival 1990 was given very wide publicity) meant that the debate too often became polarized as one between rigid and simplistic alternatives. Murdoch himself set the tone at Edinburgh, aligning deregulation directly with anti-élitism:

14

> Much of what passes for quality on British television really is no more than a reflection of the values of a narrow élite which controls it and which has always thought its tastes are synonymous with quality – a view, incidentally, that is natural to all governing classes.[17]

Under such direct attacks, which questioned their very commitment to democracy as well as raising sharply that most sensitive of issues in discussion of British culture – the question of minority class taste – it is not surprising that the broadcasting community should act as defensively and as nervously as it did. Clearly, many of those who had supported a defence of public service values (academics, producers, the viewers' association etc.) had been concerned previously about this very issue, and had often made their own complaints about the existing system, focusing on lack of access, patrician attitudes and the rigidity of the existing structures for producing innovative programmes. In the early 1980s, such complaints against the established 'television institution' had played a key part in the wide ranging debates about the funding and function of Channel 4.

Programme-makers were particularly prone to being caught up in contradictions within the new, more polarized and conflictual, climate of debate. While they were concerned to promote competition (and what they often saw as the benefits of the breakdown in restrictive industrial practices), they were also committed to protecting their own position as producers of various genres of programming which appeared to be at risk within the more aggressive 'free market' perspectives now being put forward. As an example of this, we can note the position of Stuart Prebble, one of the founder members of the Campaign for Quality Television. Prebble, head of regional programming at Granada, was previously editor of Granada's current affairs series *World In Action*. While he was willing to agree that a lively independent sector was good at 'starting people off', and that competition was very effective in producing the best talent, this was tempered by a concern that an unstable organizational base could endanger the production of programmes that required sustained planning and research:

[If] 26 minutes of *World In Action* takes nine months of production, then the availability of time and money is going to be crucial.[18]

So, although Prebble supported the application of market principles in some measure, he continued to be concerned about the insecurities of independent production, and was wary of a market that seemed all too likely to be dominated by the cheap. 'Cheapness' was portrayed, by other broadcasters as well as Prebble, in terms of both economic *and* cultural value. The notion of 'cheapness' itself already carried connotations not strictly related to cost – implying vulgarity, lack of imagination and an incipient flashiness that was somehow 'nasty'. The 'cheap and nasty' of television was exemplified as a potential tidal wave of game shows and of foreign-produced, imported programmes, which often meant soap operas and the more sensationalist chat shows.

A further subset of contradictory tensions grew around the idea not of 'broadcasting quality' but of 'broadcasting standards'. Underlying arguments using this notion there was often a fear about an erosion of public morals as a result of what was perceived as television's irresponsible 'license' in reproducing, with increasing frequency, offensive images and language. While this was a concern for many public service supporters (the Viewers Associations were particularly active here) it was also a concern for some individuals (specifically Conservative politicians), who might otherwise have been unproblematically in agreement with the free market deregulators. After all, arguments about the need to uphold moral standards by firm regulation are more traditionally associated with groups holding a conservative political perspective. Not for the first time, nor indeed the last, the moral-authoritarian strand of the new British conservatism was in sharp contradiction with its economic neo-liberalism. Occasionally, this was openly commented upon by those on the Right. Samuel Brittan, anxious about possible compromises in the progress toward de-regulation, identified the 'internal' problem which made them likely:

> In principle, Mrs Thatcher and her supporters are all in favour of deregulation, competition and consumer choice. But they are also even more distrustful than traditionalist Tories of policies that

allow people to listen to and watch what they like, subject only to the law of the land.[19]

These concerns were articulated in two different ways. Firstly, moral standards were officially 'protected' by the creation of a public body – the Broadcasting Standards Council – which had a specific remit (but no official power) to patrol the perimeters of 'taste and decency'. Secondly, an anxiety about 'standards' often appeared as yet another aspect of the generalized concern for 'quality', leading to argumentational slippage between a programme's ethics, its aesthetic worth and its production values.

Conclusions

We can see, then, that argument about 'quality' actually drew on a number of separate if related issues, and did so in a way which served mainly to conflate and confuse these issues. As a public 'debate', it was notable in the extent to which participants so often failed to comprehend one another's positions, let alone engage with them. But, with few exceptions, 'quality' was what participants declared themselves to be *for*. As one commentator remarked: 'Quality is one of those things that it's very hard to be against.' Popularity and profitability weren't, *on their own*, seen to be decent enough as reasons for changing national television. As we have shown above, those who chose to think otherwise received a corrective lesson when the franchise decisions of the ITC were announced.

'Quality' became a key idea in the debate about the future of television because of its accommodating ambiguities. Although it carries the ring of a simple and self-evident meaning, in fact it was used to widely different purposes and effect within a range of fundamentally conflicting perspectives on television's future. Initially inflected in the direction of a defence of established public and cultural values, it was quickly serviceable as a term to describe the improvement of product which, it was argued, would follow the introduction of a new, more competitive, television system. This is not surprising when we consider its pedigree of usage, both within the long-standing debate about 'minority' and 'mass' taste, and within the newer language of managerial efficiency and consumer satisfaction. As a term of real argument it is chronically inadequate and as a principle it is vacuous. However, as a talismanic abstraction, it provided a token point of common reference for a conflict between views which often found it convenient to leave their own real groundings and principles unstated and unexamined. This ritual use has been continued in the BBC's response to the current government review of its future.

Our brief study suggests strongly that argument about the future of national television needs to engage much more directly with the distinct component issues which 'quality' succeeded so often in confusing and mystifying. Such argument also needs to pay more attention to the political and cultural context within which television operates and is used, instead of focusing almost exclusively on programmes themselves, as centres of reified value. Nervousness both about explicitly addressing the real divisions in people's preferences in entertainment and dramatic fiction, and about an open discussion of the public requirements that might be made upon broadcast journalism, have worked against such a broader view. Quality arguments about television-as-art (distinctive forms, generic excellence etc.) and about television-as-industry (efficiently manufactured value for money etc.) have a reductive tendency to exclude consideration of the values of television as the primary agency of national, political and cultural life, and as a key agency for the education and self-development of individuals. Arguments about programme *kinds*, about *different audiences*, about proper *diversity* about public informational *needs*, indeed about how viewing preferences are *formed* in a society characterized by economic and educational inequality, need to be set within these broader contours. Otherwise, despite any best intentions, the present focus on 'quality' from all sides may finally turn out to have been little more than a convenient cover for a play-off between old privilege and new opportunism. The real terms of this play-off, and the real range of options available for change, will almost entirely have escaped sustained public attention.

Notes

An earlier, shorter version of this paper was published as 'British Television and the Quality Issue' in *Media Information Australia* Number 68, 1993.

[1] See for instance G. Mulgan (ed), *Questions of Quality*, British Film Institute, London 1990, and C. Brunsdon, 'Quality in Television', *Screen* Volume 31, Number 1, 1990.

[2] P. Bourdieu, *Distinction*, (tr. Richard Nice), Routledge, London 1984.

[3] See J. Corner (ed), *Popular Television in Britain: Studies in Cultural History*, British Film Institute, London 1991, for discussion of this in relation to specific genres.

[4] R. Williams, *Culture and Society*, Chatto, London 1958 (also Penguin, Harmondsworth 1961).

[5] R. Williams, 'Culture is Ordinary', 1958, reprinted in R. Williams, *Resources of Hope*, Verso, London 1989.

[6] See J. Corner, 'Debating Culture', *Media, Culture and Society*, Volume 16, 1994, for more on this point in relation to cultural theory.

[7] Home Office, *Broadcasting in the '90s: Competition, Choice and Quality*, HMSO (Cmnd 517), London 1988, p1.

[8] S. Hood and G. O'Leary, *Questions of Broadcasting*, Methuen, London 1990, pxvi.

[9] Home Office, *op.cit.*, 1988, p21.

[10] Hansard, House of Lords Official Report, 502 (11) 13 December 1988, quoted in W. Stevenson and N. Smedley, *Responses to the White Paper*, British Film Institute, London 1989, pp7-10

[11] M. Brown, 'Television 1990-91' in *Film and Television Handbook 1992*, British Film Institute, London 1991, p45.

[12] ITC, *Invitation to Apply for Regional Channel 3 Licenses*, ITC, London 1991, p31.

[13] K. Schroder, 'Cultural Quality: Search for a Phantom' in K. Schroder and M. Skovmand (eds.), *Media Cultures*, Routledge, London 1992. Schroder argues for this position from a media research perspective.

[14] Home Office, Report of the Committee on the Future of Broadcasting, HMSO, London 1977, (Cmnd 6753), p19.

[15] Quoted in S. Brittan, 'The Case for the Consumer Market' in C. Veljanovski (ed.), *Freedom in Broadcasting*, Institute of Economic Affairs, London 1989, p25.

[16] *Ibid.*, p14.

[17] R. Murdoch, McTaggart Lecture delivered at the Edinburgh International Festival, 25 August 1989.

[18] S. Prebble, personal interview with Karen Lury in 1990 quoted in K. Lury, *Quality and Television*, unpublished M.Phil. thesis, Liverpool University, 1991, p139. Prebble subsequently took charge of documentaries at the ITV Network Centre.

[19] S. Brittan, *op.cit.*, p40.

Public Service in the 'New Broadcasting Age'

Brian Winston

Late in 1992 the BBC appeared to win a famous victory for the principles of public service broadcasting. But the appearance was deceptive. For this was a victory only if one were to accept that the BBC constitutes the sole embodiment and ultimate expression of what public service broadcasting is or could be. In fact, what the BBC won was not so much a defence of principle but rather a triumph for the continuation of its own particular forms and structures.

The reason was simple. Despite Conservative hostility to the Corporation as an anomalous, privileged, publicly-funded entity (in general) and as a perceived ideological enemy (in particular), the government had boxed itself into a corner on broadcasting issues. The artillery it had mounted against the old commercial television structure was in the process of misfiring even as its other guns were trained on the Corporation. The licence auction mandated by the 1990 Broadcasting Act had produced considerable instability in ITV, for what was already seen in the first days of the new dispensation as little or no gain. This failure then became the BBC's best protection. It was as if Her Majesty's Government, having had the misfortune to lose one half of the old system was eager not be accused of carelessness by losing the other. The result was spiked guns which left the BBC more or less free to stand pat.

But, arguably, the BBC and the principles of public service broadcasting were not well served by this. Indeed it could be that all such victories in the public debate on broadcasting in Britain, at least since the Pilkington Report in 1962, have paradoxically weakened the BBC by drawing it farther and farther away from its essential mission. If, as now seems probable, there is no real debate about the public service principle in the run up to the BBC's Charter renewal, (or, perhaps, a new Act), then the Corporation will certainly survive until the next century: but it will likely be in much less good health than it would otherwise have been had such a debate taken place. Instead of an opportunity to reassess the concept of public broadcasting seriously, we had what might be described as a false agenda laid before the public by both the government and the BBC.

The False Agenda

The Government's U-turn from the position taken in the mid-1980s was remarkable. There was, quite suddenly, no real question but that the BBC would continue essentially as before. This was made quite clear in the Government's Green Paper, *The Future of the BBC*. It queried but backed away from any significant proposals about the strategic issues – the BBC's size, its governance or its financial base.

On the first of these points, size, the government discussed a number of scenarios which could remove or significantly alter the BBC's programming and distribution capacities, only to conclude that: 'The government's present view is that these options would detract from the BBC's ability to compete effectively as a broadcaster.'[1] The maintenance of the BBC's current size was thus implicit, e.g.: 'The BBC might be expected to ensure that national events were accessible to audiences throughout the United Kingdom'; or: 'The BBC might be expected to continue to broadcast radio and television services for people in Scotland, Wales and Northern Ireland',[2] and so on. The explicit question of downsizing was then raised in a context which made it moot: if the BBC was not expected to provide pop music, it could lose two national radio channels; if it were to become exclusively an educational television broadcaster, it could lose one TV channel; if it did not have to broadcast to the Celtic fringe or locally it could shrink yet further. But since it 'might be expected' to continue to do all or most of these things, it therefore followed that it could not get very much (or even any) smaller.

The same cautious tone was deployed in considering the role of the BBC's Governors. The Governors currently function as both regulators and supervisors. Some suggestions were considered about splitting these roles and having the Governors either regulate or supervise. If they were to do the latter, there could then be a new regulatory structure altogether, either as part of the existing mechanism for commercial television or as a new public service broadcasting overseer.

The most extreme options were that the Governors be directly elected by licence holders or, following Peacock, that a new Public Service Broadcasting Council not only regulate but collect the licence fee to fund the BBC and perhaps some rival public service broadcasters or rival public service programming on the commercial channels. However, as before, these options were dismissed as unworkable. Confusion of responsibility as between parliament and Governors could result if the latter were also elected, the Green Paper stated.[3] A Broadcasting Council with power to distribute money 'would clearly be unacceptable if this power led to the imposition of a single cultural or editorial viewpoint'.[4]

As for the licence fee, the government's view was that this had worked 'since 1927 and so far no-one has devised a better system'.[5] This was at the heart of the U-turn. Advertising as an alternative revenue source was already dead in the water because there was now, post-Peacock, a clear understanding that there was simply not another £1000 million of advertising to be had out of the British economy. This alone had blunted the Thatcherite attack.

A new realism was now displayed. Alternative funding sources such as the general tax or a levy on equipment were dismissed, the one because it would cost half a per cent on VAT, the other because it would add £300 to the price of a TV set. Combination plans (licensing plus advertising) got similar short shrift: 'experience in other countries suggests there are difficulties'.[6]

Subscription, the favoured solution to the problem of the licence fee, was recommended by the Peacock Committee and endorsed by a Home Office study six years ago. Both felt the time was not yet ripe, however, for a switch over. *The Future of the BBC* reveals that the government still felt the same way in the winter of 1992/3. This did not mean that there could be no tinkering with the licence fee – decriminalizing evasion, abolishing the black and white TV licence, charging per set rather than per household – but, as with size and governance, nothing radical was suggested. As the very language of the Green Paper confirmed, the Thatcherite attack on the BBC was ending not with a bang but a whimper.

There was, for instance, an interesting contrast in the use of the words 'could' and 'might' in the document. Supposedly open (that is, tactical) possibilities were 'coulds'; more closed (that is, strategic) ones were 'mights'. It was the 'mights' which worked to preserve the status quo.

Thus the BBC 'could' concentrate on providing only what commercial broadcasters do not provide i.e. 'culture'; or it could produce programmes that would not sell abroad; or it could broadcast more educational programming; or it could contract out its support services; or it could split off its commercial publishing and entrepreneurial activities, or its training role, or its research and development. On the other hand, 'The BBC might be expected' to obey the European directive that a majority of programming be Euro-originated; and, as I have just pointed out, the BBC 'might be expected' to remain a full-fledged national broadcaster.

This is not to say that all these 'coulds' were moot. Various forms of contracting out, for instance, were clearly already underway. But some of them are nothing more than 'straw' options – the élitist, educational or rigorously nationalist programming strategies, for example. All the 'mights', though, speak unambiguously to the continuation of a large organization. In contrast to the rhetoric of the 1980s, the government was now ready to concede that the BBC should continue to be a monolithic, multi-media conglomerate, funded by a hypothecated tax and governed by a quango.

The BBC was therefore quite right, in its booklet *Extending Choice*, almost to ignore the strategic questions (except funding) and to deal only with the tactical issues so that it could conclude that it would simply continue to do what it had been doing, only more so. This document promised for television such things as:

'journalism of impartiality and authority'
'a wide range of drama'
'science and natural history'
'pioneering comedy and light entertainment'
'authoritative and creative coverage of sport'
'the continued development of world service television'
'complementary scheduling of programmes across the radio and television to ensure maximum choice for viewers and listeners, particularly at peak times'[8]

And for radio, such things as:

'a continuous news service'
'pop and popular music programming of range, diversity and innovation'[9]

All this as well as continued local activity, entrepreneurial activity, research and development activity and, finally 'a transparent system of access to the BBC'.[10] In short, the Government's negative 'coulds' were dismissed and its positive 'mights' were endorsed.

Extending Choice agreed with the Government that size made for coherence, for concentrations of specialized skills and for complimentary scheduling. The booklet avoided, unsurprisingly since it bore the Governors' imprimatur, consideration of the appropriateness of the BBC's increasingly quango-style of governance. It responded to the Governors' perceived recent interventionism by asking for a 'clarification' of their broad relationship with the Board of Management. The thrust was to suggest that the Governors should become regulators, and that therefore there was no need for any other form of regulatory authority to be placed over the BBC. Arguments as to why this should not be imposed were outlined, echoing those of the Green Paper.

This did not mean, though, that the BBC document was entirely conservative in nature. For one thing, some of these continuing or expanding activities were quite controversial, the 24 hour radio news service, for instance. For another thing, the BBC did mount one strategic argument, albeit obliquely, in defence of its funding arrangements. That it was doing so was not obvious. At first sight, on the licence fee, *Extending Choice* seemed to argue, as it had on size and governance, for continuity with only tactical changes being suggested. The Corporation promised more internal efficiency, depending primarily on the introduction of an artificial internal market to achieve it. It also promised to 'continue energetically to explore additional revenue streams' from sales of programmes and publishing, joint ventures in the new distribution technologies, the World TV Service, sponsorship of the arts and sport and public monies for Gaelic.[11]

But more significantly, the BBC deemed it necessary, although the Government had not really attacked it, to mount a disguised, rearguard defence of the licence fee *as a principle*. The method chosen to do this was, paradoxically, to couch the entire stand-pat strategy as a response to radically changing external circumstances. The Corporation's framing rhetoric in *Extending Choice* was therefore of a 'new broadcasting age', as the booklet's subtitle had it.

There has long been a perceived relationship between the legitimacy of the tax and BBC's overall domestic audience reach – what might be called 'the BBC Proportion'. Although the government was in too much disarray to question the licence fee, nevertheless the echoes of the earlier 1980s debate were still sufficiently loud for the Corporation, in *Extending Choice*, to attempt the (formally unnecessary) renegotiation or re-insurance of some form of 'the BBC Proportion'.

The 'Proportion' had been that, in a duopolistic situation, 100 per cent of the fee was justified, crudely, by reaching 50 per cent of the audience. *Extending Choice* essayed the difficult task of arguing that 100 per cent of the fee would still be justified even if the total audience fell below 50 per cent. Hence the paradox: to achieve this, the BBC couched its entire tactical, essentially conservative case in the context of a strong rhetoric of a new (and threatening) broadcasting environment.

This upheaval was occasioned, the BBC suggested, because the duopoly was metamorphosing into a triopoly, with new distribution systems, direct-broadcasting satellite (DBS) and cable, as the third leg. Almost entirely ignoring the critical role of governmental policy-making, these technologically-determined developments were deemed to be the engine that the BBC thought (or purported to think) was driving 'the new broadcasting age'.

At the outset, in its very first paragraph, *Extending Choice* boldly stated, *as a matter of fact*, that by the year 2000 the majority of households would have access to at least twenty television channels and five radio stations. Moreover, a few lines further on it was asserted with equal confidence that the spending per household on broadcasting equipment and services would rise by 45 per cent in the same period while broadcasting revenues would be doubled.[12] £6 billion (in 1992 £s) would be shared between these three parties, commercial broadcasters, subscription broadcasters using new technologies and the BBC. However the licence fee would only account for 25 per cent of this total. The changed technological environment, for which the BBC could not be held responsible, would inexorably reduce the audiences to as low as 30 per cent, in the opinion of the new Director General, John Birt. But even then the BBC would still be efficient: it would deliver one third of the audience for a quarter of the available money. Therefore the audience share could be allowed to fall below 50 per cent without 'the BBC Proportion' being destroyed. The legitimacy of the tax would be maintained.

While the political cleverness of this argument cannot be faulted, the ploy can nevertheless be criticized. There were serious flaws in the BBC's assessment of the basic technological situation. These flaws, though they do no more than reflect current received opinion, need to be examined carefully.

The BBC's authority for the assertion on projected increases in spending was anonymous ('It is expected that'), but let us assume for the moment that it proves to be correct. Then, how can the first confident statement as to channel expansion also be true, especially as regards television?

Extending Choice assumed five terrestrial and fifteen subscription channels. In the scenario it presented, the terrestrial television channels and fifteen radio stations would share 35 per cent of the £6 billion – £3.9 billion while the fifteen new television channels made do with the balance. Assuming radio continued to absorb about 25 per cent, then each of the television channels would have something in the order of £600 million in revenues per annum, and this is without considering the extra revenues to be earned by programme originators in the secondary, world-wide, programme syndication market. The new broadcasters, on the other hand, would only have about £150 million for each of their channels, about a quarter of the revenues of their terrestrial rivals. Clearly, the 'new broadcasting age' would not mean twenty channels of traditional television.

Extending Choice suggested that there would be 'radical changes in broadcasting industry costs';[13] but just how radical could these changes be? Could they encompass, at a minimum, a 75 per cent reduction in hourly costs, which is what the new channels would need to balance their books? There is considerable reason for believing that they could not. Programming costs reflect audience expectations and audiences are in this regard extremely conservative. Currently, the world's benchmark for their expectations is Hollywood, where a filmed drama costs £1 million per hour. To spend significantly less jeopardizes production values to such an extent that the product ceases to look 'professional'.

In this context, 'professional' is a term describing an element in the public's reception and acceptance of programming. It is possible to produce audio-visual images for practically nothing with a Boots camcorder in a Basildon living room. But this does not mean that such images are 'television' in the sense of being of interest to the general public, much less being of sufficient interest to persuade audiences to *subscribe* to them. Therefore, although it is true that production money can be saved, it is equally clear that these savings would not be so great as to allow new channels to operate as full competitors with traditional broadcasters.

This, of course, does not matter for the BBC's strategic purposes. If the competition does not materialize (and audiences levels do not fall) then the case for maintaining 'the BBC Proportion' is even stronger. If the newcomers prosper and the falling-off occurs, then the BBC is again protected by the one quarter: one third proportion. Birt, apparently unwittingly, has put the BBC into a 'win-win' situation. However, because the received wisdom about new technology is so awry as to cloud the possibility of reasonable discussion, I will digress with a further argument as to why these assumptions about the new environment in general are wrong.

The BBC (and others) claim to believe, then, that these new competitors will use alternative programming strategies. Given the inherent conservatism of the audience, it might be thought that such alternative strategies would be difficult, if not impossible, to develop; but *Extending Choice* pointed to 'growing international experience' of a 'revolution' along these lines. The most important evidence of a twenty television channel world, typographically signalled in the booklet by being printed in bold, came from the United States.[14]

In the light of the stress placed on the American evidence in the 'new age' case, it is of some significance that *Extending Choice* made a number of seemingly minor errors when talking about the United States. It claimed, for instance, that the average American household can now receive fifty channels when in fact US cable (even after forty years of activity and despite the assistance poor broadcast reception gives it) only reaches six of every ten homes, and with only thirty-seven channels.[15]

These channels include re-transmission of broadcast signals and alphanumeric services of the sort available in the UK on teletext. Most basic cable channels are, economically, loss-leaders relying heavily on recycled, cheap, or in the case of the music channels, free programming. (I should add that MTV's cumulative audience does not exceed one per cent of all households, less than a million.) Beyond basic, movie and some sports channels (for which additional subscriptions are charged) are taken up by only half of all cabled households.

Having failed to take over from the broadcasters, the cable industry now claims that services can be provided for audiences as small as 200,000; but, it must be noted, this can only be possible if almost all programming on the service is virtually cost-free and endlessly repeated – even then it is still a questionable claim. The audience tolerance for this sort of television can be seen in the fact that all these basic channels together command attention for less than fifteen minutes in any hour. Most American TV sets, are still tuned to the broadcasters for most of the time.[16]

Another significant fault in the BBC's account of the US situation is the omission of any reference to the regulatory environment which, for instance, allows cable to re-broadcast the networks and the broadcast independents at virtually no cost, and prohibits the networks from owning their own programming. *Extending Choice* made much of the fact that the networks are no longer profitable, without taking these regulations into account. Confusingly, it also reported the rise of Murdoch's Fox Network without explaining why, if the network business is such a bust, Murdoch wants to be a part of it.

The answer is that the technology is not responsible for the networks' current economic position; the US government is. As soon as the networks can show themselves to be in really serious difficulty – and the quickest way of doing that is by crying 'woe' – the regulations will be rewritten. Already, cable is being constrained by having its rates once more regulated by the municipalities. The American system is not technologically determined, much less a real market. As the imposed unprofitability of the networks shows, it is an artificial creation, a complex web of regulations which has allowed a proliferation of relatively impoverished channels without those channels cumulatively replacing the broadcasters (networks and independents) as the main deliverers of audiences to advertisers. And all this is in a country with a broadcasting market currently five times larger than that which the BBC is projecting for the UK in the year 2000.

About the United States one can therefore argue quite the opposite case to the BBC's. Far from America demonstrating the inevitability of the coming of twenty TV channels in the UK, American experience actually can be used to show the economic impossibility of such a proliferation in the UK. The truth of the changing American environment is that it has changed less than people seem to think, because new channels do not produce new audiences, new programming and, above all, new revenues at anything like levels necessary to create a true extension of choice. As *Extending Choice* (again, confusingly) acknowledged, US experience suggests that people will not and, indeed as long as work and sleep exist, cannot watch more than eight to ten channels regularly. The American experience suggests that they cannot watch more *at all*.

Beyond 24-hour news, weather and sport, a premium movie channel, rock videos and, perhaps, a children's channel, the new technologies offer little challenge.

Thus the BBC was being disingenuous to suggest that 'Nobody can predict with any degree of certainty what will be the "natural limit" of broadcasting supply in the UK.'[17] While prediction is a dangerous business, a combination of time available for consumption and the *culturally-determined* economics of programme provision can give one some fairly clear ideas about where those limits lie. In fact, the current range of alternative satellite channels (domestic and imported) are almost certainly already beyond the 'natural limits' of the range which *Extending Choice* suggested.

The sum for twenty channels in the UK simply does not work out, even if satellite continues to grow at nearly a million homes a year. Since satellite is currently a predominately C1-C2 phenomenon, that growth projection requires DBS to be diffused by higher socio-economic groups emulating the consumption patterns of lower ones. Obviously this would not be an impossible development.

Finally, looking beyond the year 2000, the current research agenda into high definition, digital television which *Extending Choice* presented as a centrepiece of the BBC's Research and Development efforts, is unlikely to help the economics of further channel proliferation since the introduction of such technology will send infrastructural production costs soaring again. It might well also raise above-the-line costs by making the epic image possible for the first time on TV.

Yet, as I have said, none of this matters. For whatever good internal and external political reasons, the BBC chose to get most of this technologized case wrong. But, as they did not intend to act upon this analysis anyway, the damage to their strategic response is minimal. To repeat: the BBC's answer to the 'new broadcasting age' is to suggest doing more of the same. This is almost certainly the right strategy since doing the same means spending money to maintain traditional broadcasting norms – that is, spending money on programming at a level 'new age' rivals cannot hope to match.

Since the Government has allowed the corporation to keep the licence fee *and* its entrepreneurial profits (while seriously carpet-bagging the revenues of its main terrestrial commercial broadcasting rivals), and since the new distribution technologies have yet to achieve rapid diffusion or even a viable economic basis for competitive programming should such diffusion ever take place, the BBC is thus set fair, with its protected revenue stream (significantly augmented by its entrepreneurial activities), to be the one player who can most easily continue to programme at levels acceptable to the public – and cope with high-definition if and when that happens.

In fact, the BBC could ensure its victory at least until the end of the century by deliberately using a 'Star Wars' strategy. They are well placed to outspend their rivals, both terrestrial and celestial, forcing them into programming bankruptcy. But it would not be honest to thus set this strategy down for it reveals the central importance of licence fee. Which, of course, brings us to the real agenda: whether or not there should be a licence fee?

The Real Agenda

Put another way, the question of the licence fee is whether or not the concept of public service broadcasting is a viable one for the twenty-first century? That is the central issue of the real agenda.

The idea of media as a species of public servant goes to the very beginning of the history of the newspaper press. In the seventeenth century, the novel demand of the rising mercantile class for the sort of information that had previously been the sole province of princes was met by the simple expedient of the princes' establishing a monopoly of supply over that information. In other words, to the well-established impulse for state control of the press was added the fresh notion that news might also be a staple of the state. The state monopoly was relaxed only to allow printers to retail *foreign* intelligences, which could, after all, usefully support and supplement the state's own sources of overseas news. Domestic news remained a crown, or rather a state, staple; for, after the anarchy of the Civil War which saw a sudden flourishing of proto-newspapers, the monopoly was re-imposed.

The newspaper existed in the crease between the impulse to censor and the need to disseminate information to ease and aid effective public participation in the emergent mercantile capitalist system. This confusing set of objectives meant that, at the Restoration, the Surveyor of the Press became both the chief censor and the producer of the news – both Sir David Calcutt and Rupert Murdoch, as it were.

There is, therefore, historical warrant for seeing the provision of news as an infrastructural public service, like the provision of the post, of roads, or (more pertinently) of places of public recreation such as the patented royal theatres or royal (i.e. state) lands as parks.

Beyond the effects of general policing inefficiency, two forces worked to erode this state monopoly over the press. First, as I have said, not only was the press (and theatres and other places of recreation) of social value, but these very institutions could themselves operate as enterprises. The press was a capitalist tool but it was also (albeit only potentially so in the eighteenth century) itself a capitalist enterprise. The more expensive it became to produce and distribute newspapers, the more stable and reliable (from the state's point of view) became the press' proprietors. At the end of this process of capitalization, in the middle years of the nineteenth century, the proprietors were able to argue that the last vestiges of control, the taxes on newsprint and advertising, were unnecessary so respectable and trustworthy were they as men of capital.

There was a second impulse eating away at the principle of state control. The very same collapse of state power in the Civil War which had allowed for the first proliferation of newspapers also allowed for the initial assertion of freedom of expression as a right. This was part of a broader set of arguments about liberty which embraced the idea of freedom of expression as a necessary element in the struggle for freedom of religious expression. As such it was seen as a very important, if not paramount, freedom: 'Give me liberty to know', cried Milton, 'to utter, and to argue freely according to conscience, above all liberties.'

Although the needs of capital were the major forces driving the development of the 'free press' in the nineteenth century, nevertheless this secondary liberal impulse was also of considerable power. When the press was eventually 'freed', this was condoned in liberal, political terms traceable back to the seventeenth century radicals. Thus, it might be that, in reality, this 'freedom' was allowed because the press was too valuable a tool for enterprise and too profitable an enterprise in itself to be totally controlled. But, all the same, 'liberty' was another factor in its emergence.

This is not to say, though, that the received 'Whig interpretation' of British press history, which sees the entire story in terms of a successful struggle for freedom, has much merit. If the issue had really been liberty then the tale would have ended not with the removal of the 'taxes on knowledge' but with the passage into law of a right to publish. This last has yet to happen in the UK, although it did occur in the eighteenth century at the next available revolutionary juncture – in the revolted American colonies. There, what had been nothing more than a sentiment in England, was enacted as a legal principle fundamental to a democratic constitution: 'Congress shall make no law abridging freedom of the press ...'

Graham Murdock has reminded us of the line that runs from this centuries-old debate about the organization and function of the press to more recent arguments about the organization and function of broadcasting.[18] By the turn of this century, the contradiction between the importance of the press as an essential institution in a modern democracy and the sometimes conflicting requirements of the press as a species of capital-intensive enterprise was becoming glaring. Murdock pointed out that for some American thinkers, newspapers were public institutions 'which (as one of them wrote) ought not to be controlled by irresponsible individuality'. Another felt that, just as the march of time had revealed the inadequacies of commercial loan libraries, parks, schools, swimming baths etc., so the inadequacies of a privately-owned press were now being exposed.

Obviously, given the tradition of non-governmental interference with the press, enshrined in that country's constitution, the solution could not be municipal or state control. Instead, the idea of newspaper trusts was mooted. These were to be run by 'the great and the good' for the purpose of producing corrective newspapers which would avoid the sensational, and eschew crime and gossip. There is no question, for all that it was swept aside by the imperatives of commerce, but that this idea influenced the debate about broadcasting in America in the 1920s.

Over British broadcasting the forces of commerce were less triumphant, not least because they had prevailed in the United States with (temporarily) disastrous results. The essential idea of some form of 'public trust' was mooted and, along these lines, the fledgling broadcasting system was wrested from commercial hands and placed in the care of the state. Not only did the British state not share its American counterpart's inhibitions as to the inappropriateness of government activity in these areas; but the military connotations of the technology, arising out of radio's role in World War I, aided this development both in general terms and specifically in the matter of instituting the licence system.

The BBC was created to be run by 'the great and the good', and its finances secured by a hypothecated tax in the form of this licence. It was established as a public servant much as the Restoration Surveyor of the Press had been. The state had seized it, just as the state had seized the press and the theatres centuries before; but this was a liberal state and therefore the nature of the seizure was complex and sophisticated. It took this up-to-date public trust form that was being suggested in some quarters for the reform of the newspapers. Yet the demands of 'liberty' were also met, as it were. Just as the now-safe press was sold as a 'free press', so with broadcasting the structure was declared to be 'independent'.

It is noteworthy that the model of a Government Board, a more modern method of control much in vogue in the war, was not used for the BBC. Instead 'liberty' demanded that the contradictions between the reality of structural control and simulacrum of independence be fudged by the use of a medieval governmental device, the Royal Charter, to govern the system and by the creation of the concept of 'public service broadcasting' to explain its mission.

Tom Nairn has argued that the crucial function for the British intelligentsia in general has been to press for social integration entailing 'the preservation of rule from above by constant adaptation and concession from below'.[19] Certainly, it requires no great effort to read the history of the BBC as a perfect example of this process in action. John Reith's handling of coverage of the General Strike in the Corporation's founding moments, whereby the BBC so conducted itself that official censorship was deemed to be unnecessary, is but one example of how the BBC's history illustrates Nairn's thesis.[20] The destruction of Talks Department which was in danger of becoming a potential source of dissident voices and opinions in the 1930s would be another example of this.[21] Best could be the presence of the Secret Service officer in Broadcasting House vetting every last appointment for political rectitude.

Yet on the other hand, it would be wrong to dismiss out of hand as illusory the BBC's sense of 'liberty'. The independence of the BBC might well have been, by reason of governance and finance, a myth; but it was a myth believed by a large proportion of the political class and by the BBC. It was thereby given a not inconsiderable substance. Reith's unfortunate strategy of being seen as the government's mouthpiece during the General Strike was abandoned. In its place, a number of emblematic crisis events (e.g. Suez, *Yesterday's Men*) reinforced the idea that the liberal concept of freedom could apply to the BBC.[22]

This substance was manifested by the internal culture of the Corporation, which read the emblematic rows as evidence of independence of government; by successive Postmaster-Generals refusing to intervene in programming arguments; and by the Governors of the Corporation being chosen by governments of all political persuasions from the usual list of 'the great and the good'. Finally, the idea of the BBC's independence was further bolstered by the reality of its financial position.

The charter-structure had been established to give the BBC a distance from the government. Once the Corporation was established, the only necessary point of contact, and therefore of potential improper leverage, was at the periodic setting of the licence fee level. However, since penetration grew annually and new technologies (TV, colour TV) engendered new licences, the opportunity for such leverage was less than it appeared to be. With the principle established that new services required new licence fee levels, the system essentially supplied the BBC over many decades with an ever-increasing revenue stream – even without basic levels being raised.

It is possible to read the radical account of the BBC's perfidy as evidence that, at the very least, lip service was being paid, however cynically, to the idea of its independence. It is also possible to go further: to suggest that the incidents of servile submission to external authority are the exceptions that, certainly after World War II, prove the rule of everyday integrity.

However one chooses to interpret the history, there can be little question that the peculiar concept of public service broadcasting flourished. Within the liberal British state, the BBC, its revenues protected and its 'independence' valued, laid down the bench marks for British broadcasting. Between the Charybdis of, say, American commercialism (where thousands of radio stations failed to provide a single minute of drama, childrens' programming or even serious news analysis, and hundreds of TV channels and stations fought with homogenized programming for the same maximal audience demographic) and the Scylla of, say, western European state control (where underfunded services dully defended a limited vision of official bourgeois culture), British broadcasting steered the middle course of public service. Thanks to this concept, it was 'the least worst broadcasting system in the world' exactly because it delivered more acceptable programming to more of its population than did other systems. Nevertheless, in the radical upheavals of the 1980s, all this was to count for naught. Under the government's attack, the always fragile BBC myth of independence was drained of potentcy. A number of factors contributed to this.

First there is the running sore of Northern Ireland. If truth is the first casualty of war, then for British broadcasters, integrity has been the first casualty of this undeclared war. Northern Ireland has been the basis of an attack, unprecedented in its openess and crudity, by the government on editorial freedom. This highlighted previously implicit assumptions about broadcasting's servile political role in extreme conflict situations.

In one sense the government's demand for such control was not exceptional. Indeed, historically, the BBC has on numerous occasions acquiesced to state interference at the time of such crises. In other senses, though, the Northern Ireland rows were new because they were conducted in public. The government clearly felt that aversion to the IRA would overcome any public sentiment for the principles of free expression and editorial freedom.

The recurrent problems arising out of the coverage of Northern Ireland then opened the door for further public attacks on other areas of output, all of which battered the BBC's sense of independence. This was a government so confident of its support and so contemptuous of the liberal tradition of 'liberty' that it saw no advantage in preserving the BBC, even as its own creature.

The second factor also arose from this contempt. Thatcherite disdain for 'the great and the good' brought to the business of state patronage the different criteria of loyalty and political partisanship. The BBC Governors were not immune from this development. The era of rule by appointees whose main qualifications were that they were 'one of us' has worked to delegitimise the Governors to the point where the BBC, at this level at least, shows all the signs of being just another quango. The fact that the current Director-General, John Birt, was appointed in defiance of established BBC usage, without even the due process of an open board, is a most glaring instance of this new culture.

Finally, and this is in large measure the BBC's own fault, the financial situation has also worsened to the point where the setting of the licence fee assumes a far more critical importance than it did previously. I say this is the BBC's fault because the Corporation had argued successfully before Pilkington for a massive expansion of its operations into local radio, a second national TV channel and colour TV at exactly the moment when the curve of ever increasing licences were finally leveling off because of nearly 100 per cent penetration by both radio and television.

The BBC has always been notoriously inept at sums, but this was a most grievous error. The licence fee bonus for colour, for instance, would take years to accumulate while the expenses were immediate. The imperialist expansion sanctioned in the early 1960s involved massive expenditures which could only be funded by going to the government for substantial, and therefore politically unpopular, increases in the licence fee. To make this argument required demonstrating not just that households bought licenses but that they listened and watched the BBC's output with regularity. Thus was born 'the BBC Proportion'. Within a decade, that is by the mid-1960s, 'the BBC Proportion' required taking BBC 1 downmarket to maintain share.

Adopting the emerging entrepreneurial rhetoric of the day was not necessarily a salvation either. To make some money from publishing, co-productions and the sale of programming was to raise questions about making all the needed money from such sources. It was in a weakened financial state – for these other revenue streams remained marginal – that the BBC then faced, for the first time in its history, a government ideologically hostile to liberalism, virulently opposed to public enterprises, and apparently uncaring about the culture of freedom.

The BBC survived this attack, as I have argued above, by the skin of its teeth and, more importantly, not because of anything it had or had not itself done. The government neutered itself. But this does not mean that the injured liberal vision of public service broadcasting can now heal, as if these attacks and erosions had not taken place. It is too damaged for that. The real agenda, therefore, ought to be concerned with addressing the problem of the future of public service broadcasting. If the concept of public service is drained of even the simulacrum of independence and integrity, as I believe it has been in these last years, then this future has to be debated in terms far broader than it has been debated thus far.

I do not mean by this just that the current debate is inadequate, although that is clearly the case. Rather, it is that the BBC is now in serious danger of becoming irretrievably the government today that its radical critics, erroneously as I have suggested above, have always claimed it to be. From their viewpoint the debate is utterly sterile: Who cares whether or not the BBC has a rolling news operation if that news is the creature of Westminster? Who cares if the BBC Governors supervise or manage when those Governors are nothing but the lickspittles of the party in power? Who cares how the thing is funded if it is nothing more than an operational arm of the Ministry of Truth? Best were it for the BBC to die!

But to wish this is to ignore the fact that public service broadcasting – that is, crudely, non-commercial broadcasting – brings advantages for viewers and listeners that cannot simply be thrown aside. In other words, while it is true that the BBC was and is an institution insufficiently distanced from government, even by the standards of the liberal tradition of free expression, it nevertheless has constructed a broadcasting culture which, by every measure, better served more of its public than would have been the case under commerce. For it is quite simply a fact that the market-place in broadcasting, however it is organized, has not provided a comprehensive range of programming, wherever it has been tried. It always has to be augmented non-commercially to fill, even partially, the cultural space available for broadcasting. (Yesterday's argument, that what the market cannot provide has no place in national life is, at least in the cultural realm, too asinine, impoverishing and blinkered to require rebuttal. And the argument of the day before, that a third alternative, viz. that the state itself, when properly constituted, can provide all is, in my view, too utopian to be addressed, especially in these weasel times.)

However, I am far from here recommending that we must always keep hold of the BBC as nurse 'for fear of finding something worse'. I am suggesting that we need and can do better than that in finding arguments in support of the public service broadcasting concept. The concept needs to be reassessed so that its strengths can be preserved and its weaknesses, indeed its dangers, obviated. Since the major danger is that public service broadcasting can be suborned by authority, the central issue to address is how that might be prevented.

To answer this, I make an assumption that no amount of tinkering with the current organizational arrangements would offer sufficient protection against authority. Therefore, the preservation of public service broadcasting requires a more fundamental approach. In fact, any reassessment of the concept must take place within the context of the general question of the future of the British state. In essence, for non-commercial, state-funded broadcasting not inevitably to mean state control requires, as a first essential, that freedom of expression be constitutionally guaranteed.

In the British context that means the demand for public service broadcasting is another constitutional demand. Without constitutional guarantee there is no conceivable structure that can isolate the broadcasters from improper pressure; there is no arrangement for the appointment of the Governors that cannot be corrupted; there is no funding system that cannot be abused – in short, without such a guarantee there can be no independence.

To illustrate what a fundamental difference such a guarantee would make, let me revisit these three strategic areas of size, governance and funding, and look at some of the suggestions that have been put on the table from time to time. In each case, a 'right to broadcast' – which, given that broadcasting is subject to the law, is actually only a right to be free of prior constraint – transforms the potential of the suggestion.

The principle of plurality of voices has never been applied to the BBC in part because of an old argument that monolithic size was in some way a protection against improper interference. Were there to be competing public broadcasting organizations, each would be smaller and more vulnerable. Events have now shown that the BBC's size is no protection and therefore the argument has lost its force. The BBC's other arguments in favour of size – complementary scheduling and concentrations of expertise etc. – are equally suspect, and at best smack more of convenience than principle. The constitutional guarantee of free expression would allow for plurality – competing and/or specialized public service entities – without the danger of autonomy being eroded.

Similarly, on the second strategic issue, governance, guaranteeing the autonomy of the broadcaster transforms the argument. Take for instance, the Green Paper's dismissal of the suggestion that the Governors might be elected: 'this might result in confused responsibilities between the Governors, as representatives of the BBC's audiences, and parliament and the government, representing the general public'.[23] Were the broadcaster's guaranteed autonomy, the possibility of confusion would be removed. 'Responsibility', essentially to create a balance against free expression by holding the broadcasters accountable to their public service mission, would unambiguously rest with the Governors as the representatives of the general public. Anyway, what business does the state have, in a modern democracy, claiming 'responsibility' for organs of expression beyond its own information and publicity apparatuses?

The Green Paper's attempt to distinguish between the audience and the general public is a residual whiff of the anti-licence fee argument. But by buying the principle of the licence fee the Government is, as it were, condemned to a *de facto* acknowledgment that the general public are one and the same as the audience which must at any given moment include potential as well as actual viewers and listeners, all of whom are perforce licence holders. This brings us to the third strategic issue: funding.

It is exactly the tax that allows the government to adopt this improper talk of 'responsibility' while also allowing broadcasters to benefit from it as a non-commercial source of funding. A constitutional guarantee would inhibit the dangerous consequences of a tax-funded system. Protection could be afforded by making the level, collection and disbursement of that tax as formulaic as possible.

I offer the above simply by way of illustration of the importance of a fundamental alteration in favour of freedom of expression. This would have consequences not just for the BBC, nor just for broadcasters, but for all the media. On this broad front I would argue that it is time Britain made the great leap forward into the late eighteenth century and acquired a constitution which gave the citizenry rights, including the right to publish or broadcast. The demand for such a right has to be the central agenda item in any meaningful discussion of the future of public service broadcasting.

Notes

[1] *The Future of the BBC: A consultation document*, HMSO, London, November 1992, (Cm 2098) (cited as *The Future*) p25.
[2] *Ibid.*, p19.
[3] *Ibid.*, p39.
[4] *Ibid.*
[5] *Ibid.*, p31.
[6] *Ibid.*, p35.
[7] *Ibid.*, pp11, 34; see also *Broadcasting in the '90s: Competition, Choice and Quality*, HMSO, London, November 1988, (Cm 517) p8.

[8] *Extending Choice: The BBC's Role in the New Broadcasting Age*, BBC, London 1992, (cited as *Extending*), pp28ff.

[9] *Ibid.*, pp45 *et. seq.*

[10] *Ibid.*, p76.

[11] *Ibid.*, p67.

[12] *Ibid.*, pp10 *et. seq.*

[13] *Ibid.*, p12.

[14] *Ibid.*, p14.

[15] Prunier, John et al, *Veronis, Suhler and Associates Communications Industry Forecast*, New York, Veronis, Suhler 1993, p117.

[16] *Ibid.*, p82.

[17] *Extending, op. cit.*, p10.

[18] Graham Murdock, 'Citizens, consumers, and public culture,' in *Media Cultures*, Schroder, (eds.) Michael Skovnand & Kim Christian, Routledge, London 1992, *passim.*

[19] Tom Nairn, 'The Twilight of the British State', *New Left Review*, February-April 1977, *passim.*

[20] John Cain, *The BBC: 70 years of Broadcasting*, BBC, London, p15.

[21] Paddy Scannell, ' "The Stuff of Radio": Developments in Radio Features and Documentaries Before the War', in John Corner (ed.) *Documentary and Mass Media*, Edward Arnold, London 1986, pp7ff.

[22] Cain, *op. cit.*, p111.

[23] *The Future, op. cit.*, 39.

Television, Audiences, Politics

Mike Wayne

This book is primarily concerned with issues and developments in the sphere of production, but processes going on 'behind the screen' impinge on and are affected by what is going on in front of the screen – in other words we must also attend to the question of audiences. Broadcasters and programme makers have paid relatively little attention to the way in which people watch television. They have been concerned with how many people see a programme, rather than the way audiences interact with the images on the screen: what they absorb, what they challenge and what they discard. This is perhaps understandable since the way people watch television is difficult to record or 'prove', nevertheless, some conception of this process is crucial in evaluating the cultural role or 'effect' of television. This absence of analysis has allowed the right to keep a constant threat of censorship hanging over programme content with the essentially élitist claim that viewers will be 'corrupted' or in some way 'led astray' by violent or extreme images (it is always other people who are deemed to be 'vulnerable')[1]. Thus we have moral guardians such as the Broadcasting Standards Council, which monitors representations of violence and sex and concerns itself with matters as universal and easily defined as taste and 'decency'.

The roots of these assumptions and anxieties about the effects of the media can be traced back to a whole range of sociological, political and cultural work done in the early part of this century. What became known as 'the mass society thesis' proclaimed that 'the people', or 'the masses', who were at that time being drawn into the expanding cities, were rootless and cut off from tradition and communities. They were therefore considered to be suggestible and open to manipulation by the media and communications industries that were consolidating themselves into various and powerful oligopolies, like Hollywood. This tradition of thought had left exponents (e.g. the Frankfurt School), liberal exponents (e.g. F.R. Leavis and later Richard Hoggart) and right advocates, whose contemporary descendants are attempting to police television today.

There is a peculiar *disjunction* between these rightist moral guardians and what is actually happening to audiences, courtesy of the global transformation of television by the very market forces which the right supports. With the two additional terrestrial commercial channels initiated in 1956 and 1981, and more strikingly, through the new technologies of satellite and cable, audiences for television can no longer be conceived of as a 'mass' in thrall to a single supplier. Further technological developments on the horizon, such as the displacement of national or regional television schedules by personalized schedules, which could be called up on the telephone and pumped down fibre optic cable, makes the future for our would-be moral guardians look very precarious indeed.[2]

However, the mass society conception of the audience is not the only game in town. There have recently been strong populist challenges to that tradition. Broadly, the argument is that cultural consumers, diverse in terms of class, gender and ethnicity (as opposed to a homogeneous 'mass') are making a plethora of heterogeneous meanings from various symbolic resources (texts), and that these meanings are linked to their own value systems and experiences. It does not take an ironist to see that the largely progressive, leftist roots of this position are in a peculiar *conjunction* with the corporations who insist that developments in delivery systems are going to empower the consumer by giving them more choice. Many questions remain, however, about the desirability of the current and envisaged transformations of television, questions that are often marginalized in the name of an inevitable technological progress.[3]

In this context then, the current populist paradigm for audience studies needs to be approached as critically as 'the mass society thesis'. There is too much at stake to make unqualified endorsements of popular culture and the people who consume it – not least because 'the people' have hardly been invited to participate in the decision-making processes that will continue to transform the 'end product' which they receive. In what follows I will sketch the connections between two left traditions of mass society cultural criticism, looking at their problems but also insisting that they were asking the right questions. I will then look at some recent work in the field of audience research. The key question that needs to be addressed in order to negotiate the twin traps of élitism and populism, is how to reconcile the conflicting claims that, on the one hand, texts have 'effects' and, on the other, that audiences are active participants in the production of meaning. I will finish by looking at the way that the construction and struggle for audiences at the production end has an effect on the texts themselves.

Distance from the Popular: Two Traditions

Theodor Adorno was a key figure in the Frankfurt School. Adorno argued that culture under twentieth century capitalism is just another commodity, indistinguishable from anything else on the production line. Formula, and those clusters of formulas and conventions that we call genres, provides the culture industry with the opportunity to plan and calculate the product for a known, predictable and quantifiable effect. Thus culture becomes broken down into so many interchangeable parts that can be swopped about and assembled according to the market designs of the planners. Far from being the realm of 'escapism', popular culture is an extension of the controls and disciplines which capital exerts in the sphere of production:

> ... mechanization has such power over a man's leisure and happiness, and so profoundly determines the manufacture of amusement goods, that his experiences are inevitably after images of the work process itself ... What happens at work, in the factory, or in the office can only be escaped from by approximation to it in

one's leisure time. No independent thinking must be expected from the audience: the product prescribes every reaction ... Any logical connection calling for mental effort is painstakingly avoided.[4]

Here is an example of Adorno's (dialectical) totalizing method in which the production and consumption of popular culture as a leisuretime pursuit is related to, indeed determined by, the general characteristics of work in advanced capitalist societies. The power of the proposition resides precisely in the way that it locates culture within the totality of society. At the same time we sense how, in Adorno's thinking, all possibilities for resistance are squeezed into oblivion.

There are some interesting analogies between Adorno and the tradition of film theory that emerged in the late 1960s and 1970s. It is against this tradition of film theory rather than the Frankfurt School, that the recent work on television and its audiences has reacted. The central concept for film theory, at least in so far as it referred to the point of reception, was, as Annette Kuhn has pointed out, the spectator rather than the audience.[5] As Kuhn notes, these are not easily reconcilable concepts. The spectator is understood as the position which the viewer is invited, by the text, to occupy in order to make 'best' sense of the text. Of course, the 'best' way of reading a text will be deeply bound up with values and beliefs about the world, and this is particularly evident in the way a text invites us to evaluate a character's motivation and behaviour, whether we are to be sympathetic to them or not, and so on. Since the spectator is an 'effect' of the text, all or most of the determining power in the production of meaning is awarded to the text, with the viewer's role being largely one of taking up their allotted position. Writing in *Screen*, the journal that pioneered this new film theory in Britain, Stephen Heath argued, rightly, that without a theory of textual 'effects', the film becomes

a malleable transparency ... to the determinations of the individual or audience, thus removing in the end all real basis for supporting through political-cultural analysis any film or films against any other or others.[6]

46

Yet a stimulating article on *Jaws*[7] in the 1980s finds Heath, in Frankfurt School fashion, constructing the text and indeed the whole industry of commercial cinema, as a pleasurable and inescapable prison for the spectator (the totality as closed system again). This highlights the difficulty in weighing up the relationship between text/spectator and actual audiences.

Another point of contact between Adorno and film theory of this era is that Adorno's combination of Marxism and psychoanalysis prefigured the renewed interest in these theories that film theory was to show. However these two intellectual traditions and practices have been institutionalized, both have been the inspiration for critiques on the apparent rationality of society, and so it is hardly surprising that mass culture, so evidently integrated with that society, should be seen as complicit with its facade of rationality. For film theory, the concept of the spectator allowed text-based analysis to link up with models of larger general processes, whether social and critiqued from a Marxist perspective, or psychoanalytic and Freudian/Lacanian in understanding. Moreover the period of Adorno's intellectual formation (the 1920s and 1930s) saw the hopes of international revolution in the aftermath of the First World War recede as capitalism consolidated itself. Similarly, as the wave of political radicalism and optimism of the late 1960s and early 1970s receded, intellectuals were left trying to account, as Adorno had done before them, for the role that mass culture played in subverting the historical process of transition (from capitalism to socialism) that Marx had outlined.

Given such historical moments, left intellectuals may be drawn (with the attendant danger of élitism) to those cultures that are produced and circulated outside popular culture, as a stick with which to beat the latter. Adorno, for example, used bourgeois high culture as a standard of cultural resistance, since mass/popular culture, as he saw it, simply supported the status quo.[8] In his comments on film, Adorno again prefigured later positions by arguing that the medium's construction of the perfect *illusion* of the world (immeasurably advanced by the coming of sound), encouraged an uncritical acceptance of that world.[8] In a similar strategy, film theory (and independent film practice) chose to align

47

itself with the anti-bourgeois tradition of modernism. Self-conscious aesthetics foregrounding of the processes of audio-visual production marked their work off from the illusionism of dominant cinema. Yet this alternative mode of consumption was deeply marked by a political ambiguity, pulling simultaneously in conservative and radical directions. On the one hand, the deployment of such self-conscious aesthetics could be read as encouraging a more 'sophisticated' kind of consumption than that demanded by mass culture (the élitist and therefore conservative pull). On the other hand, it could be understood as a mode of consumption which, in being aware of its relationship to the text, was seen to be analogous and contributing to, the raising of consciousness in a political sense.

Engaging with the Popular

Frankfurt School Marxism and the dominant strand of 1970s film theory converge, then, around a set of questions, each of which has the potential to drive theory into an impasse: how to think the relations between culture and society without turning that relationship into a seamless, uncontradictory 'system'; how to think of texts as having an impact on audiences without turning the latter into a passive product of the former; how to adopt a critical distance from the popular without succumbing to bourgeois elitism. That these should remain central issues despite their intractability, is only re-inforced by the historical pattern to be discerned when we turn to consider the pro-popular tradition.

The distance which intellectuals have assiduously constructed between themselves and the popular has occasionally been bridged at those historical moments when the struggle between contending classes can be declared dead by various ideologies of capitalism. Then, new groups of intellectuals or reconstructed members of the older generation, rush to embrace the popular and the people as rational creatures of market capitalism. The 1950s culminated in Daniel Bell's famous book *The End of Ideology*. Admittedly left intellectuals remained wedded to one form or another of the mass society critique (see for example Richard Hoggart's *The Uses Of Literacy*), but there did emerge in reception theory a corollary to Bell's celebration of the market-led, post-industrial, information society which (according to Bell and others) would transcend the class conflicts initiated by the Industrial Revolution. It was known as 'the uses and gratifications theory'. Here, 'information' products such as film and television were approached purely as resources, so that the uses identified by the researcher were assumed to be the product of the audience meeting its own needs.

Today, the brief period of working class and student militancy which eclipsed the 1950s ideologues of capitalist society, recedes, for the moment, from view. As it does so, the process repeats itself; new Daniel Bells emerge to proclaim in one way or another the 'end of history'[10] and to prepare, with a kind of *fin de siècle* delirium, to waltz with consumer capitalism.[11] Only this time the political retreat of the left coincides with the expansion of the media, including publishing, and the expansion of media studies in higher education. Thus the old messages return with an amplified force.

It is in this context of political retreat, that the 1980s has seen a range of audience studies stressing the active role of the social audience (not the passive spectator) in the production of meaning with the day to day texts of popular culture. As we have seen, 1970s film theory constructed its critique around the text/spectator. There is a key question that concerns us in regard to the new enthusiasm for audience research: what political purchase is available on the evidence of audience responses when the meanings of texts are collapsed into the meanings which audiences make of texts?

One immediate consequence of the dissolution of the text as an object of study, is the tendency for the question of politics to get ducked altogether in favour of notions of audience creativity. In *Public Secrets: Eastenders and its Audiences*, David Buckingham stresses the heterogeneity of responses which a sample of young viewers had to the serial. Buckingham's work is in dialogue with the modernist aesthetics which underpinned earlier film theory. However, instead of the valorization of self-conscious texts, he stresses the *viewers'* consciousness of *Eastenders* as a fictional construct, composed of narrative and generic conventions which are acknowledged, rejected and sometimes ignored. Buckingham concludes by summing up the relationship between serial and audiences as a kind of game 'in which viewers themselves are the major participants'.[12] Here Buckingham evokes and appropriates the metaphor (i.e., the game) which is often used to describe the modernist text's invitation to the reader/audience to co-operate in the production of meaning; he imports it into the relationship between popular consciousness and its cultural resources. Buckingham accepts the terms of the debate that dominated 1970s film theory in which the question of realism was equated with illusionism and the 'reality effect'. Having demonstrated the irrelevance of such notions to a television audience who do not (surprise, surprise) mistake the serial for 'reality', a key question is avoided: namely: how do these texts speak to audiences' political experience and understanding of the world?

Essentially, Buckingham's work amounts to a new furrow in the field of uses and gratifications research. The same is true of other contemporary writings on cultural consumption. Hobson's work on *Crossroads* is very similar to Buckingham's,[13] while David Morley's interests move him even further away from the question of the text as he inserts cultural consumption into the wider context of everyday practices in the home.[14] John Fiske focuses specifically on the texts, but he uses a theoretical framework that conceives of television output as being in a state of semiotic flux, thus allowing meanings to be assembled according to the energies and preferences of consumers.[15]

Such audience studies provide empirical evidence that audiences are not inevitably 'looking through' the forms and conventions of culture, that they are aware, or can be aware, of its constructedness and are not naively persuaded of its absolute legitimacy as a 'true image' of the world. However, it is equally true that audience studies, Buckingham's included, continually find the category of 'experience', and therefore some conception of 'the real', to be a measure by which audiences assess representations.[16] The question is then, how do these two different types of criteria, aesthetic criteria (which acknowledge a radical difference between representation and the real) and 'realist' criteria (which assume that some comparison with the real world is part of the process of meaning-making), come together in actual readings?

From the 'old' school of uses and gratifications research, Liebes and Katz have attempted to address this question by mapping audiences' use of cultural knowledge (aesthetic criteria) and lived experience ('realist' criteria) in the consumption of culture.[17] They insist that the sophisticated viewer should be seen as a commuter between aesthetic and 'realist' criteria. In other words they are not interested in simply recording and celebrating the cultural knowledge displayed by audiences. Liebes and Katz's explicit aim is to assess the defensive capabilities and vulnerabilities of audiences to the 'message' of the programme.[18] Yet, although they are concerned with the question of textual 'effects', like Buckingham, they do not discuss the text itself. Is there a contradiction here?

At one point Liebes and Katz argue that an overly aesthetic appreciation of a text is likely to 'lower the barrier to the penetration of unchallenged messages'.[19] The researchers suggest that this is the case with American viewers of *Dallas* for whom the serial is 'pure' entertainment with any sense that the programme might relate to the real world (the 'realist' criteria necessary for the sophisticated viewer) largely subordinate. Yet they do not suggest what the 'message' of *Dallas* is or may be. We then have to ask how such 'penetration', in the case of American viewers *vis-à-vis Dallas*, can be assessed if one deals *only* with the meanings the audience are making. So then, there is no great political purchase available on the evidence of audience responses when the meanings of texts are collapsed into the meanings which audiences make of texts.

Of course it could be argued that *Dallas* has *no* meaning until an audience engages with it. In that case one can no longer work with any notion of texts having effects. This is one reason why we cannot altogether let go of the idea that texts imply a reader/spectator as a necessary device to get them through the process of constructing meaning. It is the gaps and fissures between the implied reader, necessary for the text to have constituted itself, and the real reader or viewer, constituted by a whole range of other historical, social and cultural forces, which is at stake. However, I want to argue that the reader implied by texts may not be the most powerful level at which texts have a determining effect on their audiences. For such an argument, audience research is indispensable, but so too is textual analysis.

Texts, Effects and Audiences

The field of audience studies has provided a wealth of examples which demonstrate the lack of fit between the texts of television and the meaning making activity of audiences. But, as the quote from Stephen Heath earlier reminded us, unless some notion of textual effect is retained, any question of cultural intervention (theoretical or indeed at the level of cultural practice) is jettisoned; one text or set of texts is conceived of as being as good a starting point for audiences as any other. There are two points to be made about the concept of the spectator. Firstly, the spectator positions which texts construct are interpretations which the critic offers rather than objective facts. But secondly, and more importantly, these interpretations are premised on readings which incline towards a holistic understanding of the cultural artefact. The question of how the signifying parts relate to the whole, the totality of the fictional world(s) in question, does not necessarily lead to monolithic readings. On the contrary, it is only by theorizing the text or texts as totalities, that we can understand the character of diverse readings in practice; readings that are generated when audiences resist the wholly integrative logic of the text; readings in which audiences choose to accentuate particular clusters of signs over others, and thus begin to disturb the total organization of signs and meanings which the text offers. But, so that audience studies' preoccupation with the reworking of texts does not then become a version of the uses and gratification model, it must be demonstrated how such reworkings, while breaking with specific spectator positions, fail to transcend the ideological parameters *initiated* by the text. One such parameter may be the relation between the individual and society.

Let us take an example. Valerie Walkerdine has investigated the cultural consumption of films of a single working class family in the domestic context.[20] This is how she explains the husband's obsession with the *Rocky* films:

> fighting is a key term in a discourse of powerlessness, of a constant struggle not to sink, to get rights, not to be pushed out. In that lived historicity fighting is quite specific in its meaning, and therefore not coterminous with what fighting would mean in a professional middle class household.[21]

According to Walkerdine's account, a series of texts that could be read using a left mass culture perspective as celebrating the 'American way', are for this viewer a way of *registering* not effacing, social inequality. What *is* celebrated is not so much America, but the body as a sign of resistance, survival and advancement in a society in which the 'odds' are stacked against you. This viewer's reading is anchored in a more concentrated focus on the body than a textual analysis might have registered if it focused solely on the implied spectator, (on the text as totality). Walkerdine makes it clear that, this is due to the particular intersection of class and gender that underpins this viewer's sense of identity.

To recap the discussion so far, we can make two observations regarding Walkerdine's interpretation of this reading by the *Rocky* fan. Firstly it requires extensive knowledge of *Rocky* as a multiple text phenomenon. This is an example of the aesthetic criteria which Liebes and Katz suggest the sophisticated viewer needs if they are to recognize culture for what it is: a construct, and thus something that can be re-constructed. Secondly, this aesthetic reworking registers a certain dislocation from the world as it is. In other words some comparison between representation and the real is being made. So the *Rocky* fan displays the 'realist' criteria which Liebes and Katz suggest the sophisticated viewer must also deploy.

However, I would suggest that we need to refine the notion of 'realist' criteria still further, for there are two kinds of comparisons to be made between text and 'experience'. We have already identified one kind, that which registers dislocation from the world as it is. But we can also identify another type of comparison, one which places the social world beyond the possibility of change, thus persuading the individual to find their place, albeit grudgingly, within it. And this consciousness is also evident in the *Rocky* fan's reading, and is indeed encouraged by an ideology of personal autonomy which the texts themselves are articulating.

The term ideology, refers, in this context, to the process of imaginary reconciliation of contradictions.[22] An ideology of personal autonomy reconciles the individual to the social by investing the former with the meaning, purpose and significance that the social arena, degraded by the atomizing, fragmenting and alienating effects of late capitalism, can no longer offer. But of course it is an imaginary reconciliation of contradictions because only changes in the social structure can guarantee fulfillment of the personal in genuine and fundamental ways. Thus it is an *ideology* of personal autonomy when the *Rocky* texts offer the body, and the version of masculinity constructed for it, as an adequate response to socio-structural inequalities. The *Rocky* fan is offered a form of social Darwinist individualism (survival of the fittest). This lends the fan's reading of the texts a rather conservative form of resistance in so far as it seems to accept competition as the basis of social relations (hence the appeal of an indestructable masculinity which *Rocky* offers) even though it also recognizes (and this presumably is the class identity coming through) that it is not 'fair' competition.

Walkerdine's research was carried out in Britain, and in the context of a de-regulated television industry sucking in more and more imported, and primarily American, films, it has an added relevance. One can think of other Hollywood films which may elict similar kinds of readings (other Sylvester Stallone or Arnold Schwarzenegger films, for example). The implication is that what is going on at the point of consumption is more complex than simple notions of cultural imperialism can account for. In a similar vein to Walkerdine, Dick Hebdige has discussed how, in the post-war period, American mass culture provided British working-class youths with a means to articulate their resistance to a society in which they were located somewhere near the bottom.[23]

Nevertheless, Walkerdine's research also suggests that, while audience involvement in the production of meaning is theoretically possible and empirically verifiable, this is hardly grounds for complacency. We ought to know from history that the inflection of grievances suffered by 'the people', can be a starting point for reactionary politics as much as for the left. And indeed the social Darwinist ideology evident in *Rocky* made an alarming return to the political agenda on both sides of the Atlantic during the 1980s. The reason for this paradox lies in what Antonio Gramsci, described as the dual consciousness of subordinate classes. Like the *Rocky* fan, workers of all kinds generate conceptions of the world from their practical engagement with it, but these are combined, Gramsci argued, with the ideas and values (social Darwinism, for example) of the ruling classes and their apologists. In the case of the *Rocky* fan, this fissured consciousness is yoked together by a particular ideology of the individual.

The working through of ideologies of personal autonomy by texts is facilitated by an emphasis on the narrative trajectories of individual characters which is one of the most pervasive features of popular culture. It is worth speculating whether the domestic context of consumption for television helps to encourage readings that are less attuned to our social and collective identities. With the prospect of multiple channels, and even the dismantling of scheduling as we know it, the possibilities of confirming a shared experience of television-viewing through oral culture may further diminish, thereby increasing the atomization of audiences and the individualized nature of their readings.

But whatever the future for television, the total individualization of readings is difficult to conceive because, as various philosophers of language have stressed, meaning – including that of individual identity – is always the product of shared experiences and perceptions. The trick of popular culture is to draw on and allude to the social dimensions of signs and meanings and then, in a sleight of hand, fill up those meanings with notions of individual agency and responsibility. It is this tendency which is embedded in the text in a more fundamental way than the specific spectator positions that the text might offer but which the audience can refuse. The distinction is important I think because those studying audiences frequently point out the disjunction between the meaning of the spectator inscribed into the text and what a social audience makes of the text. From there, questions of textual effectivity are rapidly downgraded altogether.[24]

An example from the soap opera *Eastenders* may illustrate the tensions between specific spectator positions, audience readings and, in this case, an entrepreneurial ideology of personal autonomy. The petit-bourgeois class structure of its fictional world – almost every character is self-employed – produces that serial's particular approach to exploring the genre's essential subject: women. Sam's attempts to become a model, Pat's at trying to set up her own taxi service, Sharon's at running a pub, these endeavours all make sense, at least to the women characters, against a background of small-scale entrepreneurial zeal and self-employment by the male characters. Yet these assertions of independence are continually greeted with dismay by the male characters. Not surprisingly for a genre pitched primarily at a female audience, these assertions of independence are frequently achieved, though sometimes with considerable ambivalence on the part of the text. This is particularly so in the case of Sam and Ricky. There is often a strong sense that Sam has transgressed. For example, when she does some topless modelling and the photographs get printed in a magazine, Ricky comes home late and collapses: cue for Sam to find an empty bottle of whisky on him and a copy of the magazine. In another episode, Ricky's elaborate plans to celebrate their wedding anniversary go awry because Sam is too busy on a modelling shoot in and around Albert Square. (Tellingly, the BBC announcer introduced a preview of the same evening's episode with the words, 'Is Sam enjoying her work too much?') In such instances the text appears to be soliciting a spectator position that is disapproving of Sam. However, it seems reasonable to speculate that it would not take too much for women viewers to 'force' another reading, choosing perhaps to focus on Ricky's insecurities as the problem rather than Sam's ambition.

On what basis could such a reading be 'forced' by a hypothetical viewer? At the level of aesthetics it could be argued that there is less pressure on the viewer to align with a particular viewpoint when the narrative is composed of multiple, episodic and loosely interlocking stories. In dominant cinematic narrative, character action (say, a women's 'transgression') immediately produces effects which press for assessment in line with the whole story's strong forward momentum. So, armed with an acquired knowledge of the soap form, and mobilizing their own experience, the adept viewer can reassess the position they are apparently being urged to adopt, in this case, on Sam's ambitions.

Stuart Hall has offered a model for audience studies to use in mapping the politics of audience readings. In an article focusing on news and current affairs, Hall outlined three hypothetical positions that audiences can take up in relation to texts.[25] Firstly, there is the dominant or preferred reading. Here the meanings which the actual audience generates, correspond closely to the spectator posited by the text in the process of its construction. Secondly, there is the negotiated reading in which audiences bring to bear their particular experiences to modify or alter texts. Drawing on Leibes and Katz's work, we can add that sophisticated negotiation also requires the use of aesthetic criteria, which would exploit contradictions between the text's forms and conventions on the one hand, and its preferred readings, as in the already cited *Eastenders* example.

Yet the negotiated reading, Hall argues, still takes place within the 'mental horizon' of the preferred reading. Although it may have a more contradictory relation to the preferred reading, indeed it may break with it at specific and 'local' points, the negotiated reading still takes for granted 'whole sector[s] of relations in a society or culture'.[26] We can relate this to the *Rocky* fan, for example, who finds in the protagonist, the star and the motif of boxing, an image of economic competition as an inevitable fact of life. The hypothetical reading of *Eastenders* already discussed would also fit into this category. At one level the reading exploits the potential contradiction between the pluralistic soap form and specific spectator positions but, as with the *Rocky* fan, it anchors its reading in the individual character. It contests the soap's judgement of Sam, but not the structure of assumptions which systematically offer such judgements across the range of characters. In other words, the viewer may disagree about a specific judgement, or even each and every judgement, but remains complicit with the continual game of judging the shifting behaviour and motivations of characters as individuals.

The third kind of reading outlined in Hall's model is the oppositional kind. This breaks down the organizational assumptions of the text and re-totalizes them within another frame of reference. It is an open question, however, to what extent oppositional readings are possible to sustain in relation to fictional texts. The battery of narrative strategies deployed by fictional texts encourages a far more intense engagement and investment than the news programmes that Hall is writing about. Thus, while one can imagine the viewer 're-totalizing' notions of economic 'efficiency' into a discourse of exploitation and class conflict, it is arguably difficult to see how audiences can consistently perform an analogous feat, with say *Eastenders, and* continue to find it a source of pleasure, something that is 'worth' exchanging scarce leisuretime for. For example, to 're-totalize' the character of Mandy in terms of the lack of welfare structures that have determined her life, cancels out the pleasures of watching her feed her own bitterness with her incessant scheming. If it is the case that to engage with such texts necessarily requires some complicity (even if negotiated) with its ground rules, then there is a debate to be had, and there are things at stake between different kinds of texts and modes of representations. I want to return to this question later.

The Struggle for Audiences

A recent anthology of audience studies concedes in its introduction that,

> The most serious lack in the audience studies presented here is the integration of a political economics perspective.[27]

Yet in the last ten years or so, economic competition for audiences has been growing increasingly intense within British television. The BBC has contradictory obligations to fulfil in this context. It must on the one hand win an audience share large enough to justify the levying of a universal license fee. Yet the BBC must also invest in programmes that may not win massive audience ratings but will demonstrate the Corporation's public service profile (also the basis on which its license fee depends). The latter kind of programmes might include authored drama, documentary and innovative and indeed politicized scheduling such as BBC2's *One World* season and *Black and White in Colour*.

ITV can risk far less with a programme in terms of audience ratings because it is funded on the basis of the airtime it can sell to the advertisers around each programme (or series). But at the same time it has an interest in 'quality' television (that is, programmes that have some sort of prestige value) because these attract sections of the audience the advertisers want to target.

Consumption is intricately wedded to form. ITV's detective series *Inspector Morse* clearly constructs itself as 'quality' drama. The textual marks of this are in its use of location shooting – Oxford, infused with a sense of 'culture' and history – and its protagonist – Morse, the classically cultured and sensitive detective. The series' unusual programme length of two hours also helps to distinguish it from the day-to-day television fare, as do various stylistic touches such as opening straight into the first scene, which is then intercut with the titles. Even these are coded rather differently to the titles of a routine television presentation, with the screen given over entirely to the names of the key players on a black background, as in the opening sequence of a 'serious' feature film. The 'quality' dimensions of *Inspector Morse* are much prized by the advertisers; they ensure the series' popularity amongst the As and Bs, the wealthiest but most infrequent viewers, and thus, for advertisers, the most difficult section of the television audience to target.

Yet these audiences are not captured at the expense of others. The casting of John Thaw and Kevin Whatley helps to draw in a wider socio-economic range of viewers who are familiar with these actors from *The Sweeney* and *Auf Wiedersehen, Pet*. The roles that Thaw (as Morse) and Whatley (as his subordinate/partner, Lewis) play in *Inspector Morse* also rehearse, with comic effect, the high culture/low culture debate, presumably to the mutual satisfaction of socially disparate audiences. Thus there is a careful binding together of audiences to an uncontroversial 'quality' package that exists by marking itself off from the run-of-the-mill television norm; a phenomenon spawned by the same economic rationale that has made the run-of-the-mill norm so prevalent on ITV in the first place.

This cynical packaging of the audience compares unfavourably with the publicly-funded spaces for aesthetic innovation and political combativeness which has attracted writers and film-makers to the BBC for decades. But this small enclave of cultural potential has always marked itself off from the popular heartlands of the mainstream BBC. Popular elements may find themselves appropriated and transformed, as in Dennis Potter's *The Singing Detective* or Troy Kennedy Martin's *Edge Of Darkness*, but while this institutional space is to be defended, the principle of a division of cultural labour between the small creative enclave and the more routine popular programming helps to consign the realm of the popular to conformity and conservatism.

In the heartlands of the popular, innovation is tolerated to the extent it will construct a new market for the product. A residual public service ethos was allowed to inform *Eastenders* in so far as it combined social realism with the soap genre. However, the success of the serial as it captures a suitably large audience (peaking at 23 million within a year of its launch),[29] means that it becomes a victim of its own success. Its central place in the BBC's battle for ratings makes it unable, having won a large and loyal audience, to take risks with it, to develop itself and its audience.

Does it matter? I would argue that it does because it undermines *Eastenders'* progressive liberal intentions. For example, the conventions of speech, so central to the soap genre, have become so fixed and limited that characters do not have to confront the issues posed, they merely alternate between listening sympathetically or not, or talking sympathetically or not. A kind of ping-pong tension is thus set up. For example, when Mark Fowler tells his parents that he is HIV positive, their difficulty in understanding this, once established, is merely repeated again and again. Pauline quickly reconciles herself to Mark and acts as an intermediary between Mark and Arthur. The resolution of their more protracted estrangement is not qualitatively different because, as with Pauline, Arthur eventually adopts a paternal posture, i.e., they will stick with Mark because he is their son. For all the arguments between the characters there is no sense of a learning process about the issue of AIDS. Arthur and Pauline's initial response that Mark must have done something 'wrong', for example, is never re-evaluated; yet again, popular culture frustrates its own potential.

Some might argue that to ask for more is merely a residual élitism. Yet to accept popular culture as it is, is to miss the potentialities which make it dynamic. For example, in *Eastenders* there are often glimpses of other conventions and forms. In one episode, a beauty contest at the Queen Victoria pub gathers all the main female characters together in one room. The fixed convention that first one character is unreasonable, then relents but, too late! now the other character will not listen, etc., is abandoned. Here, in an unusually long scene the characters recall their past, particularly their past relations with men. The essential ingredient of the genre is still there – talking, gossiping, exchanging information – but it is momentarily broadened by the device of bringing them all together and using a more *vérité* style of camerawork. For a moment then, we glimpse a rather stronger construction of collective identity among the women than the serial usually allows. Such glimpses demonstrate that there are alternatives that could be explored and developed, but this would mean complicating the serial's relationship with its audience, that is, thinking of its audience in terms other than as a share of the market.

This line of argument, that mechanization or standardization blunts critical consciousness, is somewhat Adornoesque in spirit. But Adorno had such a monolithic view of cultural industries that it was difficult for him to identify difference when it did occur, or think how gaps in the machinery of production might be exploited. Despite the unpromising implications of much of the government's broadcasting legislating, the state of flux in the industry presents opportunities as well as problems for programme makers. If *Inspector Morse* and its successor, *Cracker*, represent a middlebrow synthesis of popular and 'quality' programming, there does seem to be some scope for reworking staple popular genres in more complex directions (such as *Between The Lines*). The pivotal genre for popular television schedulers – the soap – is surely ripe for just such a reworking. As a practical suggestion ...

Imagine a soap that ran for a fixed, predetermined length of time, say six months. This would help to distance it from the pressures and definitions of being 'popular' which currently hold sway over

British soaps. For example, it would open up the possibility of locating the action in the recent past, rather than being coterminous with the moment in which it is viewed (and extending interminably into the future as part of the broadcasters' audience-getting strategies). A particular historical moment, perhaps one that has been subject to ideological closure, say the 1970s, could be prized apart for re-investigation, providing an opportunity to relate day-to-day experience to its social context, using news footage, popular music of the time and so on. In the tightly circumscribed, hermetically sealed community that *Eastenders* deals with, Rachel's narrative trajectory is symptomatic of just how resistant the typical 'soap' world is to acknowledging a wider society. Rachel was the only main character to work outside Albert Square (in higher education), but lost her job to be assimilated fully into the petit-bourgeois world as a worker in the cafe and finally as a market-stall trader. By contrast, the distance implied by a re-assessment of a historical period would allow explicitly political issues to be addressed, and in a rather more profound way than simply showing canvassers at election time, urging people to vote for their party. The links, however, between past and present, or near present, could be established through a flashback structure (although probably not subjectively motivated given the genre's focus on more than one or two characters). In fact all these formal strategies are mobilized by a Brazilian soap called *Rebellious Years* which is both political and massively popular.

Conclusion

My argument has been structured around two contesting traditions of thinking about popular culture. Problems within the mass culture tradition are more than balanced by the blind spots of pro-popular traditions which come through very strongly in audience studies. Here, there has been a tendency to conceive the popular as a realm of cultural self-making where 'the people' reconstruct their identities and their sense of place in the world at will. Thus questions of power and ideology are suppressed by methods which celebrate audience creativity and/or dissolve the text as an object with any effectivity.

I have attempted to sketch how the intellectual course of audience studies has been doubly determined, both internally as audience studies try to come to terms with perceived weaknesses of previously dominant intellectual models, and externally by the historical and political conditions in which they emerge. The external conditions in which television finds itself as it approaches the millenium are going to exert powerfully determining forces on popular culture and its audiences. An intellectual tradition that cannot develop the arguments to challenge these forces – and I would suggest that a theory that is consumer-led is just such a tradition, will find its own agenda shaped by those forces. The key question of how to engage critically with the popular in a way that does not dismiss it or the audience, remains. But it is a question that can only be explored by relating audiences to text(s) and relating both of these back to the production context which, in the long run, defines the popular and its audiences.

Notes

[1] G. Pearson, 'Falling Standards: A Short, Sharp History of Moral Decline' in *Video Nasties: Freedom and Censorship in the Media*, M. Barker (ed), Pluto Press, London 1984.
[2] J. Freedland, The *Guardian*, Saturday, 1 January 1994, pp 10-11.
[3] As Raymond Williams warned they would be back in the early 1970s. See his *Television: Technology and Cultural Form*, Routledge, London 1990.
[4] T.W. Adorno and M. Horkheimer, 'The Cultural Industry: Enlightenment as Mass Deception' in, *Mass Communications and Society*, J. Curran, Gurevitch, J. Woolacott (eds.), Open University, London 1977, p 361.
[5] A. Kuhn, 'Women's Genres' in *Screen*, Volume 25, Number 1, 1984.
[6] S. Heath, *Screen*, Volume 19, Number 3 Autumn 1978, p104.
[7] See Stephen Heath's article, 'Jaws, Ideology and Film Theory', in *Movies and Methods Volume 2*, Bill Nichols (ed), University of California Press, London 1985, pp 509-514.
[8] See E. Lunn's chapter on Adorno in *Marxism and Modernism*, Verso, London 1985.
[9] T.W. Adorno and M. Horkheimer, *op. cit.*, p 353-354.
[10] F. Fukuyama, *The End Of History and the Last Man*, Hamish Hamilton, London 1992.
[11] See C. Norris's critique of Baudrillard, and postmodernism generally, in C. Norris, *Uncritical Theory: Postmodernism, Intellectuals and the Gulf War*,

Lawrence & Wishart, London 1992.

[12] D. Buckingham, *Public Secrets: Eastenders and its Audience*, BFI, London 1987, p 204.

[13] D. Hobson, *Crossroads*, Methuen, London 1982.

[14] D. Morley, *Family Television: Cultural Power and Domestic Leisure*, Comedia, London 1986.

[15] J. Fiske, 'Moments of Television: Neither Text nor Audience' in, *Remote Control: Television, Audiences and Cultural Power*, E. Seiter, H. Borcher, G. Kreutzner, E.M. Warth, Routledge, London 1991, pp 56-78.

[16] For example, Paul Willis, leading an ethnographic study into the consumption of television, fashion and music, finds that: 'It is true that most television was judged in our discussion groups by criteria relating to realism. But this does not imply interpretive laziness or vulnerability to realist 'ideologies'. The exercise of realist criteria requires the active work of comparison and, ironically and contradictorily, a full working knowledge of the difference between reality and representation.' See *Moving Culture*, Calouste Gulbenkian Foundation, London 1990, p 28. Like Buckingham, however, Willis stresses one side of the equation (meaning-making as creative game) over questions relating to the politics of knowledge being mobilized.

[17] T. Liebes and E. Katz, 'On the Critical Abilities of Television Viewers', in *Remote Control, op. cit.*, pp 204-222.

[18] *Ibid.*, p 219.

[19] *Ibid.*, p 218.

[20] V. Walkerdine, 'Projecting Fantasies: Families Watching Films', unpublished paper, University of London 1986.

[21] Quoted by D. Morley, 'Changing paradigms in audience studies' in *Remote Control, op. cit.*, p 21.

[22] T. Eagleton, *Ideology, an Introduction*, Verso, London 1991, provides an excellent history of the concept of ideology and the diverse and often conflicting meanings it has had.

[23] D. Hebdige, *Hiding in the Light*, Comedia/Routledge, London 1988.

[24] See I. Ang, 'Wanted: Audiences, On the Politics of Empirical Audience Studies,' in *Remote Control, op. cit.*, pp98-99.

[25] S. Hall, 'Encoding and Decoding' in S. Hall, D. Hobson, A. Lower and P. Willis (eds), *Culture, Media, Language*, Unwin Hyman, London 1980.

[26] *Ibid.*, p 137.

[27] E. Seiter, H. Borcher, G. Kreutzner, E.M. Warth, Introduction, *Remote Control, op. cit.*

[28] G. Murdock, 'Authorship and Organisation' in *Screen Education*, Number 35, Summer 1980.

[29] D. Buckingham, *op. cit.*, p 23.

Programmes for Black Audiences

Thérèse Daniels

The history of programmes for black audiences on British television shows that the demands of black viewers, media workers and campaigning groups often conflict with those of channel controllers, the broadcasting authorities and parliament. I would argue that this position is hardly likely to improve, and is indeed more likely to deteriorate in the de-regulated television world of the future. However, any discussion of the future should consider the lessons of the past. In this chapter I will look at the evolution of black programmes since their earliest appearance on British television in the 1960s. In doing so, I want to locate the emergence of institutional provision for black audiences in the wider context of the race relations policies of the past thirty years, in an attempt to clarify the concepts of race, culture and integration on which the provision of black programmes has been based. I will, however, concentrate the discussion on the 1980s, since it was during this decade that the conflict between lobbyists and institutions was at its height.

Black Representation: The First Thirty Years

British television's initial response to post-war black settlement was slow and unco-ordinated. From 1946, when BBC television resumed transmission after closing down for the war, until the mid-1950s, there was little representation of black settlers on British television. The majority of programmes featuring black people showed American entertainers, had an anthropological theme, or were about the colonies.[1] The limited range and quality of programming was a reflection of the infancy of the medium; the television service lacked the technology and finance needed to make, for example, weekly domestic current affairs programmes or drama serials. It also lacked a clear commitment from BBC management, whose main interest was still with radio.[2]

From 1951, when the television service was re-organized, the range and quality of programmes improved. As the decade wore on, and black immigration became an increasingly contentious political issue, the black British population began to be explored on television. Studio discussions, documentaries and dramatic productions examined the troubled state of race relations. Black entertainers from the Caribbean and Africa were seen alongside the Americans. Human interest series and slots in daytime women's programmes gave people from various settler communities the opportunity to explain their way of life to (white) British viewers. There were sporadic opportunities for black voices to be heard in drama, with the production of plays by writers such as Errol John, Sylvia Winters, Horace James and Jan Carew. Educational strands dealt with issues such as the history of British imperialism, contemporary racism and cultural difference.[3]

However, although programme-makers were beginning to include black people in the content of television output, they had not yet begun to address black people as viewers. These early programmes were very much an attempt to represent or explain black communities to a white audience. It was not until the 1960s that television first began to provide programmes specifically for black audiences. These programmes were not so much concerned with giving black people a voice, as with providing them with a service. Asian settlers were considered to be most in need and the needs that were identified were for tuition in the English language, and general information on settling into British society. *Apna Hi Ghar Samajhiye*, which began on 10 October 1965, was designed to teach the English language, and was transmitted both on BBC1 and on radio on Sunday mornings. *Nai Zindage Naya Jeevan* began, also on Sunday mornings, on 24 November 1968, with *Apna hi Ghar*

Samajhiye moving to Wednesdays. *Nai Zindage Naya Jeevan* continued broadcasting until 1982.

Early 'ethnic minority' programmes were very different in concept from those that were to appear in the late 1970s. They were shaped by the prevailing politics of race, and the liberal consensus under which many institutions then operated. Liberal discourse did not speak in terms of black people having the rights of access to, or control over, institutions. Rather, it argued that cultural differences were often the source of intolerance and conflict on both sides of the racial divide.[4] The programmes for Asian settlers – the group which, among the 'Commonwealth immigrants', was felt to be most different – were an attempt to ease their transition into British society.

Campaigns Against Racism in the Media

Increasingly in the post-war years, and especially during the 1970s, a number of arguments were raised by black viewers, media workers, academics and campaigning groups expressing dissatisfaction with media representations of black people.[5] These complaints, and the political events of the 1970s and early 1980s, led eventually to the provision of a different kind of black programming. The media came to be seen as a source of oppression and site of conflict, along with other state institutions, in black struggles.

These were complaints about many aspects of the portrayal of black people. In television, infrequent but stereotypical representation was said to be the norm. Monitoring of television output showed that, excluding the coverage of foreign affairs and American programmes, there was very little representation of black people on British television. Where they did appear they were seldom in leading, or even speaking parts. If they were in leading roles they were often in problem-centred race relations dramas, or in situation comedies such as *Love Thy Neighbour*, which, though very popular, was criticized for its potentially damaging effect on race relations. It was felt that black people often appeared in a limited number of roles which were consistent with commonly held racist stereotypes. They would be seen doing menial jobs, such as those of bus conductor, hospital ancillary worker, street cleaner or factory hand, they would feature in light entertainment or sports programmes, or they would be criminals involved in illegal immigration, prostitution or robbery.[6]

In terms of drama, black actors often voiced their frustration at the narrow roles available to them in television and the theatre. They were rarely cast in classical or historical plays. Leading parts were usually only in the context of problematic race relations. They were routinely denied parts which were not specifically written as black characters.[7] One solution was to set up black theatre companies, but this did not solve the problems of representation on television.

A third source of dissatisfaction with the industry was raised by the black people who sought to work within it. Very little of television's output before the late 1970s was produced, directed or presented by black people. Reporters and presenters such as Barbara Blake and Trevor MacDonald, scriptwriters such as Michael Abbensetts, Mustafa Matura and Dilip Hiro and directors such as Horace Ove were exceptions. Away from the television industry, in the economically precarious black independent film sector and in print journalism, black practitioners had to struggle to develop their careers or even to work at all. Many of these people wanted access to television. Mainstream programming was difficult to penetrate for anybody not of the middle-class, university-educated prototype. For those black practitioners who saw working in the media as an extension of political activism, who wanted to make programmes that would address their own and black people's political concerns, and who were not interested in working in existing formats, access was virtually non-existent.

A potential opportunity for black practitioners to gain a steady foothold in the industry was recognized when proposals were aired for a fourth television channel. The Annan Report of 1977 suggested that the new channel be wholly different in character from existing BBC and IBA channels. There were two proposals in particular which offered some hope that the new channel would provide a space for black voices and satisfy the demands of black audiences. First, it was proposed that the channel's output should emphasise diversity and new ideas. A new authority, which the report termed the Open Broadcasting Authority (OBA), would control the channel. Second, this new authority would not itself make programmes but would commission them from existing ITV companies and, most importantly, from other independent producers. The role of independent producers was stressed as a means of ensuring diversity.[8]

The intense lobbying of government that followed these proposals included efforts by the Campaign Against Racism in the Media, the Commission for Racial Equality[9] and others to ensure that the interests of black audiences were adequately addressed. The structure which eventually emerged as a result of the Broadcasting Act 1980 placed the fourth channel under the authority of the Independent Broadcasting Authority (IBA). This was a disappointment to the campaigning groups that had lobbied for the OBA. On the whole, however, those groups with a primary interest in race were more concerned with content than with structure, and here, at least, although there was room for scepticism, hopes had not been dashed. The new channel had a duty to appeal to 'tastes and interests not generally catered for by ITV' and 'to encourage innovation and experiment in the form and content of programmes'.[10] It was these two clauses which gave campaigners grounds on which to argue that black programmes should figure strongly in the schedules, and that they should be made by black independent production companies.

Meanwhile, in the interim before Channel 4 began broadcasting, the opportunities within the existing industry for black media workers were marginally improved. This resulted from the independent ITV companies revamping their schedules in anticipation of the franchise reallocations due in 1980. Among other things, these regional companies decided to use off-peak slots to improve their community programmes. For the London area, London Weekend Television (LWT), whose Head of Factual Programmes was John Birt, produced a short series aimed at young black people entitled *Babylon* (1979). Birt then set up the London Minorities Unit which produced a number of series aimed at different minority audiences, including black people, gays and the elderly. *Skin* was a 30-minute documentary series which concentrated on the political concerns of both Afro-Caribbean and Asian communities. Executive producer Jane Hewland described LWT's minority programmes as having two equally important tasks:

> One was to satisfy the *minority groups* themselves that their concerns were being fairly reported, the other was to inform the *majority* audience and to dispel the ignorance and prejudice against them. Our programmes about blacks had also to interest and concern the white audience. Our programmes about gays had to do the same for straight viewers, and so on.[11]

These were not, therefore, programmes intended to be accountable primarily to their respective minority audiences. However, there was at least some awareness of the issue of accountability which had not previously been institutionalized in programming.

Skin's overriding concern with racism, and its treatment of the common concerns of both the Afro-Caribbean and Asian communities was a reflection of racial politics of the late 1970s. The heyday of multiculturalism was yet to come. These were years in which the National Front was a significant political force, both on the streets and in electoral politics. In the latter case, their strength was in galvanizing the Conservative Party into playing the race card yet again, with the debate which culminated in the British Nationality Act 1981. Racism in policing, housing, education, employment and other areas united many Afro-Caribbean and Asian people.[12]

Channel 4 was due to begin broadcasting in the autumn of 1982. The Channel Four Company came into operation on 1 January 1981, and its Board of Directors began the appointment of Commissioning Editors. The fact that black programming was built into the structure was a victory; there would be a Commissioning Editor for Multicultural Programmes. Under this generic title, black representation would be assured. This would not preclude commissions from other editors.

However, the many disappointments that followed this initial gain highlighted the fact that Channel 4, for all its seemingly radical potential, was, in one respect, just like the other channels: it was answerable to a broadcasting authority which in turn was accountable to Parliament. While viewers were the rationale for its existence, it was not *ultimately* accountable to them. Certain campaigners clearly felt that it should have been subject to much greater community control, but that was neither promised nor implied in either the Broadcasting Act 1980 or in Channel 4's terms of reference. Quite apart from the technical problems of how community control and accountability could democratically operate, the history of public service television in Britain suggests that *relative autonomy* is the only condition under which a state-licenced broadcasting authority is likely to exist.[13]

That the black 'community' would not be given control was underlined during 1982 when Sue Woodford, formerly a producer/director with Granada's *World in Action*, was appointed Commissioning Editor for Multicultural Programmes. There was fury when, after considering a number of bids for black current affairs programmes, Woodford commissioned LWT to fill the slot. The regular current affairs series would be the Channel's black flagship, taking up the bulk of the multicultural programmes budget. The award of the commission to a major ITV company was hardly likely to provide the black perspective that campaigners had sought. Even less would it provide the foothold within the industry that some black independent producers, such as the newly-formed Black Media Workers' Group, felt was their right. Woodford's justification for commissioning LWT was that there were very few experienced television producers and directors among the black population in this country.[14] A major series such as this required a company capable of delivering the work on time, to budget and to the standards required. LWT was an established ITV company, capable of meeting professional requirements, and had proved that it could address black interests. *Skin* had allowed talented but inexperienced black people to learn from the experience of white programme-makers, thereby creating for the future a pool of skilled black practitioners. Woodford's argument did not succeed in persuading her most vocal critics, who kept up their attack on her commissions for the remainder of her tenure.

71

Thus, from the very start, Channel 4's black programming was marked by bitter feuding and controversy. Although the volume of black criticism diminished during the 1980s, the underlying dissatisfaction with the institution never did. Because of the particular circumstances in which expectations were raised, it was mainly 'black', as opposed to Asian, activists who loudly and consistently expressed their grievances. Significantly, this controversy never affected black programming on other channels. Channel 4's main rival, BBC2, never faced such attacks, principally because the BBC was never expected to deliver its programming to the black independent sector, or to bypass the Board of Governors and suddenly become accountable to and controlled by the communities. Channel 4 became the subject of false expectations.

Two presenters on *Skin*, Trevor Phillips and Samir Shah, were chosen as producers of the new series, with Jane Hewland as Executive Producer. By now they had come to regard *Skin*'s attempt to address both Afro-Caribbean and Asian communities in one programme as problematic, as was its task of having to take account of a white audience. Their approach was in keeping with the philosophy behind multicultural policies that were being developed elsewhere, particularly in local government, as a response to the urban violence of 1981. In these policies the ideals of cultural diversity in conditions of enlightenment, education and celebration, which were actually proposed in the 1960s, were coming to fruition. Central government was concentrating on crisis management in the form of increased spending on the Urban Programme and increased police training in riot control and community relations. Local authorities were struggling to improve their own employment practices and service delivery, and also to educate their white communities about the effects of racism. In the spirit of the Scarman report[15], their conceptualization of the needs of the black communities became ethnically specific. Each ethnic minority had particular needs based on its language, religions, customs and so on.

The LWT producers of Channel 4's black programmes felt that the common experiences of racism was not enough to justify the two groups being lumped together for all purposes; to do so was to suggest that the groups had no history or identity of their own but existed only in relation to white people. Also, to continue this common treatment would limit the new programmes to the exploration of racism and would preclude coverage of other areas of black life, such as arts and entertainment.[16] Thus it was decided to alternate the weekly hour-long slot which Channel 4 was allocating to black audiences between Afro-Caribbean (or as they were now being termed 'black') and Asian viewers. It was decided to adopt a studio-based magazine format with a studio audience in both cases. The programmes were entitled *Black on Black* and *Eastern Eye*.

Shortly before *Black on Black* was due to be transmitted, the BBC launched a pre-emptive strike with *Ebony*. Earlier in 1982, soon after the announcement of Channel 4's programmes, the BBC had revamped and restructured the long-running *Naya Zindage Naya Jeevan*. Retitled *Asian Magazine*, the new format was designed to match the proposed structure of *Eastern Eye*. The BBC thereby signalled that it was not going to let Channel 4 walk away with all the prizes for innovation and racial awareness.

Like *Black on Black*, *Ebony* was a studio-based magazine but without the former's studio audience. It was shown weekly, rather than fortnightly, although programmes were only thirty minutes long, and it was limited to two eight-week runs per year. This gave it a lower profile than *Black on Black*, despite its peak-time showing. With hindsight it may be argued that this was probably something of a blessing. The series lacked the sense of anti-climax which heralded Channel 4's programmes. Perhaps this was why it did not at any time suffer the furore that dogged *Black on Black*. Indeed, rather than invite such a possibility, the producers and presenters went out of their way to stress that the series was not being targeted at black viewers:

> Our target audience is as large as we can get on BBC2 in the early evening. The subject matter is black and there to attract as many black viewers as it can, but we're not excluding whites. They should get from it what they want to.[17]

Black audiences generally expressed greater satisfaction with *Black on Black* than with *Ebony*. *Black on Black*, with its studio audience, was able to involve its audience in the production. The monologues by Victor Romero Evans playing the character Moves were much enjoyed. Conversely *Ebony* was often described being remote and too concerned with professionalism. However, both series were criticized for the shallowness which derived from their magazine formats, and the lack of depth in their treatment of important issues.[18]

Farrukh Dhondy was appointed Channel 4's new Multicultural Commissioning Editor in 1984. His background as a playwright, journalist, member of the Black Theatre Co-operative, former political activist and member of the *Race Today* collective, gave him much of the legitimacy which his predecessor never gained. It seemed likely that he would be able to work more effectively with black media workers than had Sue Woodford.

Dhondy announced that *Black on Black* and *Eastern Eye* would be commissioned for the last time during 1985. Despite all the attacks which had been made since they were first commissioned, there was some consternation at their being axed. Giving his reasons for the change, Dhondy cited the need to develop the current affairs output and the desire to place the responsibility for production in the hands of a black independent production company.[19] Once again the hopes of black producers were raised.

They were dashed when the commission for a weekly, hour-long series, which again would hold flagship status and require much of the multicultural programmes budget, was given to *Bandung Productions*. The directors of this company were Darcus Howe, one of Dhondy's former colleagues at *Race Today*, and political activist and writer Tariq Ali. Once again the black independent producers who had fought for the commission were furious. They argued that Dhondy was helping his friends and choosing a company which had no track record in the film or television industries.

However, the criticisms that were made of the LWT programmes – that their magazine format was shallow and haphazard, that they divided the black communities, and that they were produced by a mainstream independent – were dealt with at a stroke by *Bandung File*. The series adopted a documentary format, with fewer issues covered during the sixty minutes of airtime. Issues of relevance to the different ethnic groups which made up 'the black communities' were covered under a single umbrella. And *Bandung Productions* was an independent, black-led company.

Bandung File won praise in the quality national press.[20] However it did not please those viewers who, whatever the critics said, had enjoyed the LWT programmes, or at least felt that they spoke to ordinary people. For them *Bandung File* was too highbrow. In fact, the series attracted a largely white, middle-class audience. Since its last appearance in 1989 Channel 4's black current affairs slot has been filled by different companies under the strand title *The Black Bag*.

The Advantages and Disadvantages of Black Programming

The arguments for and against the provision of separate black programmes have by now been well rehearsed.

The arguments in favour of provision are that they provide an opportunity for the positive portrayal of black people, they guarantee funds and airtime for black voices to be heard, they provide a market for black independent producers, and they are a point of entry for black people to the major broadcasting institutions.

However, there is no guarantee that these favourable outcomes will result. First, by no means all black practitioners are interested in producing 'positive images'. Television dramas from writers like Mike Phillips, Hanif Kureishi and Farrukh Dhondy have produced an angry critical response from some sections of the black community. Speaking about the reception of his BBC drama serial *King of the Ghetto* (1986), Farrukh Dhondy has said that, as a writer, he is not interested in 'protecting the image of the community':

> [it] is, in a sense, an absurd enterprise. However, it has developed into a pseudo-science nowadays, with people saying things like 'Let's have positive images'. When Mrs Thatcher wanted a positive image of her government, she didn't ask a novelist or a television writer to do it, she hired Saatchi and Saatchi. But now

we have people who are posing as writers and protectors of the community's image and they are no better than public relations salespersons. There's no harm in that as such. If indeed there is a need for such a function, they ought to be paid handsomely for it. But, in my view, it is not the function of creative writing or film-making to indulge in that sort of activity.[21]

Positive images aside, the content and angle of some programmes have laid them open to charges of scandalous, and even racist, portrayal that is no better than that of the mainstream:

Examples include *Panorama*'s 'Underclass in Purdah' which informed us that British Muslims were largely pimps and drug dealers. The BBC's *All Black* and Channel 4's *Black Bag* series have overwhelmingly concentrated on stories about black pimps, rent boys, drug dealers and thugs.[22]

Clearly, there are no guarantees that the content of black programmes will be any different from that which is offered by the mainstream. An unfavourable response attracts charges that certain black people wish to censor the discussion of unpleasant truths, which implies that black people as a whole are unable to develop a mature response to art.

Second, there are those who argue that the guarantee of a voice and funding also has its disadvantages; black programming can be seen as a ghetto. This view is based on the belief that programmes targeted at black audience will not necessarily have any effect on the rest of television. Only black audiences will take any notice of them. Mainstream programmes will not draw on them or be affected by their existence to any significant degree. The people who produce and present them will find it difficult to develop their careers and gain wider expertise, because their experience will not be taken seriously by the mainstream media.

In fact, history provides little evidence that black programmes have become ghettos, either in terms of their effects on other programmes or on the careers of the people who work on them. Trevor Phillips and Samir Shah have reached executive positions within LWT and the BBC respectively. Others too have gone on to work in the mainstream. There is also now a black presence in many non-black programmes. Black programmes as a whole have evolved to the point where they are not spoken of principally in terms of black audiences. Programmes are, rather, described as being *about* black issues, or as representing 'black perspectives'. The audience is seen as being anybody who is interested in the issues.

The third reservation about black programming is that, whilst it does provide a market for black independent producers, there is no guarantee that black programmes will be produced by black-led companies. The arguments over commissions which dominated Sue Woodford's tenure have continued under Farrukh Dhondy, who has spiritedly defended his decisions and dismissed his critics. He appears unruffled by the arguments of members of the black independent lobby. He argues that he has commissioned a large number of independent producers.

This is true; under both Sue Woodford and Farrukh Dhondy other black independent producers have won commissions. Since 1990 these producers have also been able to offer their work to the BBC, who are now required to commission at least 25 per cent of their original television programmes from independent companies. At Channel 4 they have secured contracts from, in the main, the Arts, Drama and Independent Film editors. Indeed this last department provides some of the funding which has maintained the subsidised independence of black workshops such as the *Black Audio Film Collective, Sankofa, Retake, Ceddo* and others. However, for those independent production companies outside the workshop movement, who have not received large commissions, economic survival has been precarious. The independent sector has provided steady employment for relatively few groups. The process of more secure white-led companies employing black professionals to work on their commissions has continued, and even increased since *Bandung File* ended its run in 1988.

Finally, it is true that there is now greater access to television institutions than ever before. There are a number of training schemes, bursaries and fellowships which support the training of black people for various jobs. These go some way towards mitigating the past racism of the industry, but once again there is no guarantee of the effect this will have on output. While it is unlikely that black media workers will help to produce the stereotypes of yesteryear, there is no certainty that they will want to make committed, interventionist programmes. Indeed, they might want to work on breakfast television. It is also likely that the institutions will favour university-educated, career-minded blacks over community activists.

However, individuals and campaigning groups have often argued that black people must gain entry to the boardrooms of society's institutions. It is counterproductive to attack black media workers who wish to work in the mainstream. Their right to do so must be defended at the same time as seeking access for radical and committed work.

Nevertheless there will still be limits to the potential for such work. Public service broadcasting channels are answerable to their governing bodies, which are in turn accountable to parliament. They must necessarily apply control over their programmes. Channel 4 is intended to be more innovative than the others, but it still has to satisfy the ITC's interpretation of its duties. To hope that state-licensed television will provide black control and accountability, and programmes that are uncompromisingly critical of our political system is simply not realistic.

Public Service Versus the Market Place

The audience for black current affairs programmes since their inception has been about half a million viewers. Such an audience size might not be enough to interest advertisers should the market be called upon to play a greater part.

The Broadcasting Act 1990 makes provision for the further development of local television services. Local delivery licences will be awarded by competitive tender. As with 'community interest' radio stations, services could be aimed at black audiences. Since income would be dependent on advertising, the size of the communities would affect the viability of such enterprises. Even if such a development occurred, large established companies would again have advantages over small black independents in winning a licence. Similar commercial considerations govern cable television, where multinational companies would have greater economic power than British black independents.

So far it has been the public service ideal which has allowed black programming to develop, whether on Channel 4 or on BBC2. The argument that broadcasters have a *duty* to cater to minority interests has given black audiences the grounds on which to talk in terms of rights. Both BBC2 and Channel 4 programmes have thus far operated under conditions of subsidy, either from the BBC licence fee or from ITV revenues. Channel 4 is now having to raise its own advertising revenue, and the BBC has for several years faced threats to its future. If the BBC survives after 1996 it will probably have to look to its audience figures and deliver more 'popular' programmes. If public service, as practised so far, has disappointed black audiences and media workers in the past, the market-led philosophy of the 1990s will not make things any better.

The discussion about the future of black programming has involved groups such as the Commission for Racial Equality, black media workers, channel controllers, academics and viewers. The demands which they make often do not deal with what is possible given unpleasant economic realities.

It is not possible to predict whether in future, local or national television, cable and satellite will be able to deliver enough black programmes to satisfy the interests of a diverse population. If ever there ever was a homogeneous black community, there is no longer such a thing. Differences of gender, sexuality, religion and social class are rendering the concept of 'the black community' increasingly problematic.[23] The mixed reception given to black programmes so far, and to films such as *My Beautiful Laundrette*, *Handsworth Songs*, *The Passion of Remembrance*, *Young Soul Rebels* and others, shows this. All of the independent films mentioned were criticized for not being 'representative' enough. It was argued that they, in their various ways, did not reflect the 'reality' of the lives of most black people.[24]

It is almost impossible to accurately to reflect the lives of an increasingly diverse population within a single production. In addition, there are increasing numbers of black artists who do not want to do so. They wish to explore other avenues. Their innovative work will inevitably create offence in some quarters, but it is not in the interests of the development of black art to suppress such work. It seems unlikely that there will be room for everybody in the marketplace, but this is what we must strive for.

Notes

[1] The history of black representation in the early years of television is discussed in the BBC documentary *Black and White in Colour: Television, Memory, Race*, part 1, director Isaac Julien, first broadcast in June 1992. The publications which accompany the broadcast are Jim Pines (ed), *Black and White in Colour: Black People in British Television Since 1936*, British Film Institute, London 1992, and T. Daniels, *Black and White in Colour*, BBC Education, London 1992.

[2] Asa Briggs, *The BBC: The First 50 Years*, Oxford University Press, Oxford 1985.

[3] See references under note 1 above.

[4] In the then Home Secretary Roy Jenkins's oft-quoted phrase, government policy should encourage 'equal opportunity, accompanied by cultural diversity, in an atmosphere of mutual tolerance'. Quoted in J. Solomos, *Race and Racism in Britain*, Macmillan, London 1993, p 86.

[5] See the history of the Campaign Against Racism in the Media in P. Cohen and C. Gardner, *It Ain't Half Racist Mum: Fighting Racism in the Media*, Comedia, London 1982.

[6] P. Hartmann and C. Husband, *Racism and the Mass Media*, Davis Poynter, London 1974; Commission for Racial Equality *Television in a Multi-Racial Society*, Commission for Racial Equality, London 1982.

[7] Thomas Baptiste, *The Case for Integrated Casting in the British Theatre*, unpublished paper, British Actors' Equity Association, February 1978, quoted in Commission for Racial Equality, *Television in an Multi-Racial Society*.

[8] Lord Annan, *Report of the Committee on the Future of Broadcasting*, HMSO, London, March 1977, (Cmnd 6753); Simon Blanchard, 'Where do New Channels Come From?' in S. Blanchard (ed.), *What's This Channel Four?* Comedia, London, 1982.

[9] Commission for Racial Equality, *Broadcasting in a Multi-Racial Society*, Commission for Racial Equality, London 1979.

[10] Simon Blanchard, *op. cit.*

[11] Jane Hewland, 'Not Divisive in Context but a Necessary Filling of Gaps', *The Stage and Television Today*, 2 December 1982, p 18.

[12] A Sivanandan, 'From Resistance to Rebellion' in *A Different Hunger: Writings on Black Resistance*, Pluto Press, London 1982.

[13] J. Curran and J. Seaton, *Power Without Responsibility: The Press and Broadcasting in Britain*, Methuen, London 1991.

[14] Sue Woodford 'Replies', *Caribbean Times*, 7 January 1983, p 17.

[15] Lord Scarman, *The British Disorders 10-12 April 1981: Report of an Inquiry by the Rt. Hon. the Lord Scarman OBE*, HMSO, London November 1981, (Cmnd. 8427).

[16] See the interviews with Trevor Phillips and Samir Shah in Jim Pines (ed), *Black and White in Colour*, *op. cit.*

[17] C. Spencer, 'Black Opinion', *Stills*, Number 18, 1993.

[18] P. Gilroy, 'C4: Bridgehead or Bantustan?', *Screen*, vol.24, nos.4-5, 1983.

[19] Jane Hewland, 'Is Channel Four Poking Itself in the Eastern Eye?', The *Guardian*, 7 January 1985; Farrukh Dhondy 'Karma After the Storm', The *Guardian*, 14 January 1985.

[20] Nicholas Fraser, 'Racing Away From the Bland Centre', *Observer*, 17 December 1989, p 63.

[21] See the interview with Farrukh Dhondy in J. Pines (ed) *Black and White in Colour, op. cit.*

[22] Yasmin Alibhai-Brown, 'Sold Out by Media Wallahs', *New Statesman and Society*, 28 January 1994.

[23] The importance of this heterogeneity to black arts in Britain in discussed in P. Gilroy, *Small Acts: Thoughts on the Politics of Black Cultures*, Serpent's Tail, London 1993.

[24] The mixed responses to some of these films is discussed in ICA Documents 7, *Black Film, British Cinema*, Institute of Contemporary Arts, London 1988.

Women and Television

Jane Arthurs

Greater equality makes good commercial sense in an increasingly competitive environment. Broadcasters and programme-makers should be drawing on as wide a pool of talent as possible to enhance the quality of their output, and they should make sure that women's interests and preferences are taken fully into account because women make up the majority of the television audience. One way of achieving this is by employing more women in key decision-making roles. But it is not just for commercial reasons that it is important for women to gain greater influence within television institutions. The images of women found on television have long been condemned as stereotypical, unrealistic and demeaning: content analyses have revealed the numerical dominance of men on the screen and semiotic analyses of programmes have shown that patriarchal relations of power are reproduced in the codes and conventions of popular television genres.

Thus, television does not merely reflect gender inequality, it actively contributes to its reproduction by presenting an image of society in which men's right to dominance remains largely unchallenged. The political goals of feminism depend on changes in every sphere of social, cultural and political life, and television is one of the sites where patriarchal power must be successfully contested.

Women's Distinctive Contribution to Television

Before looking in more detail at the position of women in the workforce and initiatives to gain greater equality, I want to discuss whether an increase in the numbers of women making programmes would necessarily have any real impact on the industry. The two issues here are whether there is any potential for changes to working practices and occupational cultures within the industry, and whether woman-made programmes would be any different from the type of programming that we already have.

Arguments that stress the need for more women within television production often rest on the assumption that only women can adequately speak for women as a social group; that this task can't be delegated to men because there is an area of experience that is specific to women, that is, determined by their biological and social identity, and is therefore only communicable by a woman. If women have an identity that is in essence different from that of men, then the programmes that they make must in some way express that difference, both in the forms of signification used and in the choice of subject matter. This theoretical position is known as essentialism and is attacked for presenting a model of gender identity that is fixed and immutable. It shares this view of women with those who argue that women can never compete on equal terms with men in the workplace because they are by nature suited for their role in reproduction and the nurturing of their families.

But to deny that women are different is to risk total incorporation into a system of cultural production that is already constituted as patriarchal. Programmes are not only, or even most importantly, the product of the personal vision of the people making it, they are the product of the television institution which pre-dates those individuals. The most difficult question for women is how to transform those institutions in a way that will give a voice to their aspirations and experiences without falling back on an unchanging and undifferentiated definition of what it means to be female.

Ghettoization is one of the problems to be negotiated. When a women's committee was set up within the Writers' Guild there was opposition from some of the women on the grounds that they did not want to be separated off as a special group marginalized from the majority. The consequence of being labelled as a woman writer can be similar to that experienced by black cultural workers who complain of the 'burden of representation' that they bear. This burden is the product of a situation where a very few people with opportunities to make very few programmes have to bear the responsibility for representing a diverse and complex social group. The pressure is to try to fill in the gaps left by mainstream programming and so to concentrate on 'women's issues'. There is, in drama particularly, the pressure to present 'positive images' of women to counteract the negative stereotyping which dominates the mainstream. And most problematic of all, there is the pressure to address women as a group, a group divided by class, race and sexuality, with divergent cultural tastes and often irreconcilable political differences. Finding a mode of address that works in these circumstances is very difficult though Radio 4's *Woman's Hour* is often regarded as a successful example, despite the ongoing controversies over the feminist orientation of its approach.

Whether women programme-makers should be making programmes for and about women, or whether they should rather be regarded as programme-makers first and women second, is a question that is only relevant in a situation of scarcity. The burden of representation would be lifted were there enough women in positions of power to influence the whole range of television output, as well as providing slots designed to appeal to a variety of different types of women. This is made more possible by the imminent shift to a more fragmented market in which channels will no longer be seeking to command the attention of the majority of viewers. To address all groups of women would require a mixed economy in which the market, limited by the pressure for minority audiences to be attractive to advertisers or as potential subscribers, could be supplemented by public service channels providing for the groups that are too poor or too controversial for commercial broadcasters to be interested in.

Radical feminists argue that reform of existing cultural institutions cannot bring any benefits to women, and that the construction of alternative institutions independent of the mainstream is the only way to challenge existing patriarchal systems of production and representation. It is certainly true that the weight of institutionalized norms makes it very difficult for women working within the mainstream to resist incorporation to the point where their identity as women is immaterial to the decisions they take. A number of case studies have been published which provide

84

evidence of these pressures towards conformity, but they also provide examples of how a woman's perspective can make a difference. Change will only come by building on the knowledge gained from the failures as well as the successes achieved in these isolated cases.

The most recent study was commissioned by the BBC for the conference they held in 1991 on Women and Television. Angela Coyle and Reena Bhavnani from City University spent four months observing the production cycle for *Crimewatch UK*, chosen because it had a woman producer and predominantly female production team.[1] They were trying to establish whether women do have a distinctive contribution to make to television production. The research report concluded that there was indeed a marked difference in the management style adopted by the programme's producer which created a 'woman-friendly bubble' in comparison to the prevailing norms at the BBC. Parental responsibilities were taken into account by making working hours regular and predictable, with time away from home planned well in advance. The style of working was open, supportive and participative, using power to empower others. Everyone felt that their contribution was valued and opportunities for career development were actively supported; for instance, one of the directors on the programme was originally a production assistant.

Though these approaches to people management have been gaining widespread currency in the business world, the researchers did not find any substantial evidence of this style in other BBC managers. The Sims report in 1985 found that an aggressive 'macho' approach to management, based on fear, was often cited by women in the organization as a reason for not wanting to go into management.[2] It is still usually the case that women's progress within the organization depends on their fitting in with an established male culture. Methods of working, such as the long hours and the 'clubby' atmosphere centred around after-hours drinking, fit into the pattern of men's lives and require a person with few responsibilities outside work. Coyle and Bhavnani explain the difference in management style as a response to women's relative powerlessness in the organization, rather than as evidence of an intrinsically female propensity to co-operative and collaborative ways of working. 'Women's power and authority is less readily accepted by either women or men and women have to find more subtle, and arguably more democratic and effective strategies for taking a leadership role'.[3]

The *Crimewatch* study was unable to find any evidence of women having any significant influence on the nature of the programme itself. The format and agenda were already established and remained dependent on priorities established by the police – the emphasis on violent crime for instance. The team was able to modify rather than transform the programme; there was an incident in which a journalist's sensitivity to other people's feelings prevented her interviewing a murder victim's mother, although she felt that a 'real' journalist would have had no such qualms. The team was also keen to ensure that violence was not presented in a sensationalized way.

It is very difficult for women to challenge the accepted formats and ways of working without being open to charges of amateurism and incompetence. Doing things differently takes more time and the chances of failure are much higher. It is interesting to look back at how Channel 4, which has a specific remit to be different from the other channels, has responded to the challenge to develop programmes made by and for women. Although there have been several attempts at a weekly current affairs or magazine programme for women (*20/20 Vision, Broadside, Watch the Woman*) none have survived for more than a few months. Channel 4 does not give reasons for the non-renewal of commissions but according to Rosalind Coward they have been 'allowed to fail and have been stored away in the channel's memory as "interesting experiments" '.[4]

The case of *Broadside* (January-November 1983) illustrates the difficulties faced by women seeking to change the established ways of working in the industry and how this impacts on the programmes produced. *Broadside* grew out of a feminist collective lobbying for change in the industry. Their disillusionment with existing working practices, and their commitment to feminist politics, led to a desire to work in a non-hierarchical group in which technicians would be fully involved and would contribute to the creative decision-making.

These ideals were undermined when Channel 4 insisted that an editor-in-charge had to be appointed and tight budgets limited the hiring of crews to the essential minimum. Intentions to experiment with form were abandoned once the external constraints of working within the mainstream industry made themselves felt. There wasn't time and the consequences of failure were too great. The fact that the women had long-standing personal friendships only served to make more bitter the conflicts that arose once they were working in a traditional power structure that encouraged competitive relationships exacerbated by the job insecurity engendered by the commissioning system. 'Within television, it seems, the contradictions that exists between professionalism and feminism remains unsolved and possibly, insoluble'.[5]

The contradiction between professionalism and feminism is particularly true of news and current affairs broadcasting, which is legitimated by its commitment to impartiality and objectivity. The use of experts and official spokespeople drawn from other institutions, who more often than not are men, is an important way in which the journalist underwrites the objectivity and validity of a report. Feminism challenges this approach at a fundamental level. Feminists argue that the news presents a highly partial view of the world and, in particular, a view that excludes women's interests. They challenge the right of men to universalize their perspective and they question the very possibility of an impartial view. Baehr and Spindler-Brown's account of the programmes made by *Broadside*, acknowledges the limited successes achieved in shifting the agenda of current affairs through presenting topics such as war and its aftermath from a female perspective. This was done by using female witnesses and avoiding male experts to re-evaluate what had been said.

Current policy across all channels is that it is more important to incorporate women's issues into general news and current affairs programming than to form 'ghetto' slots for women. However, there is little evidence of any change. A study by Loughborough University's Media Unit on the 1992 election coverage monitored the BBC's *Newsnight* and *The Nine O'Clock News*, Radio 4's *Today* and ITN's *News at Ten*. They found that women politicians appeared only thirty-seven times out of 1,031 total appearances by politicians, and of those twenty-eight were by Margaret Thatcher.[6] On election night the BBC coverage was presented by an all-male team. Behind the scenes there is the same male dominance; a recent study of Independent Television News by University of Westminster management students found that female employees earned on average nearly £10,000 less than their male colleagues, and that men were twice as likely to win promotion.[7]

In some ways the programme-makers can be justified in arguing that all they are doing is reflecting the real world of politics in which women have a very low participation. But a counter-argument is that they then have an even greater responsibility to represent the interests of the 50 per cent of the population who are so woefully marginalized. Television current affairs could have a campaigning role, in which it helped to change the priorities of the political agenda. Radical change can only come by jettisoning the journalistic safeguard of drawing on the agendas set by the male-dominated institutions in public life. Small shifts may result from initiatives such as the availability in Belgium, Ireland and Holland of directories for programme-makers listing women with expertise, so that programme-makers no longer have the excuse that they couldn't find a suitable woman to consult.

Research undertaken in 1990 found that in a sample of 500 TV advertisements, 89 per cent used a male voice-over; that men in advertisements outnumbered women by a ratio of nearly 2:1; and the proportion of men judged to be over thirty outnumbered women by 3:1.[8] The same ratios were found to be true of actors appearing in TV Drama and Light Entertainment, in research conducted for *Equity* in 1991.[9] Not surprisingly, the same report found that male actors worked more and earned twice as much as female actors from the mechanical media, and that they continued to be busy up to their 40s whereas women's careers started to decline after they had reached thirty.

The decision as to whether a part should be played by a male or female is, in the majority of cases, decided by the writer, though the story editor or producer would have more influence over the casting of soaps and series. In the United States, quota casting has been used to ensure adequate representation of ethnic minorities, but the idea that this could be used to increase the number of female roles in this country was considered by the respondents in the *Equity* survey to be an unacceptable attack on editorial freedom. The majority thought that if there were more women writers, there would inevitably be more and better parts for women. However, Jill Hyem, an experienced television writer, points out that without more women producers, script editors and commissioning editors there is the likelihood of men making 'creative' decisions that disadvantage the type of material written by women.[10]

Jill Hyem is an ex-actress who, like many other women television writers, began writing for television because of the dearth of good parts for women. Her own extremely successful *Tenko* (ITV series in 1981, 1982 and 1984, and a Christmas special in 1985) about a women's prisoner of war camp, was originally rejected on the grounds that 'No one'll want to know about an all-woman cast looking their worst' and she had to resist attempts to soften her scripts to bring them into line with conventional notions of an acceptable femininity.[11] In Hyem's experience 'The words "depressing", "cosy" and "feminist" recur with monotonous regularity in ... rejection letters' and there is a tendency to judge situations written from a female perspective as of 'limited appeal'.[12]

A few key successes in the early 1990s gives the impression that the tide is turning. At the start of its new franchise in January 1993, Meridian Television announced the appointment of three women in their team of six football reporters. Two documentary series, *Move Over Darling* (BBC, 1991) and *Rude Women* (Channel 4, 1992) addressed feminist and women's issues in a popular style. In sitcoms there is the success of *Roseanne*, an American product shown on Channel 4, whose star breaks all the rules of conventional female leads by being fat, working class, a less than perfect mother, and most significantly, by having creative control over the show. *Prime Suspect* (ITV, 1991) written by Lynda La Plante (another ex-actress) with Helen Mirren as a chief inspector in charge of a murder inquiry was hugely popular (16 million watched) and received enthusiastic critical acclaim despite having an explicitly feminist theme. But after the earlier success of *Widows* (ITV, 1983 and 1985), La Plante's first role-reversal gangster serial, it is surprising that she had to wait six years for another major TV serial, and in numerical terms the male dominance of sitcoms and crime fiction continues unabated. A cynical view of the reason for these occasional series with women in the lead roles is that old genres need a new twist to sustain audience interest; a form of popular feminism is one of the available variations. It is also the case that the second series of *Widows* and of *Prime Suspect* constructed their protagonists as far more conventionally feminine than in the first series. The struggle to try to resist this process in the production history of *Cagney and Lacey* (when the actress playing Christine Cagney was replaced in order to make the character more conventionally attractive) gives further evidence of the pressures towards ideological conformity that exist in television institutions.[13]

Current Position of Women in the Industry

The classic model of a television company is a large vertically integrated company in which the workforce is ordered into a hierarchical pyramid; horizontal divisions are based on specialized skills. These demarcations between levels and types of job are sustained not only through the allocative power of management, but also through the closed shop system of union power which polices the wage differentials between grades of jobs and restricts entry to the industry through a system of controls over who is allowed to do different types of work. This is the type of company organization that dominated television broadcasting in Britain up to the latter half of the 1980s.

Within this system, women have been thought to be suitable for some jobs but not for others. The jobs that are predominantly done by women are systematically less well-paid, have lower status, and are less likely to lead to promotion than the jobs that are predominantly done by men.[14] The most recent survey of employment patterns across Europe in relation to sexual equality, *Women and Men in Broadcasting: Prospects for Equality in the 90s*, gives the following impressionistic account before going on to a detailed statistical analysis:

> Walk into any broadcasting organization in the European Community, and the first person you will meet is likely to be a woman: the receptionist, the secretary, the personal assistant. If your appointment is with a manager in sales, personnel or public relations, this person may also be a woman. But if you are heading for the technical department, you will probably walk past 15 or 20 men before seeing a single female face. If the object of your visit is to discuss a programme proposal with a senior executive, the person behind the desk is much more likely to be male than female. And if you have come to see the Director General, your chances of meeting a woman are minimal: throughout all the major broadcasting companies of the European community, there is only one female director general.[15]

The 1990 survey of seventy-nine broadcasting originations, including radio, in the, then, twelve Member States of the European Community found that:

- Women form 36 per cent of the total broadcasting workforce (a higher proportion in radio than in television).
- Out of the six major categories of occupation (Administration, Production, Technical, Crafts, General Services and Specialized Services) two areas of disequilibrium stand out: 69 per cent of those employed in Administration are women, and 93 per cent employed in Technical are men.
- Within every occupational category, women's share of jobs is greatest at the bottom of the hierarchy and least at the top, and their share of jobs is progressively reduced at each step of the hierarchical ladder. Women account for only 11 per cent of those in the very top management jobs. For men, the situation is exactly the reverse.
- Women account for only 10 per cent of those involved in the key internal and external decision-making bodies (such as in Britain, the BBC Board of Governors or the Independent Television Commission (ITC)).

These figures give only a very general overview of a complex situation, masking significant differences within the general occupational categories, which cover a very wide range of specific jobs. For example, in Britain, women in the Production category are overwhelmingly represented in the badly paid, low status jobs of production assistant, continuity girl, vision mixer and production secretary, whereas women form less than 10 per cent of staff in the better paid jobs of camera, sound and lighting. There are also considerable differences between organizations; for example 32 per cent of the producers and directors in the BBC are women, compared to 16 per cent in ITV. Within each organization some programme departments employ more women than others: women are particularly under-represented in Sport, Light Entertainment and in News and Current Affairs, whereas they form a higher percentage of the workforce in Children's and Education departments.

Until the *Skill Search* report by the Institute of Manpower Studies in 1989,[16] there had been no industry-wide attempt by the British film and television industry to collect information on the composition of the workforce, so historical information is patchy and irregular. Comparisons are made difficult by the lack of an agreed classificatory system for the hundreds of different types of job within the industry. A report published in 1975 by the Association of Cinematograph, Television and Allied Technicians (ACTT) did reveal that women's position in the industry had actually deteriorated in the 1960s and 1970s during the time of television's greatest expansion. Until the Sex Discrimination Act of 1975 a whole range of technical production jobs were closed to women, but even when this became illegal there was very little change in the pattern of sexually segregated employment. There has been campaigning for changes within the industry from women's pressure groups such as the Women's Film, Television and Video Network (WFTVN) and from minority voices within the ACTT, and there have been some significant but isolated initiatives, such as at Thames Television in 1979, funded by the Equal Opportunities Commission, which instituted a whole range of positive action measures. But although many companies have had a formal policy of equal opportunities for many years (the BBC since 1975), little happened as a consequence of this until the latter half of the 1980s when support for equal opportunities became more of a priority for the European Community, the Government and at top managerial levels in broadcasting.

Equality Initiatives

Research presented to the European Commission in 1985 highlighted the entrenched inequalities in European broadcasting companies.[18] In order to promote change by influencing the climate of opinion, a Steering Committee for Equal Opportunities in Broadcasting was set up in 1986, which brought together senior representatives of Europe's major broadcasting companies. They have since produced a guide to good practice within broadcasting institutions and have instituted a prize, the Prix Niki, aimed at promoting a better image of women in television programmes. It is part of a much wider European initiative to promote equality for women which recognizes the importance of the media's role in influencing attitudes.

In Britain, the Broadcasting Act of 1990 made it a requirement that the Channel 3 licence-holders must promote equal opportunities, and that this would be monitored by the ITC. Where the Act falls short is in the exclusion of independent production companies from this requirement, just as their proportion of broadcast programming is to increase to a minimum of 25 per cent. So far only the BBC has given any consideration to the use of contract compliance clauses, which require independent companies to implement equal opportunity practices as a precondition for their being given a programme commission. Channel 4 has always refused to do this on the grounds that they have neither the resources to monitor the companies, nor the desire to constrain their ability to make decisions on commercial grounds.

Several British broadcasting companies now have equal opportunity policies, workforce monitoring, equality officers, and improved arrangements for maternity leave and child-care, but in the current climate of mass redundancies, equality issues have been sidelined in the face of a more general erosion of the rights, pay and working conditions of the whole workforce. There is at the BBC, however, despite this retrenchment a renewed determination to improve the position of all under-represented groups in the organization, including women. They have taken on the responsibility for leading the way after trailing badly in the past. The manager in charge of implementation is quoted in the BBC equality newsletter as saying: 'We must be a leading role model for society on this because you won't change what's on screen unless you change the BBC's workforce. Equal opportunities are now beginning to have an effect and I've noticed a real improvement in our on screen portrayal over the last two or three years.'[19] Portrayal monitoring is designed to check on this assertion and requires programme-makers at the BBC to record and submit to their departments the number of women, ethnic minorities and disabled people who appear in their programme, and in what type of roles. A high profile conference on 'Women and Television' was organized by the BBC in 1991, and in 1992 they were selected as one of the top twenty companies for women by *Company* magazine because of their positive action policies, particularly in the field of training for women. For example, they offer *Women in Leadership* courses for senior women managers, *Managing My Career* courses, directing courses for Production Assistants and training attachments for women in targetted departments such as Sports. This is backed up by general equal opportunities training for all managers, and specific training in *Fair Selection*. Of greatest significance is the involvement of senior management in taking responsibility for implementation and the setting of organizational targets for promotion, so that by 1996 women should hold 30 per cent of senior management positions (they held 8 per cent in 1989 and 16 per cent in 1992) and 50 per cent in all grades by the year 2000.

Training Initiatives

Until recently, routes into the industry have been based on informal, loosely defined entry requirements in which patronage, the right background and persistence have played a major part.

Learning on the job has taken precedence over pre-entry training, particularly in the technical areas of production. These procedures have tended to reproduce the status quo, both in terms of the make-up of the work force and in terms of their attitudes. Getting in and on was a question of whether you 'fitted in'. These systems have already started to breakdown. Some companies are now looking for ways in which to recruit staff from under-represented groups; strategies include forging links with inner-city schools, and reviewing entry requirements, so as not to unfairly disadvantage women without science and technical qualifications for jobs where their relevance is largely a matter of tradition.

A major change is about to take place as a consequence of the setting up of the *Industry Training Organization* (ITO) for film, TV, video and radio. As part of a Government initiative to improve training, the ITO's brief is to develop common standards of competence in the industry, to be certified by National Vocational Qualifications (NVQs). Their publicity leaflet says 'it is no longer a question of who you know, but of what you can do'. The ITO has a stated commitment to equal opportunities and hopes to promote it in the following ways:

- The ongoing monitoring of employment patterns and training in the industry (the ITO grew out of the needs identified by the 1989 *Skill Search* report).
- A training fund for freelancers and people working in the independent sector.
- Provision of careers information for young people and a database on available courses and training.
- Liaison with, and financial support for, selected college courses, and helping in co-ordinating work placement schemes.

Dinah Caine, the director of the ITO, believes that the availability of agreed standards of competence and certification will reduce discrimination against women that is based on the under-evaluation of their skills. It will also give women the opportunity to gain multiple skills as a way of enhancing their employability. This may be true, but the problem with the NVQs is that they are based on a skills concept of training which marginalizes more conceptual and critical discourses. The committee overseeing the implementation of this scheme has only one education representative. Rather than a narrow focus on skills there is a need for a broader critical education to ensure that the new entrants do more than reproduce existing representational and working practices. More women in the industry does not guarantee different programmes unless those women are able to think critically about the industry as it is currently run.

Continuing Obstacles: Occupational Culture

Despite the formal acceptance of the need for equal opportunities in the television industry, there are still enormous obstacles standing in the way of women's progress. The main weakness of all these initiatives is that they are based on a liberal ideology which assumes a rationalistic and meritocratic model of capitalist society. There is an assumption that skills training, childcare support and an overhaul of formal appointment procedures will achieve sexual equality. What is left out of the equation is the continuing existence of a society that is structured by gender, class and racial divisions, and the importance that work has in maintaining those divisions. 'Work hierarchies are the place where gender identities are lived out daily'.[20]

The chief characteristic of the social relations of gender is that both masculine and feminine identities are formed through the power that men assume over women. Thus male jobs have to be seen as empowering, whether through access to technological know-how or through the power invested in managerial authority, whereas women's jobs are systematically defined as non-technological and linked to servicing functions that assume subordination to male authority. Women pioneers who break through into male jobs, such as directing or camera operating, find themselves in an exposed position where they have to be able to withstand hostility and ridicule. Those that adapt by taking on masculine values, find that the qualities that are valued in men are not necessarily acceptable in women because it challenges the norms of femininity. Those that seek to incorporate feminine qualities into the job may find these regarded as unacceptable and a sign of weakness. This is particularly true of the occupational culture found in television in which aggressive, competitive and coercive approaches to social relations are the norm.

It is within this context that sexual harassment assumes great significance. It is one of the ways in which women are reminded constantly that their sexual identity defines their work role, and that an important element in that is to re-inforce men's sense of their power over women. Whilst this is a problem that has now begun to be recognized in, for example, the setting up of helpline and counselling services for victims of sexual harassment at the BBC, little can be done to solve it until the power relations between men and women are redefined.

The sense of being an alien in a male culture produces a feeling of resignation in many of the women working at the bottom of the hierarchy. They see no option but to seek satisfaction from their lives outside work. Comments from the 800 women who filled in diaries of their working day for the BFI *One Day in the Life of Television* project in 1988, reveal that a common survival strategy is an attitude of ironic and amused detachment, coupled with an astute awareness of the ways in which they are undervalued.[21] Unfortunately, most women only discover the lack of career opportunities by experiencing them: many school-leavers and graduates think that a secretarial job is a way into a career in television production. Research at the BBC found that over a five year period only 16 out of 589 women in secretarial and clerical grades had moved into other jobs.

The persistence of male domination of the workplace is illustrated by two examples of ways in which institutions adapt to the introduction of equal opportunity initiatives. One form of adaptation is the split between what is formally supposed to take place and what actually happens in an organization. Vogel and Zaid's research on the television industry found that where women had moved into managerial positions, informal types of decision-making, from which the women were excluded, took over from the formal decision-making committees.[22] Another form of adaptation is the systematic deskilling and lowering in status of jobs which become feminized.[23] There are signs of this happening already in television production. Just at the point where women are gaining more access to a wider range of production jobs, wage levels have been depressed, working conditions have worsened and their status undermined by demands for a multi-skilled workforce. Programme-makers are being sidelined at the top of the hierarchy in favour of general managers with accountancy backgrounds. A possible future for programme-makers is that it will become a low paid, insecure and dead-end job except for a privileged few, as a consquence of the move towards a casualized work-force described in the next section. Business acumen will be the sought-after quality, and in this area women are even more disadvantaged than in programme-making.

Move to Independent Production and its Consequences

The industry is currently experiencing far-reaching changes in the way it is structured. The large, vertically integrated companies described above are rapidly responding to political and economic pressures to be more flexible and cost-effective by shedding permanent staff (between 30-40 per cent since 1988) and increasing the proportion of programme-making and attendant services bought in from independent companies and freelance labour. Even the BBC, in response to pressures exerted by a dwindling licence fee and a need to placate government in the run up to the 1996 charter renewal, are shedding staff at an equivalent rate. The move towards a publishing model of broadcasting, begun in 1982 with the setting up of Channel 4, has been accelerated by the awarding of the Channel 3 franchises in 1991 to three new companies operating on this model (Carlton TV, Meridian and TSW).

The consequences for women of this restructuring are contradictory and it is too soon to know whether, on balance, women as a group will gain or lose. On the positive side, women stand to gain from the destabilizing of established male power bases and new opportunities for working as independents. The ACTT (now BECTU) restrictions on new entrants no longer apply, thus allowing more women into the industry. The cost-cutting trend towards multi-skilling allows women to move into new areas, even if they start off in traditional female ghettoes. At a company level, Carol Haslam of the Independent Programme Producers Association (IPPA) points out that women are just as likely as men to hold management positions in independent companies, and there is potential for forming more women-friendly company cultures.

There are some jaundiced views about the benefits of the greater freedom brought by working outside the large companies: it often amounts to a greater freedom to be exploited in a situation where intense competition between companies for available work has exerted a downward pressure on production costs, and where it is predicted that at least half of the existing companies will go out of business within the next five years. The move towards a casualized workforce further reduces the number of women who will benefit from the equality initiatives within the broadcast companies. Already there is a larger proportion of women working as freelancers; they form two-thirds of the sector, as compared to only one-quarter of the staff in the broadcast companies.[24] The equality officer at BECTU is concerned that pregnant women and new mothers are being disproportionately selected for redundancy. Freelance workers are much less likely to qualify for maternity rights and the unpredictability of working to short term contracts is particularly difficult for people with caring responsibilities. A casualized labour force is much more difficult to monitor or influence, and the importance of 'contacts' outweighs any formal appointment procedures. Significantly, the people with the power to commission the independents are almost exclusively men: out of a list of 132 names of people with commissioning powers, distributed by IPPA in 1991, only thirteen are women.

Conclusion

As in any time of great change it is difficult to predict eventual outcomes. For women in the television industry there are great opportunities to be seized in the current upheavals: entry into the industry has opened up, attitudes towards women are changing for the better, there is a growing recognition of the case for positive action to enhance women's position in the industry. Set against this, is the weight of institutionalized norms in programme-making that can only be challenged and changed with great difficulty, and the threats posed by the casualization of the industry. If women really are going to make a difference to television they need to have an understanding of feminist critiques of the television that we have. Women also need to understand the politics of the industry in a way that allows them to fight for positions of power within it. More women in the industry is not enough: there need to be more women with a politicized understanding of the ways in which women's subordination is currently reproduced, and with the will to change it.

Notes

[1] Angela Coyle and Reena Bhavnani, *Watching the Crimewatchers: Women, Gender and Differences in the BBC*, Paper presented to *Spot the Difference* conference, London, May 1991.
[2] Monica Sims, *Women in BBC Management*, BBC, London, 1985.
[3] Angela Coyle and Reena Bhavnani, *op.cit.*, p 5.
[4] Rosalind Coward, 'Women's Programmes: Why Not?' in Helen Baehr and Gillian Dyer, *Boxed In: Women and Television*, Pandora, London 1987, pp 96-106.
[5] Helen Baehr and Angela Spindler-Brown, 'Firing a Broadside: A Feminist Intervention into Mainstream TV', in Baehr and Dyer, *ibid.*, pp 117-130.
[6] Reported by Lesley Abdela in the *Guardian*, p 5, 20 November 1992.
[7] Reported by Paul Nathanson in The *Mail on Sunday*, 7 June 1992.
[8] Guy Cumberbatch *et.al.*, *Television Advertising and Sex Role Stereotyping*, Broadcasting Standards Council Working Paper, 1990.
[9] Helen Thomas, *Equal Opportunities in the Mechanical Media*, Equity, 1991.
[10] Jill Hyem, 'Entering the Arena: Writing for Television' in Baehr and Dyer, *op.cit.*, pp 151-163.
[11] *Ibid.*, p 153.
[12] *Ibid.*, p 154.
[13] Julie D'Acci, 'The Case of Cagney and Lacey', Baehr and Dyer, *op.cit.*, pp 203-226.
[14] For a detailed account see Jane Arthurs, 'Technology and Gender', *Screen*, Volume 30, Numbers 1 & 2, 1989, pp 40-59.
[15] Margaret Gallagher, *Women and Men in Broadcasting: Prospects for Equality in the 1990s*, Commission of the European Community, 1990, p1.
[16] Carol Varlaam *et.al.*, *Skill Search: Television, Film and Video Industry*

Employment Patterns and Training Needs, Institute of Manpower Studies, 1989.

[17] Sarah Benton, *Patterns of Discrimination Against Women in the Film and Television Industries*, London, ACTT, 1975.

[18] Angela Coyle and Jane Skinner, *Women and Work: Positive Action for Change*, Macmillan Educational, London, 1988.

[19] Cliff Taylor, *EqualiTV*, BBC Equality Newsletter, June 1992.

[20] Angela Coyle 'Behind the Scenes: Women in Television' p76 in Angela Coyle and Skinner, *Women and Work*, 1988, pp58-79.

[21] Janet Willis and Tana Wollen, paper presented at the *Spot the Difference* conference, BBC, London, May 1991.

[22] Quoted by Angela Coyle, *op.cit.*, p 76.

[23] Angela Coyle, *op.cit.*, p 70.

[24] Carol Varlaam *et.al.*, *op.cit.*, p 9 and p 28.

Channel 4 Television: From Annan to Grade

Sylvia Harvey

In November 1992, as Channel 4 celebrated its tenth anniversary and its 10 per cent share of the audience, it seemed as though it had always been there, a venerable landmark, taken for granted and helping to shape the contours of contemporary British television.

But, of course, it is a relative newcomer; and its birth was a complex affair. In order to understand its emergence as an institution, we need to unravel some of the complex threads of historical change and development in the relations between British broadcasting and the state; and to have some sense of the relative weight of individual passions, political priorities and economic realities in the unfolding of that relationship. This institution did not drop from the skies in response to a few lines in the British Parliament's Broadcasting Act of 1980. It was pushed into existence by many people, acting sometimes together, sometimes at cross-purposes, and under more-or-less favourable conditions. Its birth was no accident, its upbringing carefully planned, and its financial needs were secured in advance. It did not always fulfill the hopes and dreams of its progenitors, but a considerable achievement it nonetheless was. It was probably the only television channel in the world to combine a legislative requirement to *experiment*, to *innovate* and to *complement* the service offered by the existing commercial television channel, and all of this on an income guaranteed in advance by its parliamentary god-parents, under the direction of a Conservative government.

The Political Context

The Channel Four Company was incorporated in December 1980 as a wholly owned subsidiary of the Independent Broadcasting Authority – the body then charged with regulating commercial radio and television. The date is significant in signalling the birth of a new decade whose social, cultural and economic character is often associated with the values and beliefs of the 'New Right' and of the new, Conservative Prime Minister, Margaret Thatcher. One of the continuing problems for British Conservatism in the 1980s was to be that of resolving, or attempting to resolve, a conflict between the values of the 'old' and the 'new' right, between a paternalistic and often authoritarian cultural conservativism, and the demands of economic innovation, of letting the market 'rip'. If the one demanded cultural continuity and respect for heritage and the 'great tradition' (in broadcasting as elsewhere), the other proposed the values of a new enterprise culture, the development of more competitive and cost-effective forms of production, and the absolute sovereignty of individual consumers making choices in the market-place.

This tension between the twin poles of heritage and enterprise can be seen to characterize the formulation of Conservative Party policy in the two Broadcasting Acts (1980 and 1990) that mark the beginning and end of the decade.[1] There is a sense in which Channel 4 bears the marks of both tendencies. The idea of public service and public duty, reaching back well over a century into the ethics of the Victorian civil and colonial services, is manifest in the 1980 public service requirement that the new television channel should serve a variety of audience tastes and interests, encourage innovation in programme making and show a suitable proportion of educational programmes. Such detailed specification of programme categories, and the emphasis on complementarity – that new tastes and interests should be served by the new channel – had become almost a hallmark of British broadcasting policy. Certainly up to and including the 1980 Broadcasting Act there had been support from both the Conservative and Labour parties for careful forward

103

planning to ensure choice of programmes not just choice of channels. This commitment to 'public service' principles and to the fostering of a cultural heritage had historically overridden demands for a 'free market' in broadcasting, and sharply differentiated the British approach from that of the United States, where channel proliferation within an essentially commercial or free market framework had been the outcome of a different sort of public policy.

The enterprising tendency, on the other hand, is manifested in the mode of production selected: the Channel Four Company was to commission or 'publish' programmes, not to make them itself. Programme making was to happen predominantly out-of-house in the new lean, fit and flexible independent sector, called into being as a consequence of this policy. The old 'vertical integration' that had characterized the industry, allowing the same organizations to both produce and broadcast, would no longer be the only model for production. The new independents, it was argued, would have more innovative attitudes to doing business, and lower overheads than the lumbering giants who were their parents: the BBC and ITV companies. The newcomers, motivated by an anxious desire to deliver programmes at competitive prices, would ultimately transform the industry as a whole, replacing permanent contracts with freelance employment, and doing away with 'over-manning', along with the company pension schemes, subsidized canteens and childcare facilities, that had indirectly increased the costs of production. From a New Right perspective this newly enterprising sector would (quite apart from the more publicly advanced arguments about freedom and diversity of expression) challenge and ultimately change traditional production practices in television.

Before Annan: The Pre-History of Channel 4

The Annan Report of 1977, produced under a Labour government, has been seen as a kind of watershed in the history of Channel 4. It argued the case for a 'third force' in British broadcasting to break the duopoly control then exercised by the BBC and ITV. But the outcome of the 20 year battle between those who argued for the creation of an ITV2, and those who wanted something completely different, was to be a compromise, formulated by a Conservative government, and expressed in the brief but careful wording of the 1980 Broadcasting Act. In this section we shall explore the 'pre-history' of Channel 4, considering the people, the institutions and the interests which in both conflict and combination, between the time of the Pilkington Report in 1962 and the Broadcasting Act of 1980, provided the framework for the creation of the new channel.

The BBC monopoly of the airwaves was broken in 1955 with the introduction, by a Conservative government, of the first privately owned television in Britain. This advertising-financed Independent Television (ITV) provided a popular alternative to the existing BBC service, and was placed under the control of a new regulatory body: the Independent Television Authority (ITA). It is perhaps worth remembering, as a preliminary to the lengthy debates about the creation of a fourth channel, what arguments led to the ending of the BBC monopoly. Sir Frederick Ogilvie, a former Director General of the BBC, stated the case in a letter to *The Times* in 1946:

> Monopoly of broadcasting is inevitably the negation of freedom, no matter how efficiently it is run, or how wise and kindly the board or committees in charge of it. It denies freedom of employment to speakers, musicians, writers, actors and all who seek their chances on the air. The dangers of monopoly have long been recognised in the film industry and the Press and the theatre, and active steps have been taken to prevent it. In tolerating monopoly we are alone among the democratic countries of the world.[2]

In the 1960s and 1970s a number of distinguished television programme-makers (including figures like Robert Kee, Ludovic Kennedy, Donald Baverstock, Alastair Milne and Jeremy Isaacs) had attempted to set up independent production companies, and discovered how hard and financially unrewarding it was to work outside the BBC/ITV duopoly.[3] Many of these figures, concerned about the cultural protectionism of the duopoly, saw the need for a 'third force' in broadcasting in the 1970s.

The 1962 Pilkington Report had been critical of the achievements of ITV, and had advocated that the proposed third television channel be allocated to the BBC. This recommendation was accepted by the Conservative government and BBC 2 began broadcasting in 1964. However, in its evidence to Pilkington, the Independent Television Authority (ITA) had spoken up in favour of both competition and the interests of the ITV sector, arguing against the BBC's claim on the new channel, and noting:

> ... the third service should be independent of the first and second ... in a free society, control of the means of communications should be diversified not centralized.[4]

This also reflected the view of the ITV companies, among whom the belief in breaking monopolies and introducing increased competition had, at least initially, been strong. Pilkington also envisaged the creation of a fourth channel and believed that this should, in due course, be allocated to independent television. However, this should only be on the basis that it would provide a complementary service (not competition for the same audience through the provision of similar types of programmes). Speaking in the House of Commons in June 1963, the Conservative Postmaster General came under concerted pressure from MPs who sympathized with the ITV case, and indicated the government's intention to issue a licence for 'ITA 2' within the next two years. However, the debate about the uses of the fourth channel did not gain momentum again until 1971-72. The election of a government less favourable to private ownership (Labour came to power in 1964), and a crisis in television advertising revenue, which dropped by five per cent between 1969 and 1970, were to intervene.

Slowly but inexorably, under the pressures of finance and self-interest, the ITV companies, followed by the ITA (with its particular concern for the quality of programmes), came round to the view that 'ITV 2', far from being separately owned and controlled in order to bring increased competition to the system, should in fact be under the control of the existing ITV contractors. In 1970 the Conservatives returned to power after a six year interval, and a flurry of both public and confidential memoranda came to rest on the desk of the new Minister: Christopher Chataway. An early indication of the change of heart among the ITV companies came from Hugh Thomas, Managing Director of Thames Television. Writing in a staff newsletter in 1971 he noted:

> ... we should want to use ITV 2 as a try-out ground for programme experiments and for new concepts and ideas ... It is essential that ITV 2 should be operated by the existing contractors.[5]

In their submission to the Minister in December 1971, the ITA accepted, in essence, the view of the ITV companies, proposing that the existing contractors should sell advertising for the new channel in their own areas, and that scheduling should be controlled by a board consisting of all the ITV Programme Controllers together with representatives from the ITA. Two important additional points were made. Firstly, that the smaller ITV companies should have guaranteed rights to make programmes for the new network, thus diminishing the power of the 'Big Five' (Thames, LWT, ATV, Granada and Yorkshire). Secondly, that there should be some unspecified amount of airtime made available for programmes produced by outside, independent producers. However, the ITA took a rather lofty and somewhat patronizing view of the abilities of independent producers:

> It would be useful also to see how valid is the proposal that there should be freer access to the medium by particular sections of the community who feel that they have some special message or viewpoint. There are dangers of amateurishness in production and difficulties in incorporating such programmes in a national television service without sacrificing impartiality and editorial control.[6]

Criticism of these ITV 2 proposals came from a wide range of sources; principally from the broadcasting trade unions, especially the BBC Association of Broadcasting Staff (ABS), and from the Association of Cinematograph, Television and Allied Technicians (ACTT) which organised within ITV. In November the ACTT published its own document prepared by Caroline Heller: *TV 4: A*

Report on the Allocation of the 4th Channel. This drew upon some rather pessimistic data of a 1970 study conducted by the Prices and Incomes Board. The PIB noted that the now slow rate of growth of the television audience meant that ITV was facing if not a decline, then at least no increase in advertising revenue. The resultant squeeze on income might make it difficult to finance a second, wholly advertising-supported channel. ACTT members within ITV feared the possible de-stabilization of the existing commercial system, and the report argued that both job security and programme standards could suffer. Other ACTT freelance members were, however, less sceptical about the new channel and looked forward to its introduction.

Opposition to an ITV-controlled fourth channel was most sharply focused and expressed through a new organization, established in November 1971: the TV 4 Campaign. There was by now growing concern on this issue (at least among a media-oriented minority). *The Sunday Times* had published a leader in the previous month expressing its own reservations on the subject:

> Any suggestion that ITV 2 would resemble BBC 2 should be treated with the blackest scepticism. This is not because the men promoting that idea are dishonest or even because there is necessarily a shortage of talent or idealism. It is because commercial television operates within narrow and demanding constraints, which give priority to profit.[7]

The TV 4 Campaign followed this up with even stronger language and a stinging attack on the ITA proposal: '... it represents an arrogant and bland ignorance of the needs of the public.'[8]

The TV 4 Campaign was a lively and loose coalition of television producers, media journalists and academics, trade unionists, politicians and advertisers. Advertisers, of course, wanted lower prices through competition for the sale of airtime on ITV and the proposed fourth channel; they therefore opposed the concept of an ITV 2 controlled by the existing ITV contractors with a continuing monopoly which they believed would keep the cost of airtime artificially high. Others were moved to attend meetings and write papers with more culturally based motives.

The Campaign was agreed upon the following two objectives: 'that a public enquiry should be established as soon as possible ... and that the fourth television channel should not be allocated to the present independent television contractors'. This view was expressed in an Early Day Motion in the House of Commons where it attracted the support of about 100 MPs (2 December, 1971). The government, however, was more concerned to press ahead with its plan to introduce local commercial radio (finally achieved in the summer of 1972 with the Sound Broadcasting Act) and in January 1972 Christopher Chataway put an end to speculation by announcing that the government did not propose to proceed with the allocation of a licence for the fourth television channel.

Despite this apparent end-of-story, the serious debate was only just beginning. The first major contribution was made by Anthony Smith who had left the BBC in 1971 to take up a two year research Fellowship at Oxford University; in 1979 he was appointed Director of the British Film Institute and subsequently joined the first Board of Channel 4. In a letter to the *Guardian* in April 1972 he outlined, in brief, his ideas for a National Television Foundation (subsequently worked up as a submission to the Annan Committee).

The Foundation, with a very small staff, would act as a kind of publishing house of the air, buying in and broadcasting programmes from a wide variety of sources. It would be open equally to independent programme makers with fully worked out ideas, and to individuals or organizations who had a particular point that they wished to get across to a larger public. Smith argued that the existing broadcasting institutions had become vast and bureaucratic centres of power, corrosive of creative work, inclined to over-careful self-policing and absorbed in the project of their own institutional survival. Faced with the old-fashioned caution of the duopoly he argued for something completely different:

> What has to be achieved is a form of institutional control wedded to a different doctrine from existing broadcasting authorities, to a doctrine of openness rather than to balance, to expression rather than to neutralization.[9]

Moreover, in a pre-figuring of the language of minority television (or of 'niche marketing' in the terms of advertising), Smith identified the possibility of television going beyond the mass audience and towards the discovery of specialized publics, of particular communities of interest.

The philosophy of the Foundation, with its sharp critique of the perceived inadequacies of contemporary television, acted as a rallying point for many who had become disenchanted with the bland or censorious nature of the medium. However, its address to the issue of funding was regarded as problematic in some quarters, relying as it did upon a mixture of sponsorship, grants from educational and other sources, block advertising and government subvention. Others from within the world of television, and moved by similar concerns, were to develop rather more pragmatic proposals in respect of finance.

In a submission to the Minister in 1973, David Elstein and John Birt (then at LWT) argued that the new channel should be developed by the Independent Broadcasting Authority (which had replaced the ITA in 1972) who would appoint a programme controller. The existing ITV contractors should be allowed to sell the advertising airtime for the fourth channel within their own areas, but not be allowed to control the schedule. They would compete with other independent producers to supply programmes; programme ideas would be selected on merit alone. These would be paid for by a levy on the additional advertising revenue, collected by the IBA. Broadly similar proposals were made by Jeremy Isaacs, then Controller of Features at Thames TV.[10] What Isaacs, Birt and Elstein shared with Anthony Smith was a desire to liberate the creative people in television from the often stifling effects of bureaucracy, and to find a way to ensure – *systematically*, not, as it were, by accident – that new things could be said in new ways. If they lacked the institutional radicalism represented by the National Television Foundation proposal, they nonetheless shared its aims, and understood some of the practical means to achieve a greater pluralism and diversity of the airwaves. The best of causes require resources and allies in order to be realized, and their quietly effective memos to the Minister acknowledged two key factors: the importance of advertising revenue for the new endeavour, and the need to seek accommodation with (but not surrender to) the barons of ITV. In the absence of a government with a radical, public service bent and money to spend, their pragmatism was ultimately to win the day.

The Annan Report and the Open Broadcasting Authority

In 1971 the TV 4 Campaign had argued for a public enquiry into the possible uses and structure of a new channel. While this call had not been accepted by the Conservative government of 1970-74, neither had the latter acted to bring a new channel into existence. It was left to the incoming Labour administration of 1974 to invite Lord Annan to chair a committee reporting to Parliament on the future of broadcasting. Labour was to remain in power from 1974-1979, though the recommendations of the Annan Report, not available until 1977, were not to be implemented by them. Implementation, as it turned out, was to be the work of the new Conservative government of 1979, which accepted parts of the Report while rejecting others.

The committee's brief was wide and demanding and required it to investigate all aspects of British broadcasting. It met, deliberated and took evidence over a period of two and a half years. We shall consider here only those parts of the final Report and its recommendations relating to the fourth channel.

Strongly influenced by one of its members – Phillip Whitehead, a Labour MP who had been active in the TV 4 Campaign – and by Anthony Smith who had been denied membership of the Annan team,[11] the committee outlined four general principles. In their view British broadcasting should be characterized by:

- 'accountability through Parliament to a public which is given more chance to make its voice heard'
- 'diversity of services'
- 'flexibility of structure'
- 'editorial independence'[12]

Diversity and programme (as opposed to merely channel) choice were key concepts for the Report, and the preamble to the final recommendations took on board one of the ideas that had been developed by Smith: that television should not only be about reaching mass audiences. In a 1977 article Smith had argued:

> Beneath the façade of the homogeneous mass audience the cement is cracking ... a television channel can do something more than try to get the same message across to millions of people ... it can direct a programme at a highly specialized level, at a large audience of like-minded people.[13]

There is, of course, a continuing problem in an advertising-funded system of making programmes for 'like-minded people' who are not, in economic terms, of interest to advertisers. In the past this problem has been solved in Britain by giving regulatory authorities the power to ensure the meeting of broader 'public interest' criteria in the making and transmission of programmes. By the 1990s, the almost hegemonic power of 'niche marketing' arguments, combined with the removal of scheduling powers from regulatory bodies, have put in question the future effectiveness of this solution.

The Annan Committee recognised the need to create a space for minority audiences:

> ... we do not want more of the same. There are enough programmes for the majority ... What is needed now is programmes for the different minorities which add up to make the majority.[14]

However, not foreseeing the storm of free market arguments shortly to be unleashed within British political and cultural life, they perhaps failed to confront the issues of cost and control as these relate to serving the interests of minorities, and the implementation of diversity in programming.

In making their recommendations for the fourth channel, the committee effectively combined Anthony Smith's model of a National Television Foundation with the structural radicalism of Phillip Whitehead's concept of a new type of broadcasting authority. Thus it was that the Report proposed an Open

Broadcasting Authority[15] (OBA) as the institutional midwife who would deliver Channel 4. The OBA would act as a kind of electronic publisher offering an outlet to programmes from a wide variety of sources, some of which, in the words of the Report, '... would not be acceptable or appropriate on the existing channels'. While charged with achieving 'overall balance ... over a period of time', it would have much greater freedom than the existing regulatory body, the IBA.[16]

The OBA's programmes would fall into three broad categories: education (including the Open University, though the idea of an exclusively educational channel was rejected); programmes from the ITV companies; and those from independent producers. The committee attached particular importance to this third category as a 'force for diversity and new ideas'.[17] The language of the Report on this potential new sector of production helped to create a new discursive field within broadcasting policy; one that went well beyond the fear of parvenu amateurs hinted at in the 1971 ITA submission.

Philosophically, the proposed fourth channel was conceived as more than just a new line in the existing emporium of British broadcasting. The general conclusion of the Report stated:

> We see the fourth channel not just as another outlet or even just as a means of giving a more varied service to the audience. It should be the test bed for experiment and symbolise all the vitality, the new initiatives, practices and liberties which could inspire broadcasters.[18]

Cost was the great unresolved issue. In general a diversity of funding sources was regarded as desirable, but the Committee recognised that a combination of grant-aid, sponsorship and block advertising might be insufficient, in which case some government subvention might be required. Moreover, in recognition of the difficult financial climate, they recommended that the new channel should not be established '... until the nation's economy will permit the kind of services we have outlined'.[19] Only in Wales, where other political imperatives had emerged, might there be an exception to this gloomy caution. Here the Report recommended that some priority should be given to establishing a fourth channel, broadcasting programmes in the Welsh language.

From Annan to the 1980 Broadcasting Act

The Labour government was uncertain about the Annan recommendations and took over a year to decide to support the OBA proposal; this support was formalized in the 1978 White Paper on Broadcasting. However, no enabling legislation was formulated and Labour was defeated in the 1979 election. For those who had believed the announcement by a government Minister, back in 1963, that Channel 4 was imminent, the whole affair had been marked by delay and disappointment.

However, the new Home Secretary in the incoming Conservative administration – William Whitelaw – had taken a particular interest in the fourth channel project and was sympathetic to some of the aims, if not to the institutional means that had been outlined in the Annan Report. The Queen's Speech of May 1979 announced the new government's intention to proceed with a fourth channel, to be developed under the aegis of the IBA. The volume of debate and the intensity of campaigning immediately increased.

A new Channel 4 Group had emerged, replacing the old TV 4 Campaign, and this was now joined by the Independent Film-makers Association (IFA), an organization representing experimental and arts grant-aided film-makers who had, until then, regarded themselves as definitively excluded from the world of television. A wide range of film and television programme-makers, together with journalists, trade-unionists, critics, politicians and media policy makers, now made common cause to ensure a crucial safeguard: that of cultural independence for the new institution, arguing that the ITV companies should not control this initiative. In addition, the IFA in a pamphlet circulated at the 1979 Edinburgh Television Festival raised the issue of the relationship between broadcasters and their audiences:

One of the main aims of TV 4 must be to lessen the gulf between

114

the professional communicators (including ourselves) and the public we observe, question and on whose behalf we speak.[20]

The IFA also drew upon aspects of the Annan Report which had advocated provision for the needs of people living in the regions of Britain by calling for the new channel to fund regionally-based, experimental film workshops.

In a speech delivered at the same Television Festival, Jeremy Isaacs (soon to become Channel 4's first Chief Executive), outlined his views on the subject:

> We want a fourth channel which extends the choice available to viewers ... which caters for substantial minorities presently neglected; which builds into its actuality programmes a complete spectrum of political attitude and opinion ... a fourth channel that everyone will watch some of the time and no one all the time. A fourth channel that will, somehow, be different.[21]

Isaacs had, as we have already noted, communicated his views on both a purpose and a practical structure for the institution in a memo sent some six years earlier to one of William Whitelaw's predecessors. Whitelaw's own views, now the views of government, were outlined at some length in a speech made to the Royal Television Society Convention at Cambridge in the autumn of 1979.

Whitelaw's speech reassured many observers that government was committed to providing 'new opportunities to creative people' and 'new ways of finding minority and specialist audiences'.[22] Moreover, IBA control was to ensure that Channel 4 was not simply the creature of ITV. In response to strong lobbying from the independents (later to develop their case for 25 per cent of programming on all terrestrial channels) the IBA would be required to ensure that 'the largest practicable proportion of programmes' would be supplied from organizations that were not ITV companies. The reward for ITV was the continuation of their monopoly in the sale of advertising. The existing contractors would sell airtime on the new channel, but the IBA would ensure that this income – and if necessary more than this – was made available to meet Channel 4's own costs. It only remained for a change of name to mark the shift of control away from ITV. This happened as the draft Broadcasting Bill made its way through Parliament in the course of 1980. Phillip Whitehead succeeded in changing the reference to 'Service 2' to 'the Fourth Channel Service'.

Only in Wales was Whitelaw's speech met with deep hostility, for it had reneged on the Conservative Manifesto pledge to create a Welsh language channel. A tremendous campaign was developed in Wales as a consequence of this, involving both widespread refusals to pay the television licence fee, the raiding and temporary closing down of transmitters and, finally, a threat of hunger strike made by the venerable and respected President of the nationalist party, *Plaid Cymru*. In the face of such angry and widespread protest, the government returned to its original promise, amending the Bill in September 1980 in order to create a Welsh Fourth Channel Authority, *Sianel Pedwar Cymru* (S4C). It would be the task of S4C to create the first prime-time, Welsh language channel in Wales, drawing its programmes from the BBC, HTV and from a soon-to-be-created and vigorous independent sector. The IBA was to ensure that S4C received an adequate amount of advertising revenue: approximately 20 per cent of the total amount collected from the ITV companies. So, for example, from a total of £313.5 million received in 1991 in subscriptions from the ITV companies, £58.4 million went towards the costs of S4C.[23]

The key provisions of the 1980 Broadcasting Act can be briefly summarized (these provisions, with the exception of the ownership arrangements, were carried over almost unchanged into the 1990 Act). The IBA was required to ensure that the Channel 4 service would contain '... a suitable proportion of matter calculated to appeal to tastes and interests not generally catered for by ITV' and a '... suitable proportion of programmes ... of an educational nature'; it was also to '... encourage innovation and experiment in the form and content of programmes'.[24]

It was left to the IBA to decide upon the appropriate institutional form for Channel 4 and to collect an annual subscription from all the ITV companies to meet its costs. In return the ITV companies were allowed to sell the advertising airtime on the new channel within their own regions, thus maintaining their monopoly control of airtime sales. This last arrangement had been the method advocated by Birt, Elstein and Isaacs himself, back in 1973. It would change only with the 1990 Broadcasting Act when Channel 4 was established as an independent Trust (no longer a subsidiary of the IBA) with board members to be nominated by the ITC, and with an obligation to meet the costs of its programming by selling its own airtime.

It is clear from the wording in the 1980 Act and, more importantly, from the associated financial, administrative and ownership arrangements (Channel 4 was initially to be incorporated as a wholly owned subsidiary of the IBA) that the new institution, if not an 'Open Broadcasting Authority', had the potential to fulfill many of the objectives of innovation and difference proposed by the Annan Committee.

Channel 4: The First Ten Years

A Changing Cultural Context

Channel 4's programme transmissions began in November 1982, the month after the Falklands/Malvinas victory parade and a year after the riots in Brixton and Toxteth. With the wisdom of hindsight, it is possible to see the Falklands victory parade as in some sense a signal for the passing of an old order. No amount of Prime Ministerial rhetoric about Britain being 'great again' in the wake of this war, could stop a growing public recognition that the country had lived through its last days of imperial glory, and needed to discover a new economic centre of gravity and a new role in world affairs.

Channel 4 was to grow in, and try to reflect, a climate of accelerating social and cultural change, with new attitudes to national identity, family life, public services, sex and money. In attempting to pull within the frame of television what had previously been either excluded or treated in a bland or simplistic way, it had to represent (in both factual and fictional programmes) a range of contemporary issues from rising female expectations and a rocketing divorce rate, to a growing number of home owners as well as of homeless people. Its difficult task, with the liberal encouragement of the new Broadcasting Act behind it, was to give a voice to the new pluralism of the 1980s: that explosive mixture of racial hatred with new multi-racial and multi-cultural tolerance, of the quest for sex equality with the consolidation of new forms of male supremacism, of a new tolerance in matters of sexual orientation with outbursts of homophobic hysteria, of a commitment to the welfare state with the argument that its existence was incompatible with the principle of a free market.

The development of the new channel beyond the moment of its legislative conception, was to be fashioned by a culture both more pluralistic and more stratified than that of the two preceding decades: a greater variety of ideas and lifestyles, sharper extremes of wealth and poverty, more ferocious political and ideological disagreements, together with a general lessening of public interest in official politics.

In its early days, a greater frankness about the varieties of human sexuality and a more realistic and relaxed representation of everyday speech, got Channel 4 into deep trouble with sections of the mass circulation press. The tabloids attacked the showing of a programme exploring gay lifestyles, *One in Five*, scheduled for New Year's day, 1983, and the *Sun* ran what it called a 'filth count' of the language used in the Channel's first month of broadcasting.[25] Subsequently (in 1986) the broadcaster was to experiment with the use of a small red triangle in the corner of the television screen, to indicate material that might be offensive to some. This experiment was discontinued when puritan campaigners persuaded major advertisers to avoid such programmes. But the Channel's willingness to engage with its audience's interest in sexual matters, whether in *Out on Tuesday* (1988) or *Sex Talk* (1990), was to expand the horizons of what was possible in television in general. Without its new, often forthright, witty and imaginative approach it would be difficult to imagine the appearance of Carlton's *The Good Sex Guide* on mainstream ITV at the beginning of 1993. In this sense Channel 4 affected the whole ecology of British broadcasting, extending the range of subjects that might be dealt with by television.

In the representation of working life other less sympathetic cultural and political forces could be seen at work. The programme for trade-unionists, *Union World* (1984-85), was to disappear in the course of the 1980s. It was not to be replaced by a similar strand.

In political and ideological debates, in respect of 'balance' and 'impartiality' and in the representation of historical and current affairs material, the Channel was also to cause offence to some powerful (and less powerful) people. *The Friday Alternative* (1982-83) which had been set up to provide a critical commentary on the week's news from a variety of viewpoints, was axed after less than a year on the grounds of consistent left wing bias. Jeremy Isaacs recognised a distinction between 'one-off' opinionated programmes and *series* which consistently advanced the same opinions, and could therefore be taken to undermine the requirement of balance. The first chairman of Channel 4's board, Edmund Dell, was highly critical of *The Friday Alternative* with its irreverent, witty and 'straight to the point' attack on traditional news values and approaches. Though, interestingly, one outcome of the cutting of this series and of several bruising encounters between the Channel's Chief Executive and its chairman, was the policy assertion by Isaacs that:

> We have firmly established the notion that television programmes from a variety of sources may express explicit opinion, without upset to the body politic.[26]

This advocacy and representation of strong opinion was to be furthered through two long running programmes slots: *Opinions*, a 30 minute slot, usually given to well-known speakers, and *Comment*, a three minute slot after the evening news, given to anyone who had a point of view to put across. One notable blow for opinionated pluralism was struck shortly after the Channel went on air, when the socialist historian and anti-nuclear campaigner E.P. Thompson was awarded the *Opinions* platform, having just been turned down for a series of lectures by the BBC.[27]

In other areas too, the taken-for-granted centrism of British televisual life was challenged: in the development of caustic comedy, whether *The Comic Strip Presents ... The Strike* (1988) or *Crimestrike* (1990); in programmes by women: the original Broadside current affairs series of 1983; or in feature films like *Hush*

119

A Bye Baby (1990) delicately considering the issue of unwanted pregnancy in Catholic Northern Ireland; or *Dream On* (1992) exploring the defiant attitudes of working class women coping with constant crisis on Tyneside; in positive and witty explorations of gay life, *Out on Tuesday*, 1989; in the presentation of fact and fiction from the 'Third World' (the *Africa on Africa* season of 1984, the series *South* in 1991), and in a rich variety of films by black British film makers: *Handsworth Songs* (1987), *Playing Away* (1989) and *Looking for Langston* (1990).

Some historical series were highly innovative, and difficult to fault in terms of balance. For example, *Wales: The Dragon Has Two tongues* (1984) financed by Naomi Sargant, the Channel's first Senior Commissioning Editor for Education, was a 13-part series in which two historians, one marxist and one more conservative, argued over their conflicting interpretations of Welsh history. Another major series, produced by Central for Channel 4, was *Vietnam: A Television History* (1984) exploring, among other things, Britain's difficult and close relationship with the United States. Other 'people's stories', drawing on a rich new vein of oral history in contemporary historiography, accompanied the major series: two examples of this, from Television History Workshop, were *Making Cars* (1983) and *City General* (1984). A far more controversial history, pushing many of the panic buttons of high level outrage, was *Greece: The Hidden War* (1986); this offered a critical examination of a little known aspect of recent British history, namely, the highly partisan role played by the British army in relationship to domestic Greek politics, towards the end of the Second World War. Strong complaints were made by powerful figures in the British military establishment.

Isaacs himself offers some useful comments on this novel process whereby entrenched and established views were challenged for the first time *on television*:

> I had never doubted, thinking too much television too unthinking, too bland, that Channel 4 would broadcast programmes that put, as forcibly as possible, a forcible point of view. I had not appreciated, and still find hard to understand, how offensive to some this turned out to be. People had no

objection to an opinion strongly expressed in a newspaper, in a railway carriage, in a saloon bar. Why object to opinionated television? Perhaps they only enjoyed reading their own opinions in newspapers, and not the other fellow's at all.[28]

It remains to be seen whether or not the new requirements on 'impartiality', written into the Broadcasting Act of 1990, and the subject of much controversy at the time, are used to stifle the expression of strong opinions. In 1991 the conservative Freedom Association had attempted to take Channel 4 to court over their screening of a programme putting the view of Americans opposed to the war in the Gulf: *Hell, No, We Won't Go*. The case was not then pursued on the basis of legal advice that the climate would be more favourable to a finding against such programmes after the formal introduction of the new ITC Code on Impartiality in 1993.[29]

Programmes and Scheduling

Channel 4's parliamentary remit to 'encourage innovation and experiment in the form and content of programmes', together with the view expressed by Jeremy Isaacs, that it should be for 'all of the people some of the time' seemed to provide the basis for a service that was prepared to edge well beyond the previously established limits of broadcasting expression.

The first ten year's of output can be roughly divided into the periods corresponding to the appointments of the first two Chief Executives: Jeremy Isaacs (1981-87), and Michael Grade (1988-1992). The recommendation of the Peacock Report in 1986, that Channel 4 should be given the option of selling its own airtime, can also be seen to mark a kind of watershed in the early history of the Channel. Certainly the vigorously purposeful reconstruction of the schedule, the judicious buying in of popular American series (*Thirty Something, Cheers, The Cosby Show, The Golden Girls*), and the continuing success of the Channel's own soap, *Brookside*, has helped to boost the ratings in the Grade era. Viewing figures went up from 8.8 per cent in 1988 to around 10 per cent in 1991.

It was argued in some quarters that, in the late 1980s, Channel 4 had 'lost its way' in a populist drive for high ratings.[30] While this does not seem to be confirmed by an examination of the quality and range of programmes commissioned, it might be said that Current Affairs programming dealing with contemporary Britain had lost something of the 'bite' and range of class voices characteristic of the early to mid-1980s. With the obvious exception of programmes like *The Committee* (1991) which claimed to have uncovered illegal, paramilitary unionist groupings at the highest levels within Northern Ireland, and which led to a fine of £75,000 as the producers and the Channel steadfastly refused to divulge their sources to the Court, professional distance had, to some extent, taken over from passionate enquiry. Moreover, the loss of the *People to People* slot (1988) and the ending of regional workshop funding in 1991 has tended to concentrate commissions within the metropolitan heartland of London; other voices from and versions of contemporary British life have received little airtime as a consequence. Set against this arguable under-development and retrenchment was the introduction of new peak time documentary series: *Cutting Edge, Critical Eye* and the access series: *Free for All* (1991).

However, many of the structural and generic innovations of Channel 4 remain, including *Comment*; the hour-long evening *News; Right to Reply; Brookside; Film on 4* and the work of the Multi-Cultural and Independent Film and Video departments under their Commissioning Editors Farrukh Dhondy and Alan Fountain. Dhondy has been responsible for bringing the work of critical black journalists into the intellectual heartlands of British current affairs and arts television with *The Bandung File* (1985-89) and *Rear Window* (1991). His budget also provided the crucial co-production finance for Mira Nair's feature films *Salaam Bombay* (1989) and *Mississippi Masala*.

The Independent Film and Video department with its 'Eleventh Hour' strand, has fostered experimental work both among British film and video-makers (*Video 1, 2, 3*, 1985; *Dazzling Image*, 1990) and by introducing work from other countries and cultures: the Godard season of 1985, the Latin American season of 1983 and the screening of work by Chantal Ackerman, Leontine Sagan, Jon Jost,

Jan Oxenburg and Marisol Trujillo. It has also presented and to some extent celebrated gay and lesbian culture before a wider audience in the seasons *In the Pink* (1986) and *Out on Tuesday* (1988). On the fiction front their 'New Waves' season of 1984 remains one of the most impressive collections of low budget, experimental features by British directors (including *Acceptable Levels, Burning an Illusion, Through an Unknown Land, Brothers and Sisters*, and *Darkest England*).

In the fields of arts and comedy programming, the Channel also made a significant contribution to extending the boundaries of these television *genres*. The first category was distinguished by the development of critical and analytical series such as *Signals, Without Walls* and *Rear Window*; the latter by an extraordinarily wide variety of material from *Who Dares Wins* to *Drop the Dead Donkey*; from *No Problem* to *Whose Line Is It Anyway?* and the generically extraordinary *Manhattan Cable* (1991).

The Drama department under David Rose, and subsequently David Aukin, has developed the *Film on 4* strand into what is probably one of the most internationally recognized innovations of Channel 4: mobilizing the resources of television to support a starving but still creative British film industry. The aim was to put co-production money into feature films and to encourage a cinema release where possible: building up a reputation and critical profile for the film prior to its television exposure. Where cinema screening was not feasible, an agreement with the Cinema Exhibitors Association (initially covering films with budgets of under £1.25 million) ensured that the film would not have to wait for the normal three year period before being cleared for television screening.[31] In this way a relationship of mutual support, not mutual antagonism, was developed between cinema and television.

In his first year of operation, David Rose had a budget of £6 million which, it was hoped, would make, or help to make, up to 20 films – giving an average contribution per film of £300,000. Figures have of course risen since then (by 1991 the Channel's annual budget for Drama, including Film on 4, had risen to nearly £36 million), but the proportion of money contributed to any one film budget has always varied considerably. Channel 4 contributed 100 per cent to the budget of *My Beautiful Laundrette* (1987), 52 per cent to *Another Time, Another Place* (1983), 22 per cent to *Paris, Texas* (1986), 10 per cent to *A Room With a View* (1989), 73 per cent to *Rita, Sue and Bob Too* (1990).[32]

The output of Film on 4 – 136 feature films by the end of 1991 – has been prodigious and varied.[33] 1987, the last of the Isaacs years, was one of the most memorable. In this year Film on 4 screenings included: *Letter to Brezhnev, My Beautiful Laundrette, Caravaggio, No Surrender, Company of Wolves* and *She'll Be Wearing Pink Pyjamas*; the last of these won one of the highest audiences of the year for Channel 4 at 7.5 million.[34]

Other programmes in the same year (1987) stand out as exemplary of the brief to experiment and innovate. Claude Lanzmann's nine hour study of the holocaust, *Shoah* was shown on two consecutive nights, *Network 7* began a genuinely new trend in factual broadcasting for younger people, *Cinema from Three Continents* challenged the comfortable Anglo-American and Euro-centrism of British film culture and *The Media Show* was perhaps the first properly researched, dynamically presented and adequately critical series to appear on British television which explored the medium itself.

Programme Costs, Suppliers and the Principle of Diversity

Channel 4 might be said to have had two distinct but interrelated purposes: to introduce stylistic and content innovations into British television, and to introduce new industrial structures for the production of programmes. This latter aim was accomplished by the creation of an independent sector, which has grown since the passage of the 1990 Broadcasting Act with its legal requirement that both BBC and ITV commission 25 per cent of their original output from out-of-house.

A few general observations about costs may be helpful here. Firstly, Channel 4 is a modestly resourced operation. It took around five years to break even (by 1987 the value of the airtime sold on the channel amounted to a little more than its costs). In 1991 its average hourly programme cost was £27,600, and it spent the largest single share of its income on Drama, closely followed by Entertainment, News and Documentaries (Table 3, 1991). By 1991, over half of its originally commissioned programmes were being made in the independent sector (52 per cent as against 48 per cent produced by ITV and ITN), and these were supplied by a total of 668 (mostly small) production companies. Only 28 of these companies received commissions totalling more than £1 million for the year; the majority of them (470) received commissions worth under £100,000.

In the relative disposition of commissions to the independents and to the ITV companies, it has been the case since 1984 that the independents have regularly been awarded a greater share of the costs in proportion to the number of hours that they produce. This is almost certainly because the ITV companies are commissioned, on the whole, to produce the cheaper types of programmes and not because they are inherently more cost-effective. Table 2 gives the comparative figures on this from 1984 to 1991.

While it is true that Channel 4 provides some opportunities for first time film-makers and for those who would otherwise have no access to television, the problem for the small independents is 'how to survive' in the face of radical uncertainty about the renewal of production contracts. As the individuals who make up the sector get older, take on domestic commitments and realize the benefits of secure employment, a predictable income, sick pay, paid holidays and properly resourced pensions, their commitment to working in a radically insecure sector inevitably diminishes. It is appropriate, therefore, to ask whose cultural and economic interests are served by the maintenance of this sector and this 'miniature' mode of production? And to what extent are freedom and diversity of expression safeguarded for the television audience by this system of production?

Certainly, many independent producers are experiencing almost intolerable living and working conditions, and yet this sector continues to be the preferred free market policy instrument for implementing the commitment to cultural diversity. There is a tense 'play off' here between the values of 'heritage' and those of 'enterprise', as discussed at the beginning of this essay. For that variant of broadcasting heritage which involves a commitment to cultural pluralism is under-written by the 'enterprising' methods of a dependent-independent production sector which may find it difficult to reproduce itself in the long term.

The Audience

Across the ten years of its history, from 1982 to 1992, Channel 4's voices of dissent, difference and even alarming experiment have gathered and consolidated audiences across the boundaries of class, race, gender and age. While it remained a minority channel, with its share of the total TV audience rising from 4.7 per cent in 1984 to 9.8 per cent by the end of 1991, it avoided the 'ghetto' trap of always reaching the same small number of people. This is shown by the 'reach' of its programmes, and the number of people who watch it at some time. In its early years some 50 per cent of the television audience viewed something on the Channel in any one week; by 1991 that figure had risen to 79 per cent, and it achieved a reach of 93 per cent of the population in the course of an average month.[35]

It may be useful here to indicate some overall shifts in television viewing in a period when British television developed from a three to a four channel, terrestrial system and (as the last column of figures in Table A indicates) the new media of cable and satellite have emerged to claim a small but significant share of the television audience. Table A (below) allows us to compare the broadcasting landscape just before the arrival of Channel 4, with that of ten years later. The figures can of course be read in many different ways but,

Table A:
Television viewing in the UK as a percentage of the total audience

	BBC 1	BBC 2	ITV	CH. 4	Other
1980-81	39.0%	12.0%	49.0%	–	–
1990-91	38.0%	10.0%	43.0%	9.0%	–
1992	35.8%	9.5%	41.0%	9.8%	3.9%

Sources: Seymour-Ure, 1991:155; BBC Annual Report and Accounts, 1990-91:80; Broadcast, 29 January 1993:28.

in general, it may be worth noting that Channel 4's audience has continued to grow while that of the other terrestrial channels has declined; BBC 1, BBC 2 and ITV have lost audience to Channel 4 and to the other new media.

In social class terms, as the Channel's Annual Reports regularly point out, a good proportion of its audience is within the 'upmarket' socio-economic range ABC1; it also attracts proportionately more younger viewers than ITV.[36] Whether this profile, which is extremely attractive to some advertisers, will ultimately put pressure on the Channel to cater principally to the 'upmarket' and youth audiences remains to be seen.

Achievements and Future Prospects

The 1990 Broadcasting Act preserved some, but not all, of the features established for Channel 4 by the 1980 Act. The original programming philosophy was retained. The new Act required the Channel to encourage 'innovation and experiment in the form and content' of programmes, and to 'appeal to tastes and interests not generally catered for by Channel 3'.

Outright privatization was avoided, though the Channel ceased to be a wholly owned subsidiary of the regulatory body. A new corporation was created, whose members were to be appointed by the ITC, and the umbilical link with the ITV companies was broken, as the new corporation was empowered to sell its own advertising. Although this change was designed to inject competition into the sale of airtime (and to end the role of the ITC as 'tax collector' for the Channel), nonetheless some element of symbiosis in the relationship between ITV and Channel 4 was retained through the 'safety net' provisions.

Under these arrangements, if the Channel's revenue dipped below 14 per cent of total (terrestrial) television advertising revenue, the ITV companies would be required to step in and contribute up to 2 per cent of that total amount. If, however, Channel 4 succeeded in acquiring more than 14 per cent, then any surplus would be divided evenly between itself and the ITV companies. Because of this mechanism the ITV companies have some financial interest in the success of their rival, and this is likely to ameliorate the more savage forms of competition for audiences and for the sale of airtime which might otherwise have occurred.

Separate arrangements for Wales ensure the continuation of S4C. A new Welsh Authority has been created for this purpose, receiving direct government funding of 3.2 per cent of total television advertising revenue each year. This figure is not dependent upon the amount of airtime actually sold by S4C, and the Act commits the Secretary of State to paying this amount out of public funds. If S4C had been made dependent upon the value of its own airtime sales this would have amounted to only a fraction of its costs. In 1991 the value of its airtime was £3.5 million, while the amount which it received through the ITC subscription, then collected from the ITV companies, was £58 million.[37] It is clear that this arrangement is based upon a political recognition of the demands of Welsh cultural nationalism (exemplified by the strong campaign conducted in Wales in 1980) rather than upon free market principles.

In avoiding both a private shareholding solution for Channel 4 and the creation of head-on competition with ITV (for the same audiences at the same time) the long established public policy principle that audiences should be offered programme choice, not just channel choice, continued to be upheld.

However, it remains to be seen to what extent Channel 4 comes under internal or external pressure to maximize its audience, and to prioritize the kinds of programmes that attract the kinds of viewers that advertisers most want to reach. The presence of airtime sales staff *within* the institution seems likely to affect commissioning and scheduling decisions (how could it not do so since the advertisers pay for the programmes, however indirectly). It will take considerable managerial skill and a clear cultural vision to hold onto the genuinely pluralistic programming policies established in the 1980s. In recognizing both the practical and political difficulties involved in implementing such policies, and their social importance, it may be worth remembering some comments made by Jeremy Isaacs in 1983:

It is cardinal, surely, to broadcasting in a free, pluralist society, that all sectors of society should be fairly represented on the screen. Tapping those new sources of energy, letting those voices (within an overall obligation to fairness) come through, is both Channel 4's most challenging task, and the practice that evokes most hostility.[38]

Appendix

Table 1
Channel 4 income, hours of transmission and costs 1984-91

	1984	1985	1986	1987	1988	1989	1990	1991[1]
Income from IBA/ITC(£m)	105.2	111.0	129.1	135.9	163.4	181.8	217.9	255.2
Annual transmission hours	3,185	3,593	3,913	4,160	5,106	5,818	5,245[2]	7,066
Total costs of programmes (£m)	89.3	95.4	101.3	114.1	135.1	149.5	179.5	195.2
Average programme costs per hour (£000)	28.0	26.5	25.9	27.4	26.5	25.7	26.3	27.6

Source: Channel Four, *Annual Report and Accounts*

[1] In 1991 the financial year changed from April-March to January-December. Figures for the full 12 month period have been given except where noted.
[2] This figure is for 9 months only, April-December 1990.
Note: the financial figures have not been adjusted for inflation.

Table 2
Proportion and value of programmes supplied by independent producers
and by ITV/ITN (1984-91)

	Independent Production		ITV/ITN Production	
	% of hours	(% of costs)	% of hours	(% of costs)
1984	29%	(45%)	33%	(39%)
1985	24%	(43%)	34%	(39%)
1986	25%	(43%)	30%	(39%)
1987	25%	(45%)	30%	(34%)
1988	29%	(51%)	30%	(28%)
1989	28%	(55%)	29%	(25%)
1990	54%[1]	(74%)	46%(1)	(26%)
1991	52%	(78%)	48%	(22%)

Source: Channel Four, *Annual Report and Accounts*

[1] Up to 1989 the percentage figures relate to total hours of programme transmissions. From 1990 they relate only to commissioned programme transmission hours (i.e. only to material originally commissioned for Channel Four, excluding other purchased material).

Table 3
Relative programme costs for Channel 4 in 1991

	Cost of Programmes (£m)	Number of Hours
Drama (including Film on Four)	35.9	719
Entertainment	33.3	1,190
News	21.1	638
Documentaries	18.9	494
Current Affairs	15.3	613
Education (including schools)	14.6	779
Arts and Music	13.9	364
Feature Films	9.5	1,378
Sport	8.7	569
Quiz	5.1	148
Multi-cultural	4.8	98
Religion	3.2	76

In 1991 out of a total of 7,066 transmitted hours, 4,127 of these hours were commissioned (i.e. original material for Channel Four), and 2,939 were purchased from other sources.

Source: Channel Four *Report and Accounts for the Year Ended 31st December 1991*

Table 4
Income for British television:
BBC, ITV, Channel 4 and S4C in 1991 (£m)

BBC (Radio & TV)	ITV	Channel Four	S4C
1,289.6[1]	1,357.5[2]	255.2[3]	58[3]

[1] Licence fee after costs of collection.
[2] Net Advertising Revenue after deduction of Channel Four and S4C subscription.
[3] Income received from the ITC.

Source: BBC, *Annual Report and Accounts 1990-91*; ITC, *1991 Report and Accounts*.

Notes

The dates given for films and programmes in this essay are the dates of television transmission not of production.

[1] J. Corner and S. Harvey (eds), *Enterprise and Heritage: Cross Currents of National Culture*, Routledge, London 1991.
[2] Sir F. Ogilvie, 'Future of the BBC Monopoly and its Dangers', *The Times*, 26 June 1946.
[3] S. Lambert, *Channel Four: Television with a Difference?*, British Film Institute, London 1982, pp 34-39.
[4] Pilkington, *Report of the Committee on Broadcasting, 1960*, HMSO, London 1962, para 878-880.
[5] S. Lambert, *op.cit.*, p 24.
[6] ITA, *ITV 2: A Submission to the Minister of Posts and Telecommunications*, ITA, London 1971, pp17-18.
[7] S. Lambert, *op.cit.*, p 44.
[8] S. Lambert, *op.cit.*, p 46.
[9] A. Smith, 'The National Television Foundation – 'A Plan for the Fourth Channel', evidence to the Annan Committee on the Future of Broadcasting, December 1974. Reprinted as Appendix II in A. Smith, *The Shadow in the Cave: a Study of the Relationship between the Broadcaster, his Audience and the State*, Quartet Books, London 1976.
[10] S. Lambert, *op.cit.* pp 158-60; J.Isaacs, *Storm over Four: A Personal Account*, Weidenfeld and Nicholson, London 1989, pp 200-202.
[11] J. Isaacs, *op.cit.*, p 8.
[12] Annan (Home Office), *Report of the Committee on the Future of Broadcasting*, HMSO, London 1977, p474.
[13] A. Smith, *op.cit.*, p 162-3.
[14] Annan (Home Office), *op.cit.*, pp471-472.
[15] For a useful insight into the way in which the committee worked see Lord Annan's Ulster Television lecture: 'The Politics of Broadcasting Enquiry', Ulster Television, Belfast 1981. This is cited in Lambert *op.cit.*, p68-69.
[16] Annan (Home Office), *op.cit.*, p236.

[17] *Ibid.*, p 237.
[18] *Ibid.*, p 472.
[19] *Ibid.*, p 240.
[20] S. Blanchard, 'Where do New Channels Come From?' in S. Blanchard and D. Morley (eds), *What's This Channel Four?*, Comedia, London 1982, p 17.
[21] J. Isaacs, *op.cit.*, pp 19-20.
[22] S. Lambert, *op.cit.*, p 93.
[23] Independent Television Commission, *1991 Report and Accounts*, ITC, London 1992, p 56.
[24] Broadcasting Act 1980, HMSO, London 1980.
[25] S. Lambert, 'Isaacs Still Smiling', *Stills*, Number 6, 1983, p 25, p 27.
[26] J. Isaacs, *op.cit.*, pp 82-86, p 88.
[27] *Ibid.*, pp 53-55.
[28] *Ibid.*, p 53.
[29] J. Willis, 'Vague Sense of Unease', *Guardian*, 25 January 1993.
[30] J. Miller, 'Do We Still Need Channel Four?', *Sunday Times*, 5 July 1992.
[31] J. Isaacs, *op.cit.*, p 150.
[32] J. Pym, *Film on Four: 1982-91*, British Film Institute, London 1992, pp 116-119.
[33] *Ibid.*
[34] *Ibid.*, p 64-65.
[35] Channel 4, *Report and Accounts 1992*, p 10.
[36] *Ibid.*, p 11.
[37] ITC, *op.cit.*, p 46.
[38] J. Isaacs, *op.cit.*, p 76.

Independent Production: Unions and Casualization

Colin Sparks

Like almost everything that we enjoy, television programmes are the result of human labour. Because they are extremely complex, the production of even the simplest sorts of programmes requires the co-ordinated work of a large number of people. Outside of the industry, few bother to read the credits at the end of programmes which are the visible record of the contribution that most of these people make. Beside the names of famous actors, presenters, producers and directors are those of many other less well known people, with highly developed skills from hairdressing to electronic engineering, whose efforts are indispensable to the final image on our television screens. Some of their skills are specific to television, others are versions of competencies found in a range of jobs. These skills were acquired by various routes – through apprenticeships, at college or on the job – much as anyone acquires a special set of employment skills. Sometimes they are able to use their monopoly of valuable skills and strong organization to gain high wages and stable employment; at others they have seen their situation eroded by inflation and unemployment. When they cannot find work, they depend on their savings and on state benefits like any other worker. The TV workforce is not an unusual or unique category of people: it is a small but integral part of the working class.

Socialists have always been interested in the working class. For some theorists this has been because they felt that workers were not getting their fair share of the wealth of society, but for Marxist socialists the focus upon the working class is because of the view that this social group alone is the bearer of the organising principle of the new society. The difference between the working class and other groups in society, some of whom might suffer worse deprivation or oppression, lies in the fact that the development of modern capitalism has transformed human labour into a collective activity. For example, the producers of culture in an earlier society, like poets or easel painters, could carry out their activities on their own or with just a few apprentices and contacts. A television programme is literally impossible without collective labour. Marxists argue that because of this collective nature of work, the working class in capitalist societies is characteristically forced to build collective organizations like trade unions to defend and further its interests. The necessity of working collectively, and struggling together to improve the terms of labour, give rise to a collective way of thinking about the world. It is on the basis of the collective self-identity and consciousness arising from socialised labour that a new society in which productive property is held in common can be built. The reason for being interested in the people who make television programmes, and in the fate of their organizations, is therefore that they are vital elements in any attempt to change society and to change television.

This chapter is about those workers and what has happened to them in the last few years. There have been major changes in the organization of work in television. The changes have not been the result of technological developments, as is often supposed, but rather of economic and political pressures. The changes have in turn had an effect on the wages, conditions and organization of the labour force and therefore on what the left, both inside and outside of television, needs to do in order to improve the chances of social change. It is only on the basis of a clear understanding of where we are starting from that we can hope to go forward and reach our desired goals.

The Age of the Producer-Broadcasters

There are three parts to the process which leads to the reception of a television service. The programmes have to be made, they have to be strung together into a schedule and they have to be broadcast. In terms of employment, the production of programmes is by far the most important element. Historically, British television combined all three of these functions into integrated organizations. The BBC is the clearest example of this: the organization owned offices, studios and transmitters, employed set-builders, camera-operators and telecommunications engineers. Some people, actors and many writers for example, were hired on a temporary basis, but most of the people who developed, produced and transmitted programmes, and provided the essential back-up and administrative services, were employees of a single organization. At its peak in the mid-1980s, the BBC employed more than 28,000 full-time staff, of whom more than 17,000 worked in television.[1]

The situation in the commercial sector was slightly different in that the transmitters were owned by the IBA (Independent Broadcasting Authority), which also had quite strong supervisory functions, but the main business of making programmes and putting together a schedule was delegated to the 15 franchise holders. This division of responsibility was a real one, but it did not alter the basic pattern. Once they had won their franchises, the commercial companies faced no competitors for advertising revenue. They could not be taken over without the express permission of the IBA, so they were relatively well-insulated from stock-market predators. The commercial sector was in a stable state which meant that it could be considered as a single entity. It employed around 18,000 people at the peak in the mid-1980s. This was fewer than the BBC, but all of these were employed in television. As with its rival these were mostly full-time permanent employees working for large organizations.

From the point of view of the workers, this situation had a number of advantages. Because the units were fairly large, it was relatively easy to establish strong and stable trade unions.[2]

Historically, the BBC employees were organized into a Staff Association which only slowly came to behave like a proper trade union. Because of these weaknesses of organisation, BBC staff were not particularly well-paid but they did enjoy a stability of employment and relative creative freedom. In the commercial companies, the dominant union was the ACTT, which had frequently used the standard techniques of industrial organisation to win 100 per cent trade union membership in the appropriate grades (the 'closed shop') and very advantageous wages and working conditions. Because the commercial companies had a monopoly of the sale of television advertising time, they were always able to ensure that they made high profits even when they were forced to concede good wages. Around these core unions were others like the Electricians, the NUJ, Actors Equity, NATKE and others.

It is important not to idealize the broadcast unions. Like trade unions in other sectors, they had many limitations and faults. They tended to be male-dominated. They tended to have few members from ethnic minority backgrounds. The membership often viewed the world in very narrow terms, looking out only for the interests of their own particular craft skills. Nevertheless, it was these unions which led opposition to the attacks of management and government, for instance, when there were attempts to do deals with South Africa or to ban controversial programmes or views. For example, while the broadcasters formally claim to oppose the government ban on members of Sinn Fein speaking on television, it has been the unions, and particularly the NUJ, which have organized protests and fought over the issue. To the limited extent that socialists could have any influence on the future of television, it was through their ability to influence their fellow trade unionists to take action for more general causes than their own immediate interests.

The Coming of Channel 4

In the early 1980s, the stable model began to break up. The key factor was the institution of Channel 4. This represented a radically different model of broadcast organization. The novelty lay in changes in the relations between the constituent parts of the broadcasting industry. Channel 4 was actually owned by the IBA, so at one level there was a greater degree of integration than had prevailed in the commercial organization up until then. On the other hand, Channel 4 itself merely commissioned or bought, and then scheduled, the vast majority of its programmes: it was and is a 'publisher-contractor'.

There were three sources from which Channel 4 could obtain programming. The first was to purchase completed programmes on the open market, mostly from US companies. The second was to buy or commission them from existing UK broadcasters, specifically the commercial companies. The third, and in Britain radically new, source of programmes was from companies which were not themselves broadcasters: the 'independent producers'.[3] Up until this point there had been no significant television production in Britain outside the control of the main broadcasters. The producer-broadcasters had always preferred to keep the vast majority of their programme production in house, partly in order to make sure that expensive facilities like studios were used as intensively as possible. A number of people working in and around television regarded these large organizations as stifling and conservative bureaucracies, and they lobbied very hard for a new balance for the new channel. They were successful in persuading Parliament and when Channel 4 was set up it created the independent sector from nothing. Within a few years, a large number of companies, on some estimates more than 1,000, sprang up to produce programmes first for what quickly became called 'the Channel' and then for the other broadcasters. This development was the most significant long-term fact about Channel 4 and it was eventually to transform the shape of British television production. Certainly, within a few years a diagrammatic representation of British television looked very different from the picture ten years earlier. While those employed by the BBC still worked for a single large employer, and those who worked for the commercial companies worked for a small number of relatively large employers, there was now a large number of small and medium employers with many staff employed only for single productions.

The effect of this structural transformation was for a long time masked by a number of factors. In the first place, although Channel 4 was always funded out of advertising revenues, considerable care was taken to make sure that it did not compete for funds with the existing commercial companies. The Channel was owned not by shareholders but by a public body, the IBA, which was also responsible for regulating the commercial companies. The funding was provided by a levy on the commercial companies, who in exchange received the exclusive right to sell advertising time on Channel 4. This meant that Channel 4's income was set in advance as the result of a political decision by the IBA, rather than with reference to the size or composition of its audience. Because Channel 4 was insulated from the pressures of advertisers it was possible for an advertising-funded channel to pursue a policy of attempting, however inadequately, to reach minority audiences of various kinds. Thus, while the new channel obtained its programmes in novel ways, it was carefully set up to maintain the central economic plank of British public service broadcasting: while different channels might compete for audiences, they did not compete for revenue and were thus not obliged to try to maximise audiences.

The second major factor which obscured the changeover was that the first ten years of Channel 4's operation, and particularly the latter years of the 1980s, were a period of boom in advertising revenues. The commercial companies found their incomes soaring and could thus afford to fund Channel 4 relatively generously, and the Channel itself found its incomes rising year by year. At constant 1985 prices, its income rose from £129.1 million in 1986 to £167.8 million in 1990 and production expenditure rose by 36.5 per cent in real terms over the same period. There were thus, in the first years, no serious cost pressures on broadcasters resulting from the new arrangements.

From the point of view of the workforce and their unions the new situation did not look too threatening. Channel 4 negotiated with the main unions and mainstream productions were covered by more or less standard broadcasting conditions. Those new groups from outside the industry who were enabled to make broadcast programmes for the first time, most notably the various 'workshops' around the country, were covered by a special agreement. The overall rise in advertising expenditure meant that the employers were under relatively little economic pressure to try to reduce wages and other costs. At the same time, the existence of a new channel, plus a dramatic increase in the number of broadcast hours on all channels meant that the workforce was expanding quite rapidly.'[4]

The System Enters Crisis

By the late 1980s, however, the picture looked very different. Changes in the economic and political climate acted together with the long-term effects of the creation of Channel 4 radically to destabilize employment in the television industry and to lead to major challenges to the wages and conditions of workers, and to the future of their unions.

One major factor in precipitating this crisis was the Tory government. As part of their general hostility to the public sector, they were concerned to attack the funding base of the BBC. In the conditions of constant inflation which characterised the 1980s, the BBC needed constant rises in their licence fee income in order to continue to provide the same level of service. In such a situation, to maintain funding at a constant real level in any labour-intensive industry – education, health, broadcasting – requires proportionately higher increases than the general rate of inflation. The government used its control over the licence fee to squeeze the BBC's income considerably: since 1988 it has been tied to the general rate of inflation, which is lower than the rise in broadcasting costs. This forced the management to try to cut costs, particularly labour costs, through keeping down wages and sacking staff. While the BBC remains overwhelmingly dependent upon licence fee income, the management have also tried to diversify their sources of income, through developing subscription services, increasing their publishing and marketing efforts and attempting to find other sources of funding, for example through more and more co-productions and overseas sales.[5]

The other arm of the government's economic attack on broadcasting was concentrated on the commercial sector. The re-regulation of broadcasting in the 1990 Broadcasting Act involved a number of major changes to the funding mechanisms which tend to increase the financial pressures upon the management of commercial television companies. The first of these is the introduction of competitioin for advertising revenue into the commercial sector. From the start of 1993 Channel 4 was obliged to sell its own advertising and thus entered directly into competition for revenue and for audiences with the existing commercial companies. The proposal to establish a fifth Channel, under much less stringent programming conditions than prevailed in the other two commercial channels, and the slow development of satellite broadcasting, also introduced more competition for advertising revenue, and thus direct competition for audiences.

Another major change was to submit the franchises to auction. This has had the effect of putting severe financial strains on those companies which won their franchises as the result of high bids and therefore their managements are under pressure to minimise costs. A third change is to allow takeovers of franchise holders. This means that managements have to make sure they generate sufficient income to satisfy shareholders and keep predators at bay. For some of those stations which made high bids in order to win their franchises, the combination of these pressures is likely to lead to takeovers, perhaps by franchise holders who bid lower for their own patch. Taken together, these legislative changes increased the pressures upon management to try to drive down wages and worsen conditions.[6]

However, outside of the legislative framework government policy also had an effect on the workforce in broadcasting. The potential of the independent sector was quickly noticed by the government and its ideologues. The Peacock Committee noted that:

> There are many reasons for wanting to enhance the role of the independent producer apart from the greater range of cost comparisons which greater competition would ensure. Witnesses from among the ITV contractors have stressed that the requirements for in-house production are at the root of union

restrictive practices in at least the major ITV network companies. If ITV programme makers were separate entities from ITV contractors, they could less readily be blackmailed by the threat to black channels out ... We were persuaded by the view that the independent producers could produce some programmes of comparable standard and content but at a lower cost than the BBC or ITV could achieve in-house.[7]

In line with this analysis, the Committee recommended that the BBC and TV should be obliged to take 40 per cent of their programmes from independent producers within ten years. As with many of the proposals put forward by Professor Peacock, the Government did not take up this suggestion quite as enthusiastically as the collection of businessmen and right-wing academics who packed the Committee might have hoped. However, in their White Paper on Broadcasting they said ominously that 'independent producers constitute an important source of originality and talent which must be exploited' and they moved to introduce a '25 per cent quota' on both the BBC and the commercial sector.[8] The two sets of broadcasters were obliged to commission programmes from non-broadcast producers, at a level to reach 25 per cent of their original output by the end of 1992. Obviously, this meant that the in-house productions of the existing broadcasters would fall by the same percentage: staff would find themselves without work and facilities would be under-utilized. Work, and therefore workers, would be shifted out of the large broadcasting sector into the world of the independent producers.

The consequences of this was to weaken workers' ability to organize into effective trade unions. In almost any industry it is easier to organise in large units and these provide the base for organizing in other sectors. The wages, conditions and general terms of employment agreed in the large and well-organized plants provide a guide and a standard for workers in the smaller plants. So long as television programmes were essentially produced by the broadcasters, the organizations established there could 'carry' the wages and conditions of workers in the much smaller units of the independent sector. However, if the organization in the larger sectors is weakened, it becomes relatively more difficult to hold the line in the small producers.

While it is essential to recognise the central responsibility of the government for the situation which developed in the late 1980s and early 1990s, it is also important to note that the managers and employers were in no way reluctant to attack the wages and conditions of their workers. The employers in the existing commercial companies had already launched attacks on their workforce before the notorious meeting with Mrs Thatcher in September 1987 when she called the television companies the 'last bastions of restrictive practices'. The ground had already been laid for this in the boom years. The BBC began its long attack on staff levels with the 1985 document *Priorities for the Future* and the ACTT had lost an important dispute with Thames, when the management were able to sustain a skeleton service despite strike action by technicians back in the early 1980s. By 1987 there had been a series of disputes involving Thames, Granada, Scottish Television, Tyne Tees, Ulster, TVSW and LWT, all of which had involved big changes in working practices and job losses, leading in 1988 to the collapse of the National Agreement which had provided a basis for local negotiations. On top of that, the ACTT was defeated in a long lockout by TV-AM, which demonstrated that management could not only run a service despite strike action but also so thoroughly defeat the union that at the end of the dispute it was no longer recognised.[9] Employers had already been concerned with manning levels, overtime rates and other issues even during the boom years, and if in retrospect they appear to have been relatively cautious in what they demanded that is only because they have subsequently become so aggressive. They had also, like many other employers during that period, started to look hard at the internal workings of their own organizations and to start to sub-contract jobs like cleaning, catering and security. The general, and intended, effect of these moves was to replace well organized and relatively well-rewarded workers with unorganized and much less well-rewarded workers.

Another factor in eroding the strength of the unions was the attitude of the independent producers. Many of these had in fact started out as leftists if not socialists. Certainly, the birth of Channel

4 and the accompanying growth of small production companies was seen by many on the left as representing an opening and an advance for new and radical ideas. However, very quickly, the material realities of being small businessmen and women asserted themselves over the subjective views of most of the producers. The normal laws of capitalism work with a particular intensity in television production and any producer must either accept their logic or go out of business.

There have always been more producers chasing contracts than were available and therefore there has always been fairly intensive competition between producers. In such a situation, there are three ways in which companies can respond. The first is to specialize within different sectors of the market. Due partly to the special nature of television production, in which all products, even on games shows, are at least partly different (in economic terms the situation is one in which all products either are, or approximate to, 'prototypes'), and partly to the fact that there were relatively few cost pressures since the total Channel 4 programme budget was rising, this is the route most taken during the early years of independent production. Certain companies became specialists in sports; others in current affairs and documentary; others in comedies, and so on. The companies which were most successful at this tended to have regular work, to acquire full-time staff, to use equipment for longer periods, to acquire offices and other fixed assets. In order to sustain this investment, the need for guarantees of regular work, and thus for diversification, becomes more and more urgent.

The second response open to firms is to attempt to cut costs. One way this can be done is by reducing direct costs: in television that means cutting the amount spent on salaries of production staff. The other method is to realise economies of scale: to use plant and labour more efficiently. There were, and still are, obstacles to the extent to which television production companies can take advantage of these factors. The labour-intensive character of television production means that there is a fairly direct relationship between the amount spent on wages and the quality of the product appearing on the screen. In a television system in which the expectations of both the controllers of the industry and the audience were historically set at what is, internationally, a very high level by the domination of well-funded and heavily-regulated broadcasters committed to a definition of public service which one commentator described as 'making a lot of expensive programmes', there are limitations to the extent to which quality can be reduced through cutting production costs.

In the case of economies of scale, these are best realized by large companies who can, for example, offset the cost of office rental against the budget of several programmes. There are only a few programme types in which these economies of scale operate within the commission. One important example is the game show. The studio set is the most expensive item in the production, but its costs can be spread over the whole run of the game show. In other cases, the gains from economies of scale are best realized through diversification.

If the laws of capitalism are allowed to work without impediment, there are few natural limits to the gains which could be made by larger firms. In all sectors of capitalist production there is a tendency for the market to become dominated by one, or a few, large producers because these operate more efficiently than a host of small companies. In the case of television, because of the risky nature of this form of production – one never knows whether a particular 'prototype' programme is going to be successful – there is a tendency for companies to grow larger, and to drive out small firms very quickly. Logically, the need to offset the risks of any individual production against a portfolio of products should lead to a merger of production and broadcasting, since it is in the latter that diversification can best be realized. In reality, three aspects of the UK regulatory situation modified the normal workings of the capitalist market. First, programmes were commissioned rather than speculatively produced and then offered to broadcasters. While some programmes never reached completion, and others never reached the screen, there was no risk to the independent producer once they had won a contract from Channel 4. It was the broadcaster that bore the risks of diversification. Secondly, the 'remit' of Channel 4 to provide diversity, innovation and the representation of minority viewpoints meant that it pursued the policy of commissioning very large numbers of productions from small companies and granted development money and other forms of financial support to even more. As Table One shows, the number of companies supported by Channel 4 grew continually throughout the last decade. While a proportion of these were very large – the number of companies receiving more than £1,000,000 per annum rose from seven to 28 between 1984 and 1990 – the majority were tiny companies receiving less than £100,000.[10]

Table One

Numbers of Companies Receiving Payments from Channel 4

Companies	1984	1985	1986	1987	1988	1989	1990	1991
Receiving Payment	281	313	332	360	460	491	526	668
Receiving £1m plus	7	8	8	13	15	24	28	28

Source: Channel 4 *Reports and Accounts* (1985-1991)

It thus artificially sustained a host of small producers who, if the market had been allowed to take its course, would have been driven out of business. Thirdly, the very structure of the relation between Channel 4 as broadcaster, and its programme producers who had created the 'independent sector' in the first place, meant that the largest and most successful of the independent companies remained excluded from access to the security which control of a broadcasting outlet would give them. The immediate consequence of this restriction was for a number of the largest 'independent' producers to attempt to cease to be independent, by buying into the existing commercial broadcasting companies and, more fundamentally, by agitating for the chance to become broadcasters themselves.

The final strategic response of the independent sector to the limits imposed on it by the broadcasting arrangements of the mid-1980s was to agitate for an extension to the market. This they did by organizing a successful political lobby, the 25 per cent campaign, designed to gain access to the programming funds of the existing broadcasters.

The overall effects of the whole gamut of changes from government regulatory policy through to the impact of the new independent sector upon the workforce in television was not only to weaken trade union organization but to lead to rapid reductions in the workforce in full-time employment. A workforce which had continued to expand through the slump of the early 1980s, but whose trade union organizations had shared something of the battering which had been meted out to other groups of workers, now had to face a new situation in which the gains of the boom were under very serious attack.

The Harsh New World

At the end of the 1980s there was a sharp drop in advertising revenue as the UK boom of the second half of the decade ran out of steam and was replaced by years of recession. As Table Two shows, the TV advertising spend rose in every year up to 1988, but has fallen increasingly rapidly since then.

Table Two
UK TV Advertising Expenditure at Constant 1985 Prices

Spending	1983	1984	1985	1986	1987	1988	1989	1990	1991
£M	1235	1324	1376	1620	1739	1882	1877	1774	1609
Growth	+14.3	+7.2	+3.9	+17.7	+7.3	+8.3	−0.3	−7.1	−7.7

Source: Advertising Association *Media Pocket Book* (NTC, 1991 and 1992).

This put direct pressure upon the independent sector since, for the first time since its inception, the programme budget of Channel 4, which was determined as a percentage of advertising revenue in the commercial sector, began to fall. This was accompanied by a shift of emphasis on the part of the senior managers of the Channel away from considerations of originality towards those of cost efficiency. In the boom years, the self-image of Channel 4 was very much that it commissioned programmes on their artistic merit and, while it controlled both the total budget of each commissioning editor and the agreed expenditure on each programme quite firmly, it did not chose which programmes to produce primarily on cost grounds. It was 'ideas led' in the sense that producers submitted suggestions for programmes to the Channel, rather than the Channel asking for tenders to produce programme ideas and choosing the most favourable. The financial squeeze meant that considerations of cost, and informal rankings of producers as to the ability to generate products cheaply, came to loom larger in the process. The independent companies in turn began to look for ways in which they could cut costs without sacrificing broadcasting quality.

A more indirect pressure upon overall wages and conditions was that the recession, combined with the need to accumulate large cash stocks in order to enter the bidding for the new franchises, led the commercial companies to shed labour in a quite dramatic fashion. These newly redundant TV workers joined their colleagues from the financially-pressured BBC in seeking work in the independent sector, setting up their own companies and competing for jobs. The overall picture of the shift in the nature of employment can be gleaned from a study of the composition of union membership, which shows that while membership of the ACTT continued to rise throughout the 1980s, by the end of the decade 'freelance' employment was more and more the norm.[11] This mass of unemployed and partly-employed workers, better described as casual labour rather than freelances, found themselves competing for a shrinking number of jobs.

At the same time, the advantages of independent production were becoming obvious to the existing broadcasters. Both the BBC and the commercial companies had initially resisted the spread of independent production, partly for reasons of bureaucratic inertia, partly to employ their existing establishments of staff and capital equipment, and partly out of a genuine belief that their production departments provided the conditions under which creative talent could best develop. Under financial pressure and political attack, however, both bureaucracies came to change their view. It became clear to them that there were important cost advantages to independent production. As one BBC analyst put it:

> Independents offer a unique opportunity to ITV companies to pass on the profit effects of cyclical advertising revenue down the line to production companies.[12]

The broadcasters had traditionally to maintain large establishments with big overhead costs more or less irrespective of the volume of production. Independent producers, on the other hand, could be commissioned at need and when their services were not required made no claims on the resources of the broadcasters. They, in turn, had no long-term commitment to their employees and could hire and fire more or less at will, avoiding the problems of pensions, sickness, holidays and other impedimenta with which the unions have sought to burden the entrepreneur who is the employer of a stable labour force.

Besides the need to fill their 25 per cent quota of independent production, both the commercial companies and the BBC used the existence of independent productions as a weapon against their own workforces.[13] In the case of the commercial companies, although there had been earlier threats to shift production from in-house staff to independents, it was the round of franchise bids under the new broadcasting act which provided the decisive turning point. The advantages of the separation of programme producer from scheduler and broadcaster were apparent both to some of the existing companies and to the new bidders, which included a fair proportion of the larger independent companies who were seizing this opportunity to make the shift to the more secure position of broadcaster. Those companies which bid for franchises on the basis of the 'publisher-contractor' model rather than the older producer-broadcaster model showed in their business plans very much smaller numbers of full-time employees than did those who stuck with the older model. Thus Thames, defending its London weekday franchise, slimmed down its projected workforce from 1,400 to 1,200 for its bid, but proposed to retain an in-house production facility. Carlton, the successful bidder, proposed a publisher-contractor model with a permanent staff of 400. This meant a 72 per cent reduction in permanent employment.

In the case of the BBC, it was the concept of 'Producer Choice' which marked the new situation. Under the finance arrangements which existed up until the early 1990s, the funds available for programme production had been divided between the production departments and the service departments (set construction, wardrobe, studio maintenance and so on). Transactions between the two sets were purely internal and did not involve any real market element: both buyer and seller were part of the same economic unit and prices were set by administrative decision. 'Producer Choice' directs all funds to the production departments. These are then free to contract for the provision of services either with the BBC's own service departments or with outside suppliers. Since these transactions would be 'real' for both parties, involving the actual exchange of money, and since the suppliers genuinely competed on price and quality, this arrangement means that the internal BBC departments will be obliged to match the bids, and thus the cost structures, of the independent sector.

By the early 1990s, the new shape of British broadcasting was starting to emerge. The contrast with the situation existing twenty, or even ten years, before is very sharp. Instead of large and stable units of production dominating the industry, we now have a large number of smaller and less stable companies, subject to much more direct market competition. In the longer run, the regulatory framework will control to a certain extent the trend towards monopoly, but the industry will become increasingly dominated by a small number of companies, with many others eking out an existence on the margins.

The consequences of this shift for workers in the television industry are quite considerable. The strong trade union organizations which had been built up under conditions of stable employment and a rich and expanding industry have been faced with a series of very severe challenges. The first of these is conjunctural in the sense that the fall in the value of new productions resulting from the slump in advertising revenue is almost certainly temporary: when the economy again expands, and with it advertising revenue, then the commissions will resume. While it lasts, however, the slump in production means that the number of jobs available is reduced and competition for each job increases. Up until the mid 1980s the unions were organizing in conditions in which there was effectively a labour-shortage, and they did not face an endemic problem of workers competing with each other for jobs. Those are not the conditions which pertain now. The opportunities for stable long-term employment are much fewer and there are large numbers of unemployed and semi-employed TV workers competing for each job. The centre of gravity of the industry is shifting towards a casualized labour force of the kind which characterized many manual jobs in the 19th century.

In such conditions, it can be very difficult to maintain existing union agreements, let alone organize new groups of workers. Because there are many people who have no steady work, some of whom have experienced real hardship from unemployment, competing for relatively few jobs, it becomes much more difficult to enforce union rates and conditions of employment. The employers have seized the opportunity to reduce the supplementary rates which used to be common in the industry, and to negotiate agreements which significantly worsen conditions of employment. Secondly, in a casualized industry, it is the management who decide who will get what work is going. Although there is no evidence of TV companies using the sort of 'blacklisting' agencies which are common in other industries, being known as a union organizer is not a factor which counts in favour of a job applicant.

The other thing which has changed in the present situation is structural and is the result of the shift in the employment patterns of the industry. We showed above how it is difficult to reduce the amount of labour employed in making a TV programme without visibly reducing the quality of the product. It is, however, possible to make the same amount of money spent on labour stretch a little further by means of making the workers involved work harder, or longer, or more flexibly, for the same payment. This is one of the things which has happened as a result of unemployment, but it is also something built into the nature of independent television production as currently organized. The multitude of tiny production companies whose existence is underwritten by Channel 4 are really too small to be economically viable. They exist from commission to commission and when they have no production of their own they try to hire themselves out as workers to other more fortunate companies. In order to survive as producers they are prepared to work themselves and their circle of friends and fellow workers much harder than organized workers employed by larger companies are prepared to tolerate. They are the industrial equivalent of small peasants who work themselves and their families to death in order to hold onto the tiny family plot of land long after the realities of the market place have dictated that it would be rational to sell up to a large capitalist farmer and move to the city to find paid work.

The general effect of the existence of this sort of labour is to hold down the rates of pay of those who are in paid employment can command, and to set norms of work-times and intensity which influence the whole industry. What has happened in television production over the last few years is that real rates of pay have fallen, workers have been asked to complete particular jobs for lump sums rather than being paid for the actual amount of hours worked, training and equal opportunities have suffered a major set-back. All of the worst features of casual labour which in the past provoked militancy from dock workers and building workers are emerging amongst the TV workforce. A recent issue of the official magazine of the independent producers carried a long string of complaints about employment practice in 'an independent sector utterly obsessed with price [which] is now in mortal danger of turning its "worst practice" into an industrial norm' ....[14] The inputs of very highly-skilled labour are needed in order to produce a marketable product. Whatever the short term gains of rate cutting and windfall profits are, if they become established as the long-term norms of the industry, they will surely lead to a decline in the quality of product and competitive problems in an increasingly global market for TV programmes.

Conclusion

Faced with large-scale redundancies, massive unemployment and continually eroding wages and conditions it is easy for trade-union minded workers in the television industry to fall into despair. This, of course, is amplified by the prevailing political situation. It is not, however, the inevitable response to such conditions. It is important to remember that even the cut-down BBC remains a large employer. The economic processes unleashed by the 1990 Broadcasting Act will take some time to work through the industry, but in time they will produce a tendency towards concentration into a few smaller units of production. These in turn will be open to unionization drives in the same way as an earlier generation of TV employers were. There will continue to be problems with the surviving small producers, some at least of whom will be prepared to act like the cowboys of every other industry and try to undercut wages and conditions, but the long-term experience of union organization is that if it is strongly established in the large plants then it is possible to make sure that the small sub-contractors play by the rules as well.

Television remains an industry almost completely dependent upon continual massive labour inputs and is thus very vulnerable to concerted industrial action. The attacks of the last decade changed the old BBC staff association into a genuine trade union and it has merged with other entertainment unions, most notably the ACTT, to form a new integrated union (Broadcasting and Entertainment Trade Union – BECTU) which is free of much of the deference which characterized its BBC parent and the craftist attitudes which marked its commercial parent. As recently as 1989, this union was able to confront and defeat the BBC over wages. Although trade union organization in the industry, in common with elsewhere, is much weakened and finds itself operating in a hostile legal and political climate, the possibilities of recovery remain. The main task facing socialists inside television is to work for that recovery. The task for socialists outside the industry will be to support them in the bitter struggles which will be necessary to establish once again trade organization and the decent wages and conditions which go with it.

Notes

Much of the information contained in this chapter was produced as a result of a research project at the Centre for Communication and Information Studies at the University of Westminster. I would like to thank my colleagues Bill Granger and Antonia Torchi for their contribution. While some of the arguments rehearsed here were first presented in a paper to the 1991 International Television Studies Conference ('Re-regulation and TV Production: A Comparison of Italy and the UK') jointly authored by all three of us, my colleagues are not responsible for the political analysis presented above.

[1] BBC, *Annual Report 1986*, London, BBC, p 26.

[2] The degree to which a workforce is organised into trade unions (the 'union density') in any industry, is more or less related to the size of the average plant. This is partly because in an industry dominated by small plants (catering is a good example) labour relations tend to be 'patriarchal': the boss rules through personal knowledge of the workforce and weeds out 'trouble makers' and rewards crawlers. Another important factor is that it is quite easy to set up in business for oneself, and therefore becoming a boss is a viable alternative for the energetic and able workers, particularly when they are victimized for trade union activism.

[3] The British talent for euphemism is remarkable. The commercial companies managed to sanitize themselves as 'independent' back in the 1950s. The next lot of commercial companies, coming into being to compete with the existing commercial companies also managed to sanitize themselves as 'independent'. Presumably these companies were independent of the independent sector.

[4] The volume of BBC network new productions, for example, rose 42.8 per cent between 1979 and 1991. See J. Davis, *TV, UK: A Special Report*, Knowledge Research, 1991, p 31.

[5] The attempt to force the BBC to earn advertising revenue in the mid-1980s failed to command widespread support.

[6] Another change, outside of the framework of the Act, was to the way in which the 'TV Levy' (a special tax on broadcasting companies) was determined. Instead of this being a tax on profits, it was changed to a tax on advertising revenue. This appeared on the surface a mere technical change in the way that the TV companies were taxed, but in fact has implications for programme expenditure, and thus on employment, wages and conditions in the sector. In order to minimilize their exposure to a tax on profits, the TV companies had increased their spending on programmes and shown relatively small profits. With a tax on revenue, the incentive to spend on programmes is replaced by an incentive to maximize the profit element in the amount of revenue remaining after tax.

[7] *Report of the Committee on Financing the BBC*, HMSO, London 1986, (Cmnd. 9824) p 142.

[8] *Broadcasting in the '90's: Competition, Choice and Quality*, HMSO, London 1988, (Cm 517) p 41.

[9] See C. Sparks 'The Impact of Technological and Political Change on the Labour Force in UK TV' in *Screen*, Winter-Spring 1989.

[10] Channel 4, *Report and Accounts* (1985-1991). London: Channel 4.

[11] Source of Figure Five: B. Granger *The Casualization of the Membership of the ACTT*, CCIS Policy Paper no.2, Polytechnic of Central London, London, p 51.

[12] M. Oliver, 'Deregulation and the Organization of ITV Companies' in R. Patterson (ed.), *Organizing for Change* BFI, London 1990, p 38. A similar statement could be made about the advantages to the BBC of independent production.

[13] See Sparks, *op.cit.*

[14] D. Barrie 'Lone Ranger be warned' in *Impact*, January 1993, Number 7, 5.

Money Talks: Broadcasting Finance and Public Culture

Graham Murdock

Broadcasting or Television?

In a now famous statement, Mark Fowler, President Reagan's first appointee as head of the Federal Communications Commission (the main regulator of the American media industries) declared that as far as he could see 'Television is just another appliance. It's a toaster with pictures'. He spoke for all the men in suits who reach for a calculator whenever they hear the word 'culture'. They regard television as first and last a business, and claim the right to pursue profits with minimal interference from government. Ranged against this, is a definition of broadcasting as a public service whose prime responsibility is to develop the cultural rights of modern citizenship. As the screenwriter, Dennis Potter insisted in a passionate speech to the Edinburgh International Television Festival in 1993, broadcasting 'is not a business trying to distribute dosh to its shareholders ... but something held in trust and in law for every citizen'.[1] The contest between these views is increasingly acrimonious.

In November 1991, Gerry Robinson was appointed as chief executive of the Granada Group, the conglomerate that controlled Granada Television, one of the leading companies in the ITV system. He had no previous experience of broadcasting, having made his mark as head of the contract caterers, Compass. He arrived with a reputation for controlling costs. The television subsidiary was a prime target, and after refusing to implement the measures asked for, David Plowright, the widely respected executive chairman (who had enjoyed a distinguished career as a producer) was forced to resign. For many observers, the incident dramatized the growing conflict between 'broadcasting' and 'television'. The Directors' Guild of Great Britain dispatched a letter of protest to The *Guardian* signed by many of the country's leading programme makers. It expressed dismay at Plowright's sacking, and restated their belief that he 'embodied the ideals of quality broadcasting in Britain and that this is therefore a sad day not just for Granada but for British television as a whole'. The comedian, John Cleese, was less guarded. He sent Robinson a fax which read: 'Fuck off out of it, you ignorant, upstart caterer'. Robinson faxed back: 'Reading between the lines I think I can safely say that I am a bigger fan of yours than you are of mine'. These skirmishes have their roots in the founding moment of modern broadcasting in the 1920s, and in the divergent philosophies and organizational forms that emerged then.

The advent of broadcasting coincided with two profound social changes: the rise of a mass consumer system and the advent of mass democracy; its nascent institutions had to find ways of negotiating these shifts. The American response was to integrate broadcasting into the new consumer marketplace. The stations were private companies whose main business was assembling audiences for sale to advertisers. In contrast, the British solution was built around the assumed needs of the new political system, with a view of audiences as citizens rather than consumers. This project was thought to require a public corporation, funded out of the public purse, whose creative decisions would be relatively free of pressure from either government or business, and whose productions would be equally available to everyone. The aim was to create a new kind of shared space in which the cultural rights of citizenship could be developed and refined.

In practice, this space was under continual pressure from governments wishing to secure a favourable hearing for their platforms and policies, and from restrictive definitions of broadcasting's cultural project. Nevertheless, the ideal of providing symbolic resources for citizenship offered a core rationale for public broadcasting that distinguished it sharply from the commercial logic of advertising-funded services.

It became the defining feature of the 'British way' of broadcasting, so that when the BBC's monopoly was finally breached in the mid 1950s, it was transferred relatively painlessly to the new commercial television system. The ITV stations were privately owned and supported by advertising, leaving the BBC with the full licence fee. However, the ITV companies' own 'licence to print money' (as Lord Thompson put it on winning the main franchise for Scotland) was overstamped by a series of public service obligations. They were allowed to employ tried and tested programme formulas to maximize audiences in peak hours, providing they also addressed minorities and extended diversity. Producing programmes that were unprofitable, or at least, not as profitable as the alternatives, was the price they paid for enjoying a monopoly of advertising revenue in their franchise areas. This arrangement of non-competitive funding and an overlapping commitment to broadcasting as a public service, produced what critics on the right came to see as a 'comfortable duopoly'[2] long overdue for a strong dose of market discipline. With Mrs Thatcher's election as Prime Minister they got their chance.

The old adage, 'money talks', applies with particular force to broadcasting. Who gets to speak in this central public space, to whom, about what, and in which ways, depends in large part on how the system is paid for. Funding plays a crucial role in organizing production and consumption. It has powerful effects on both the diversity of programming and its availability. The BBC's claim on the licence fee assumes that this is the 'least worst' way to maximize the range of voices in play, and to ensure that their conversations and arguments are accessible to every citizen. The plausibility of this case hinges on whether one sees the continual renewal of public culture as the most productive way to use television technology. Enthusiasts of a market-oriented view of television clearly reject this view. For them there is no 'public', only individual consumers who must be enticed to part with their money. But before we trace the rise of this ethos and the ensuing retreat from public broadcasting, we need a clearer definition of broadcasting's relation to citizenship rights.

Cultural Rights and Complex Citizenship

Recent years have seen a marked revival of interest in the rights of citizenship and their implementation, but definitions vary widely. A number of commentators operate with relatively narrow conceptions. There is, for example, the common sense view that equates citizenship with participation in the formal political process. Or there is the consumerist definition underpinning John Major's Citizen's Charter, which identifies citizenship with consumer rights in relation to public services. Applied to broadcasting, the first emphasizes the need for 'comprehensive, in-depth and impartial news and information coverage' capable of supporting 'a fair and informed national debate',[3] whilst the second, demands adequate mechanisms of accountability and redress. Both of these elements need to be included in any definition of 'public service' but they do not exhaust it. Over and against attempts to delimit the notion of citizenship, I want to argue for a general definition which identifies it with *the right to participate fully in existing patterns of social life and to help shape the forms they may take in future*. An insistence on a general right to social membership and action allows us to see citizenship in a more complex, multi-dimensional way. This core entitlement rests, in turn, on four major subsets of rights: civil rights; political rights; social and economic rights; and cultural rights.

Cultural rights are comprised of entitlements in four main areas: information; knowledge; representation; and communication. Information rights consist of rights of access to the information people need to make considered personal and political judgements, and to pursue their rights in other areas, effectively. In particular, it entails a right to comprehensive and disinterested information on the activities and plans of public and private agencies with significant power over peoples' lives. But information is of only limited use in its raw state. It needs to be placed in context, and its implications teased out and debated. Knowledge rights promote these processes by underwriting the public's access to the widest possible range of interpretation, debate and explanation.

158

The third subset of cultural right, rights of representation, revolve around the right to have the ones' experiences, beliefs and aspirations adequately and truthfully represented in the major forms of public culture. This is coupled with the right not to be quoted or pictured without informed consent. Finally, communicative rights entail the right to contribute to the circulation of public information, knowledge and representation, not simply as a consumer but as an active provider; the right to speak as well as to be spoken about.

Even listed baldly like this, it is clear that delivering these entitlements has far-reaching implications for the way in which broadcasting is organized and funded. It must be as open as possible and not subject to undue influence from any one power group. It must promote diversity not plurality, offering the widest possible range of viewpoints, perspectives and expressive forms, rather than a restricted choice in a variety of packages. And it must be available to everyone at the minimal feasible cost. As we shall see, the various branches of the emerging television industries clearly fail these tests, in whole or in part.

The Retreat From Public Service

The retreat from public service began with the policy for broadband cable services developed by the first Thatcher government. Cable was not in itself a new. The first cable systems were built in the mid 1920s soon after regular broadcast services got underway. Their business was relaying signals to areas where reception was poor or impossible. As well as BBC services, many also carried the transmissions of commercial radio stations based in Europe. This led to a running battle between the BBC, who demanded the right to control what was available over the wires, and the relay companies, who wanted to offer their customers a range of services. Their market orientation was endorsed by the Post Office, which declared in 1932 that 'the choice of programmes should be, as far as possible, regulated by the desire of the subscribers who listen to them'.[4] With the introduction of regular television services, the national broadcasters regained the upper hand and cable was relegated to the subordinate role of relaying their programming. In response, the cable operators renewed their efforts to persuade successive governments to allow them to carry additional services. There was a short-lived experiment with a subscription channel dominated by films in the 1960s, and forays into local community services in the 1970s. But at the beginning of the 1980s the cable industry was still confined to a secondary, relay role.

Innovations in technology, however, were breathing new life into arguments for adding a range of subscription services. The new fibre optic networks (using thin strands of glass) had the capacity to deliver a far greater number of television channels than the old wired systems. More importantly, they offered the possibility of developing a wide range of interactive services. It was this second feature that caught the government's attention. It fitted perfectly with their general assumption that information technology would revive the economy, and that developing its potential as quickly as possible was a national priority. Not surprisingly, given this political context, the hand-picked panel that Mrs Thatcher appointed to look into the future of cable systems gave this view their enthusiastic backing. After deliberating for seven months, they duly concluded that cable's 'main role will be the delivery of many information, financial and other services to the home and the joining of businesses and home by high capacity data links'.[5] At the same time, they realized that this push would have to wait until the general strategy for deregulating telecommunications services had been implemented. Since both industries shared the same new technologies, their futures were clearly interlinked. As a result, the panel recognized that 'cable systems will go through an initial phase when their attraction will be based on "entertainment" considerations'. [6]They also endorsed the government's growing commitment to privatization in seeing 'no need for any public subsidy to cable systems'.[7]But if private investors were going to pay to install a new cable infrastructure, they would need substantial incentives and a ready source of revenue. The panel's answer was simple: allow entrepreneurs to offer a wide variety of new television channels and get the public to pick up the bill. As they put it, 'private sector funding will only be available if the range of programmes and services permitted on cable systems offers sufficient revenue-earning potential'.[8] This meant that the public service requirements placed on broadcasters had to be suspended or substantially watered down for the new industry.

This fundamental shift towards a philosophy of 'television' was institutionalized in the 1984 Cable and Broadcasting Act. Instead of adding cable to the responsibilities of the Independent Broadcasting Authority (IBA), which regulated commercial television, the Act created a separate regulatory agency, the Cable Authority, with the clear expectation that they would apply a 'light touch' in awarding and policing cable franchises. The new body set about their task with relish. They declared in their first Annual Report that their most important duty 'was to promote cable services'[9] and that, since 'cable was not designed as a public service'[10], many of the areas that had traditionally been the subject of strong regulation within broadcasting – such as the scheduling of advertising breaks, the screening of sponsored programmes, and the amount of foreign programming allowed – 'could be left to market forces to decide'.[11]

The major exception was local programming. Since cable systems are installed in bounded geographic areas, enthusiasts had long seen them as an ideal medium for developing local television services, to supplement the programming offered by the main channels, and as a way of involving more people in making programmes. This argument was incorporated into the Cable and Broadcasting Act of 1984. Section seven required all cable operators to provide programmes 'calculated to appeal to the taste and outlook of persons living in the area' and to encourage local people and local voluntary groups to participate in their production. However, in line with their chosen role as advocates for the industry, the new Authority was quick to argue that 'it is unrealistic to expect substantial amounts of money to be devoted to these services until the basis for a successful business has been established'.[12] Given this official indifference, it is not surprising that by July 1992 only ten out of the 55 franchises then operating were providing locally made programming.[13]

This situation is unlikely to alter significantly in future for two reasons. Firstly, unlike the 1984 Act, the 1990 Broadcasting Act which replaced it at the beginning of 1991, contains no local or community obligations. Secondly, in an attempt to attract new investment into the industry, the government abolished restrictions on overseas ownership. This has allowed North American companies to move in and acquire the majority of UK cable systems. Some of these new owners are companies with interests in cable and entertainment, but most are US telecommunications companies who are using cable to break into the British market for telephone services. As *The Economist* pointed out, the fact that 'Margaret Thatcher deregulated the cable business to an extent unparalelled anywhere in the world' has allowed US firms to use 'Britain as a televisual test-tube for the sorts of programmes and services they will launch in America'.[14]

The American phone company Nynex, which had become Britain's largest cable operator by the end of 1993, is a prime example of this logic. As the firm's Chief Financial Officer has explained, they chose to focus their European efforts on the UK because it is 'one of the few countries open to US corporations and offering the potential to provide telephoney'.[15] They have taken full advantage of this 'window of opportunity', building viable geographic markets for telecommunications services by acquiring adjacent cable franchises in selected areas, and expanding them through joint ventures. Nynex's network in the Greater Manchester area is due to link up with the networks operated by other companies in Liverpool and Yorkshire to form a northern network. This will then link with networks in five other regions to provide a national telecommunications infrastructure that will enable cable operators to carry telephone traffic without connecting with either of the established telecommunications operators: BT and Mercury.[16]

These moves change the economics of the cable industry. If financial viability depends solely on establishing a mass subscriber base for entertainment services, offering local and community services can be a useful way of building good public relations in the local area. But if, in the longer term, the main profit centre shifts to telephony, companies are likely to concentrate on attracting relatively affluent subscribers who make extensive use of their telephones and are in the market for other interactive services. Certainly, telephone services are becoming a major growth area for cable operators. In 1991, the number of telephone lines they installed rose from 2,224 to 21,225, and revenues per line generally exceeded forecasts, particularly for business users. [17]The emerging inter-regional links will also enable cable companies to engage in joint programming. This move towards national networking will place additional pressure on local programming.

Ten years on from the original report on cable systems, the panel's view that they have more to do with telecommunications than broadcasting finally seems to be gaining ground, spurred on by the rapid convergence of the computing, telecommunications and screen-based industries. Cable operators will continue to offer additional television channels, but most of these will be produced and packaged by companies based outside Britain. They will not provide shared spaces for exploring 'the state of the nation' or negotiating new conceptions of the common good. On the contrary, they will fragment audiences by offering services tailored to saleable interest groups, and they will continue to exclude everyone who cannot afford the entry price. At the end of 1993, subscribers to systems operated by Videotron (one of the leading cable companies) had to pay £30.97 a month to receive all the channels on offer.[18] Even the standard pack, at £9.99, is well beyond the reach of the many poorer families.

Satellite television does nothing to address these problems. Which is not surprising since its development is marked by the same rapid retreat from public service principles.

In the spring of 1982, the government announced that it had decided to award two of the direct satellite broadcasting channels allocated to Britain by international agreement, to the BBC. As with cable, the main impetus was economic rather than cultural. The government wanted to establish a strong British presence in the emerging market for satellite technology, and the BBC's bid provided a convenient way to kick-start a national initiative. The contract to build the satellite went to the Unisat consortium, comprising the newly privatized British Aerospace, the soon to be denationalized British Telecom, and the Marconi Avionics divisions of GEC, one of the country's largest companies. Once again, there was to be no public finance, a ban which included money from the licence fee. Thus in the summer of 1983, the BBC's Charter was ammended to allow it to borrow on the open market.

The Corporation's euphoria at stealing a march on the ITV companies soon wore off as it became clear that the financial burden of the project was far more than they could comfortably carry. Partnership was the only solution, and in the spring of 1984 the government approved a new alliance between the BBC, the ITV companies and selected 'outside' interests. This soon collapsed, and in 1986 the IBA (who had assumed responsibility for the project) advertised a new franchise for commercial services on three of Britain's national DBS channels. The contract went to the British Satellite Broadcasting (BSB) consortium backed by a mix of leading ITV companies, (including Granada and Anglia) and major communications companies, notably Pearson (publishers of the *Financial Times*) and Richard Branson's Virgin group, BSB promised 'quality' programming and committed itself to a substantial amount of original production. It was to be, in part at least, an extension of public service broadcasting, an ambition which led Rupert Murdoch's *Sun* to dismiss it as 'toff's telly'. His motives for attacking the venture were soon to become clear.

Things started to go wrong with BSB almost immediately. Costs soon passed the initial projections. Then, in the summer of 1988, Rupert Murdoch announced that he was leasing four transponders on the Luxembourg-based, Astra satellite and launching a new package of television channels in Britain under the Sky brand name. By the time BSB finally went on air, some months after Sky, it was clear that the project was unsustainable. It had been planned on the assumption that it would have a national monopoly on satellite services for long enough to gain a reasonable return. It was totally unprepared for competition. However, Sky was also losing money and many commentators had already written it off. The solution was a merger. The terms were announced publicly in November 1990. Murdoch emerged with a 50 per cent share of the new group, B Sky B, and overall control. A government initiative, which had begun as a planned extension of the BBC's operations, had ended up accepting a commercial monopoly relaying transnational programming from an 'offshore' satellite under the strategic direction of an American citizen.

As with cable, these developments represent a substantial shift from 'broadcasting' to 'television'. In place of a universal service committed to diverse representation and open debate, satellite TV offers subscription channels tailored to commercially viable interests and limited to those able to pay. For some, including Rupert Murdoch, this is still a 'public service'. As he told the Edinburgh Television Festival in 1989: 'my own view is that anybody who, within the law of the land, provides a service which the public wants at a price it can afford is providing a public service'. [19]This linguistic twist substitutes a consumerist definition – that public service means offering a service that people want to buy – for a political definition which supports the provision of cultural and information resources needed for full citizenship. Mr Murdoch is not alone. Redefining 'public service' to fit with current practice has become a popular pastime with television executives, not least within ITV.

Despite a good deal of initial scepticism, commentators are now broadly agreed that after an uncertain start, cable and satellite operators have established a significant third force within British television. This new source of competition – for audiences, for advertising, and for programme rights – has combined with the impact of new legislation to hasten the retreat from public service values within the ITV system.

The reductive consumerist philosophy of the new television industries requires the established channels to renew their commitment to core public service values so that viewers are offered genuine diversity and choice. The government position, supported by influential figures within ITV, is exactly the opposite. As the 1988 White Paper on Broadcasting put it: 'As the UK moves towards a more competitive, multi-channel broadcasting market, the existing regime for ITV would become increasingly hard to sustain ... As Viewers exercise greater choice there is no longer the same need for quality of service to be prescribed by legislation or regulatory fiat ... It should be for the operators to decide what to show and when to show it'[2'] subject only to the general law and to residual regulatory requirements. In other words, the companies' economic interests in retaining audiences in a harsher competitive environment take precedence over the public interest in sustaining services that guarantee citizens' rights. An increase in the raw number of channels and programmes serves as a pretext for reducing diversity and organizing schedules around material that is safe and saleable. Regulation does not disappear in this system, it simply re-locates to the corporate boardroom. As one critic of American commercial broadcasting in its early days dryly noted: 'Business succeeds rather better than the state in imposing restraints upon individuals, because its imperatives are disguised as choices'.[21]

By removing many of the regulatory supports for diversity and minority representation, and replacing the IBA with the lighter touch of the Independent Television Commission, the 1990 Broadcasting Act gives these imperatives a good deal more room to manoeuvre. This space is occupied by a strategy that is unashamedly commercial. As Paul Jackson, the director of programmes for Carlton Television (the weekday contractor for London) put it: 'Programmes will not survive in the new ITV if they don't pay their way'.[22]

The one significant exception to this logic is regional programming. Supporters of the ITV original system's decentralized structure, which limits companies to a single franchise covering specific geographical area, have always seen it as more sensitive to regional interests than the BBC, with its metropolitan base and bias. There is more than a touch of romanticism in this view. The boundaries of the present ITV regions were drawn up on the basis of engineering convenience, to fit the transmitter system. They were not designed to correspond to organic, regional cultures. Added to which, most major ITV companies have long had offices in London and have concentrated on producing programmes for the national network. Even so, by providing spaces for the exploration of specifically local interests and issues, regional programmes at their best have added an important element to the diversity of debate and representation offered by broadcasting.

The 1990 Broadcasting Act appears to strengthen this commitment by making regional programming a statutory duty for the first time. But how far the companies will be willing to meet this obligation, and how far the ITC will penalize them if they don't, is open to question. The larger companies want to establish a stronger presence in the expanding international programme market. But regional productions don't generally travel well, nor do they fit easily into the emerging ownership structure of the ITV system. In an effort to consolidate their commercial position, the major companies lobbied for a relaxation of the rules relating to mergers and acquisitions. Their efforts met with partial success when the government decided to allow a single company to own any two franchises, apart from the two for London. Almost immediately, Carlton proposed a merger with Central, Meridian (which hold the franchise for the South and South East) bid for Anglia, and Granada moved to acquire LWT. The long predicted consolidation of the system had begun. The winners in this competition are more likely to concentrate on producing for the national and international markets and less likely to develop regional programming beyond the minimum necessary to pre-empt sanctions from the ITC. This minimal commitment could be weakened still further if major European companies take up their right to bid for ITV franchises on the same terms as UK companies. If strategic parts of the ITV system follow cable and satellite services and end up being owned 'offshore', by corporations with no allegiance to the core values of 'broadcasting', the shift to 'television' will take a further, massive, step forward.

Marketing the BBC

Given that a market-oriented view of 'television' already underpins the new screen industries and is rapidly reshaping the ITV system, a BBC committed to a complex conception of public service broadcasting is more essential than ever. However, the Corporation's ambivalent relation to the new television marketplace presents a major stumbling block.

By the early 1980s it was clear to many observers that the idea of privatizing the BBC was gathering a good head of steam among Mrs Thatcher's advisors. It received strong support from leading think tanks on the right, including the influential Adam Smith Institute. Their 1984 report on communications policy came out strongly in favour of financing BBC1 by advertising, and funding BBC2 by a combination of advertising, sponsorship and viewer subscriptions[23]. Not surprisingly, the major advertising agencies, led by Saatchi and Saatchi (who had won the Conservative Party account), were quick to endorse the call for advertising. They had been pressing for access to BBC audiences for some time. They also hoped that competition would drive down rates, which they saw as unacceptably high due to the ITV companies' monopoly on air-time sales.

Although these proposals were radical, they received unexpected and unintended support from the BBC's own moves into the television marketplace. As the Adam Smith report gleefully pointed out: 'It is wrong to suggest that [they] would unduly "commercialize" the BBC, since it is already heavily commercialized'.[24]

The BBC were faced with a severe dilemma. To compensate for the falling real value of their licence fee revenue they had to become more market oriented, selling programmes more vigorously overseas and entering the new markets opened up by the video, cable and merchandising industries. At the same time, they had to present these moves as an integral part of their public service remit. As one senior executive explained in 1980: 'These new ventures (or adventures) into profit-making activities must be seen to be, and must actually be, extensions of the public broadcaster's mission. They must ... be profitable enough to finance the development of programme services at all levels to the direct viewer'.[25] The difficulty arises when new services break with the core commitment to universal access.

The BBC's first Director General, John Reith, had made universal access a cardinal principal, insisting that 'There need be no first and third class' and that there should be no element of the service 'which is exclusive to those who pay more, or who are considered in one way or another more worthy of attention'.[26] The Corporation had renewed this pledge in 1981 in their evidence to the official enquiry into the future of cable, claiming that: 'All citizens have the right of equal access to the BBC's service of information, education and entertainment provided they are prepared to pay their license fees'.[27] By proposing subscription services, the ill-fated venture into satellite broadcasting clearly broke with this principle. It established a division between the core services, open to all and funded out of the licence fee, and the additional commercial services available only to subscribers.

In recent years, the Corporation has extended the scope of these 'secondary' ventures. In partnership with Thames Television (the country's largest independent programme producer) it has established a satellite channel, UK Gold, which is part of B Sky B's subscription package. Through its subsidiary, BBC World Service Television, it offers an advertising-funded service on the Star satellite system, which is based in Hong Kong and owned by Rupert Murdoch. And in May 1994, in its most ambitious move to date, it announced an alliance with the Pearson group to launch a series of new satellite channels around the world starting with two in Europe. It has also established its own domestic subscription services using the night time hours to transmit programming to specific professional markets. The core rationale for these initiatives remains the same: raising additional revenues to support programme making on the two core channels. But by venturing into the marketplace so enthusiastically, the BBC runs the risk of undermining its case for a continuation of the licence fee.

The all-party House of Commons National Heritage Committee which reported on the BBC's future at the end of 1993, siezed this cleft stick and brandished it with gusto. On the one hand, 'with great reluctance' they came down in favour of retaining the licence fee for the ten years after the expiry of the Corporation's current Royal Charter in 1986.[28] On the other, they urged the BBC to exploit every opportunity to extend 'its role in the market', but immediately added that 'should the BBC find a new, profitable commercial role ... it might be very difficult, if not impossible, to justify the existence of a licence fee at all'.[29] The logic of this argument has been taken a stage further by the BBC's former Head of News and Current Affairs. He argues that the BBC can only become a major player in the emerging transnational television marketplace if it is 'free to compete' as a privately owned company relying on advertising and subscription for the bulk of its revenues, topped up with grants for specific projects from a public service broadcasting council.[3'] The fact that these proposals come from a former senior insider gives them added force and re-opens the case for privatizing the BBC.

The argument for abolishing the licence fee was first given authoritative backing by the Committee on Financing the BBC, chaired by the economist Sir Alan Peacock, which reported in the summer of 1986. They rejected advertising as a means of funding the Corporation but endorsed 'a sophisticated market system based on consumer sovereignty' which gave viewers 'the option of purchasing the broadcasting services they require from as many alternative sources of supply as possible'.[31] In line with this model, they proposed phasing out the licence fee and moving the BBC's financing to a subscription base. They envisaged a new social contract in which the Corporation would deal with its audiences firstly as consumers and only secondly as citizens. At the same time, they recognized that 'There will always be a need to supplement the *direct consumer market* by public finance for programmes of a public service kind supported by people in their *capacity as citizens* and voters but unlikely to be commercially self-supporting in the view of broadcasting entrepreneurs'[32] (emphasis added). Accordingly they proposed that a new body (analogous to the Arts Council) should dispense public money to worthy programme ideas that advanced 'knowledge, culture, criticism and experiment'[33]. The BBC would be free to compete for these funds but would have no priviledged right to them.

Since John Major replaced Mrs Thatcher as Prime Minister, a general consensus has emerged that the Peacock report was the high-water mark of the push to privatize the BBC; that the case for a continuation of the licence fee as the sole source of funding for core services has now been won. This may be wishful thinking. Certainly there is likely to be fierce argument before such a provision is written into the Charter, which takes effect after 1996. Even if this battle is won, the new Charter may well usher in the final decade of the Corporation's life in the form we know now.

Whilst the government's 1992 consultative document, *The Future of the BBC*, does not lend its unequivocal support to any particular funding option, equally, it does not rule any out, declaring that 'There is no reason why all the BBC's services should be funded exclusively by the licence fee'.[34] In their own manifesto for their future, *Extending Choice*, the Corporation partially concede this case, arguing that whilst 'the licence fee remains the best available mechanism for … guaranteeing universal access and maintaining a wide range of broadcasting in the UK … licence payers will benefit if [the BBC] generates further income from secondary sources'.[35] Not only because 'taken together they can be an important supplement to the licence fee' but because they would 'form part of *a genuinely mixed funding base* for the full range of the BBC's services'[36] (emphasis added). This acceptance of mixed funding opens the way for critics to renew their assault on the BBC's exclusive entitlement to the licence fee and on their resistance to advertising and subscription.

The battle for the future of public service broadcasting then, is a battle with the BBC as much as a battle with its detractors. To win it, two things are necessary: a clear conception of what public broadcasting stands for now and why it offers an essential counter to the consumerist philosophy of 'television'; and a convincing demonstration of the need to fund this project out of the public purse. The plausibility of the second argument depends on the force of the first. Without a convincing philosophical rationale for public broadcasting, arguments about how to finance it become purely technical. Here again, however, the BBC's attempt to define its core project raises a number of questions.

Remaking Public Broadcasting

Public broadcasting must negotiate the new economics of the television marketplace, particularly the accelerated move towards a transnational image system. It also needs to respond to significant shifts in the cultural landscape represented by the new politics of difference. The fact that so much of the original rationale for the BBC centred around its role as a national agency with a special relationship to the 'national culture', places the BBC in a problematic relation to both these trends.

In its initial statement of future policy *Extending Choice*, the Corporation argued strongly that it 'should continue to develop its leading position in the international market for television programmes and related services' by promoting programme and archive sales more vigorously, and developing new ventures with partners.[37] The House of Commons National Heritage Committee underlined this point, urging the BBC to capitalize on the fact that its 'respected brand name [makes] it an international asset to the UK'.[38] The Corporation argued that further moves in this direction would produce a wholly 'virtuous circle of investment yielding high returns for licence payers by allowing domestic programme making to benefit from the additional monies earned in overseas and secondary markets'.[39]

As the Heritage Committee was quick to point out, however, this strategy poses problems of legitimacy. Transforming the Corporation 'from being a terrestrial broadcaster into predominantly a supplier of programmes for viewing on demand in the United Kingdom and throughout the world'[4'] could provide it with a secure future, but in the process it would have to change 'its role from its present structure and purpose'[41] so that 'the BBC that survived might not be the BBC the Committee admires' and 'might not even be a BBC that could argue for a public sector role'.[42] *The Economist*, with its usual commercial 'realism', drew the obvious conclusion, arguing that 'if the BBC is to compete on the world stage, it needs to be free of the restrictions that the charter puts on its commercial ventures. The best way to do that ... is to privatize it'.[43] But even if the Corporation stops short of sawing completely through the philosophical branch supporting its claim to the licence fee, there is still a problem. Any significant increase in its orientation to the transnational television system will exacerbate tensions between the requirements for selling in major overseas markets, and the need to address 'the national condition' in a situation where established categories are being challenged by a new politics of difference.

As befits a publication from the Department of National Heritage (which has taken over responsibility for broadcasting from the Home Office), the government's consultative document on the BBC's future lays considerable stress on the fact that it is in a special position to 'celebrate and enhance the national heritage and encourage people to enjoy it.[44] The BBC accept this role, arguing that they will continue 'to give special prominence to the artistic, sporting and ceremonial events that bring the nation together' and to 'reflect all the dimensions of both popular and minority culture that make us different as a nation'.[45] The problem is that much of what unites 'us' as a nation and defines the 'national culture' is based on our unique experience as a modern imperial power. It is a unity rooted in the supression of difference and the refusal to recognize the claims of 'Black Atlantic' culture[46] or the cultures of other areas of the old empire. In a post-colonial polity, notions of 'national heritage' can no longer be evoked or celebrated unproblematically. What we share cannot be taken for granted. It has to be continually renegotiated. The BBC partly recognizes this, and commits itself to portraying 'a multiracial, multicultural society' and responding 'to the diversity of cultures throughout the UK'.[47] But it is not clear what form this response will take. The issue of representation cannot be addressed in full by creating more specialist programmes for ethnic minorities. It must involve a positive engagement at all levels of programming, not only because minorities have a right to see themselves represented in diverse ways within the cultural mainstream, but because such moves are a basic precondition for negotiating a renewed conception of the common good. This same logic applies, in varying degrees, to all minorities.

The main difference between public broadcasting and 'television' is not that broadcasting pays more attention to minority interests, but that it represents them across the range of programming, showing people as full subjects, with complexities and contradictions, and not as objects defined by handy stereotypes, be they negative or positive. Public broadcasting at its best is open-ended and dynamic. It does not use overly familiar images to pre-empt uncertainty and close down dialogue. On the contrary, it offers spaces in which the claims of specific interests can be debated, and the relations between unity and difference, solidarity and separation, consent and dissent, continually tested.

This search for a renewed concept of the common good, rooted in an active engagement with difference, is at the heart of public broadcasting's capacity to underwrite cultural rights. But it cannot be pursued successfully unless programmes remain open to the greatest possible range of viewpoints and perspectives, and all viewers have equal access to all the results. This rules out funding from subscription, advertising and sponsorship.

It also requires that production draws on the full range of available forms and genres. Documentary, current affairs and discussion programmes are essential but they are not enough. Fiction and entertainment can offer unique insights and vantage points. Narratives can go behind closed doors to dramatize the workings of power. They can decentre familiar perceptions, and they can link biography to history in unexpected ways, tracing the intimate repercussions of public events and official policies. To achieve these ends, however, programme makers need to take risks, not only with new talent and new forms that engage more fully with social and cultural changes, but with audiences. They have to challenge and provoke as well as celebrate and entertain. Whether or not the BBC has the resources and spaces to do this in the future depends on how the Corporation is funded.

All forms of finance have drawbacks. But the choice cannot be based on purely economic criteria. The options must be measured against public broadcasting's central role in guaranteeing cultural rights.

Funding the BBC's Future

The case for continuing to fund the BBC's core activities out of the licence fee rests on the claim that all other major sources of funding would produce a less desirable outcome in terms of openness, independence, diversity, innovation and universal access. But how convincing is this argument?

There are four main sources of possible finance for the BBC: profits generated by commercial activities in the new television and entertainment marketplaces; revenues from advertising and sponsorship; direct payments by viewers; and monies granted by government.

There are three main drawbacks to the Corporation coming to rely too heavily on profits from its commercial enterprises. Firstly, it generates potential conflicts of interest between the Corporation's responsibility to engage with the full diversity of national life, and the search for programme ideas that have revenue earning potential in overseas and secondary markets. The danger here is that this will lead to more productions designed to appeal in America and elsewhere – by celebrating unproblematic, but saleable visions of national heritage and national life – and fewer that speak to the complex cross-currents of contemporary circumstances. Secondly, funding secondary ventures out of advertising or customer subscriptions erodes the legitimacy of claims to the licence fee, and strengthens the hand of those calling for partial or complete privatization. Thirdly, and most importantly, the introduction of subscription services undermines the cardinal principle of universal and equal access by establishing tiers of provision dependent on the viewer's ability to pay.

Consequently, although the idea of maximizing returns on the Corporation's investments in facilities and productions has obvious attractions in straightened financial times, it has the clear potential to become a trojan horse, wheeled through the gates by a government intent on phasing out the licence fee, aided and abetted by BBC personnel aspiring to be major players in the new market-places of the transnational television industry.

The other major pressure comes from advertisers wanting access to the BBC's audiences. Advertising takes two main forms: corporate sponsorship of specific programmes, and payments to place conventional advertisements in selected spots in the general flow of programmes. British broadcasters have always been highly suspicious of programme sponsorship, and rightly so. The objections are two-fold. Firstly, it acts as a powerful source of potential pressure on creative and editorial decisions which can subordinate the pursuit of diversity and openness to the requirements of corporate image-building. Secondly, and more generally, by giving one specific interest group access which other groups are denied, it reinforces the priviledges of corporate speech as against the claims of other voices, commandeering spaces that should remain open. It is therefore clearly inappropriate for a service attempting to maximize the range of viewpoints.

The pressures exerted by spot advertising are less direct but no less damaging to diversity. Indeed, its impact is greater since it has the potential to reshape general programming strategies, whereas sponsorship is confined to particular productions. Much to the chagrin of many on the right, the Peacock Committee, who were otherwise sympathetic to the case for privatizing the BBC, accepted this argument, conceding that the 'progressive introduction of advertising on the BBC is likely to have effects on the range of programmes available' and that these effects are likely to be mainly negative.[48] In making this point, they drew heavily on research they had commissioned on the impact of advertising on American television. The study's conclusion was unambiguous, arguing that a system mainly supported by advertising 'is inimical to broadcasting range. The combination of dependence on high ratings and uncertainty over what will attract large audiences ... biases programme offerings toward ... what does not strain at the leashes of familiarity and acceptability... In such a system the implicit terms of the network's "social contract" with its viewers are relatively narrow: It promises only to grab attention, excite and/or relax and facilitate escape'.[49] These features follow logically from the fact that an advertising-based system must address audiences first and foremost in their role as consumers (of the programmes and the goods advertised within them) rather than as citizens with an entitlement to the broadest possible range of representation and debate.

But, argue supporters of advertising on the BBC, Britain is not America, at least not yet, and they point to the case of Channel 4. Here is a channel with a well deserved reputation for diversity and innovation that is funded by advertising, why not extend this model to the BBC? In many ways this is an attractive argument, but it ignores two very important points. Firstly, Channel 4 is not a private corporation. It has no shareholders. It cannot be traded on the open market. It is not obliged to maximize profits. Consequently, although it sells air-time to advertisers, it is not subject to the same demands to deliver the highest possible ratings. It is further insulated from this pressure by the financial safety net provided by the ITV companies. In the present political climate, it is very unlikely indeed that any government would be willing or able to secure a similar arrangement for the BBC. The second problem concerns Channel 4's remit. This gives it a special responsibility to address areas and interests that are under-served on the main channels. The BBC, on the other hand, operates two of these channels. It could adopt significant parts of Channel 4's remit but it would also have to retain a commitment to assembling majorities, and this would expose it to advertisers' demands for audience maximization and the dynamics familiar from the American experience.

Nor is there a strong case for introducing a strictly limited amount of advertising as part of a move towards a mixed funding base. Evidence from countries where this has been tried, such as France, suggests that even a modest dependence on advertising has a marked effect on diversity.[50]

Searching for an entree to BBC audiences that avoids the usual criticism, the Incorporated Society of British Advertisers (who represent the major companies advertising on television) have proposed separating advertising from programming by 'subletting' one of the Corporation's channels at peak hours 'retaining the off-peak hours for programming financed by the licence fee'.[51] They claim that this arm's-length arrangement would give the BBC the benefit of substantial advertising revenue whilst avoiding direct conflicts of interest. They neglect to mention that it would substantially reduce the cultural space available for public broadcasting and reinforce the priviledges of corporate speech as against other voices.

There are substantial question marks too against direct funding from viewers. Some commentators have floated the idea of voluntary donations as a useful supplement to the BBC's income. But this has several major drawbacks. Firstly, the amount raised is likely to be small and highly variable, making long term planning for production highly problematic. Secondly, the likely revenues need to be weighed against the costs of operating and administering appeals to viewers: this should include the opportunity costs of pre-empting resources and broadcast time that could be used for other purposes. Thirdly, and most importantly, the principal of voluntary donation undermines the case for regarding access to public broadcasting as a universal right, to be enjoyed by all as part of an overall entitlement to adequate resources for citizenship.

The case for moving the BBC's funding over to a subscription basis, as proposed by the Peacock Committee and endorsed by a number of subsequent commentators, falls foul of the same basic principle. There is some evidence that people would be prepared to subscribe to BBC services, though the research is by no means clear cut. [52]But even if viewers did subscribe, and did so at a level sufficient to replace the licence fee, there would still be the problem that this move would abolish the principle of universal access, and with it, any principled claim to be underwriting rights of citizenship. BBC services would become another commodity to be purchased or passed over in the television market place and viewers would be recreated as consumers. Resisting this shift is particularly important now, after a decade that has seen a very significant widening of the income gap between the top and bottom of the class scale, leaving about a quarter of the population living on less than half the average income. The rise of the new television industries has been accompanied by the rise of the new poverty.

In this situation, public funding for broadcasting is a necessity not an option. But what form should it take? Some observers have suggested that the BBC could be funded partly out of the proceeds of the new National Lottery. However, this would pitch the Corporation into a continual competition with other deserving causes, again, making future revenues unpredictable and forward planning impossible. The same objection can be lodged against proposals to fund the BBC through an annual grant out of general taxation. This idea has the advantage of building in a progressive element to public payments, so that the better off pay more. However the overwhelming disadvantage is that broadcasting would become a political football to be kicked about in the annual fixture between the spending ministers and the Treasury. By opening the BBC to the possibility of more direct and more frequent political pressure, the independence on which diversity depends would seriously be compromised. If the BBC was allocated a fixed percentage of the revenues from income tax or VAT, the risk of political influence would be substantially reduced. It would also make it more likely that the Corporation's finances kept pace with rising costs.[53] However, any such proposals would meet great resistance from the Treasury, with their entrenched oppposition to any form of 'hypothecation' in which particular segments of taxation income are earmarked for specific purposes.[54]

This leaves the licence fee as the least worst option for public funding in terms of underwriting the core principles of broadcasting. It is also the most feasible politically. But it is not without its drawbacks. Four aspects are particularly open to criticism: equity; efficiency; acceptability; and adequacy.

Because the license fee is a flat rate poll tax which everyone pays regardless of income, it is highly regressive and unfair. This has lead a number of observers to suggest various kinds of exemptions (for pensioners for example) or subsidies (such as incorporating licence payments into the benefits system). These proposals are well-intentioned but flawed since they tie these additions to income to one specific purpose. It could be argued that this places unacceptable limits on personal choice, and that the problem is better addressed by raising the level of pensions and benefits.

The question of efficiency arises when the costs of collection account for an unacceptably high proportion of the revenues obtained. At present, according to one recent estimate, it costs about £3.00 per household to collect the licence fee (including the costs of anti-evasion campaigns).[55] This is less than many other charges such as telephone bills and the figure is likely to come down even further with the introduction of more flexible payment by installment schemes.

More significant, and less easily addressed, is the problem of acceptability. Evidence from other countries suggests that substantial licence fees (of over £50.00 per household) are 'generally only found in countries where the broadcaster receiving it has an audience share of a third or more'. [56]The BBC's own projections now see a 30 per cent share as the likely norm in future, given the expected growth of cable and satellite services. It could well be even less. The Corporation's case looks more positive if the figures for reach and appreciation are highlighted. These show that almost everyone sees some BBC programming in the course of an average week, and that most viewers are satisfied with what they watch. On this basis the Corporation could still claim to be providing a service that most people want and value highly, even if the figures for audience share dipped below 30 per cent. But would this argument be generally accepted? Would the majority of people still be willing to pay for a compulsory licence if they spent most of their viewing time watching other channels?

This problem is compounded by the need to set the licence fee at a level that will keep pace with costs and provide for new developments. Linking it to the Retail Price Index is not sufficient, since broadcast costs (which are mainly labour costs) tend to rise faster than the general rate of inflation. To address this, the licence fee would have to be linked to increases in labour costs in the private, service sector. [57]This would allow the BBC to maintain the full scope of its operations, and to invest in developments and innovations without depending too much on other sources of finance, which as we have seen, pose problems for the core values of public broadcasting.

This would be the least worst solution from the point of view of the BBC's ability to promote cultural rights, but it would be expensive. It would also exacerbate the problems of equity and efficiency. The alternative is to argue for a lower level of licence fee and to rely on increased income from commercial ventures to make up the shortfall. This is the BBC's present strategy. It is more acceptable to politicians and to the public, but whether it will be able to meet the requirements of complex citizenship is more debateable. But even the BBC's modest proposals are likely to meet vocal opposition from enthusiasts of partial or total privatization.

Even among those who support the continuation of the licence fee beyond 1996, there are many who see it simply as an interim solution. As the House of Commons National Heritage Committee put it: 'the BBC in its present form will not go on forever. It therefore needs enough time to consider how best to organize for, and operate in, the future'.[58] This conclusion is broadly in line with the Peacock Committee's insistence on a phased shift away from licence funding, culminating in full privatization. As the debate intensifies supporters of paying for public broadcasting out of the public purse need to insist that what is at stake is not only the future of a major public institution, but of the cultural rights of citizenship and with them the quality of democratic life.

Notes

[1] Dennis Potter, 'Occupying Powers', *Guardian*, 28 August 1993, p 21.
[2] Home Office, *Report of the Committee on Financing the BBC*, HMSO, London 1986 (Cmnd 9824), ch.5.
[3] BBC, *Extending Choice: The BBC's Role in the New Broadcasting Age*, BBC, London 1992, p 19.
[4] Quoted in Ralph M. Negrine, 'From Radio Relay to Cable Television: the British Experience', *Historical Journal of Film, Radio and Television*, Volume 4, Number 1, 1984, p 33.
[5] Cabinet Office, *Cable Systems: A Report by the Information Technology Advisory Panel*, HMSO, London 1982 (Cmnd 2098), p 7.
[6] *ibid.*, p 48.
[7] *Ibid.*, p 47.
[8] *Ibid.*, p 34.
[9] Cable Authority, *Annual Report and Accounts*, Cable Authority, London 1986, p11.
[10] *Ibid.*, p 17.
[11] *Ibid.*, p 17.
[12] *Ibid.*, p 19.
[13] Julie White, 'Survey of Local Channels on UK Cable, 1992 in Dave Rushton (ed.), *Citizen Television*, John Libbey, London 1993, p 140.
[14] 'You Say you Want a Revolution', *The Economist*, 8 January 1994, pp 27-28.
[15] Nicholas Mearing-Smith, 'Atlantic Alliance', *Spectrum: The Quarterly Magazine of the Independent Television Commission*, Winter 1993, p 17.
[16] Andrew Adonis, 'Cable companies plan rival telecom network', *Financial Times*, 5th December 1993.
[17] Independent Television Commission, *1991 Report and Accounts*, ITC, London 1992, p 37.
[18] Torin Douglas, 'Lay Your Cards on the Cable', *Marketing Week*, 12 November 1993, p19.
[19] Quoted in Ian Hargreaves, *Sharper Vision: The BBC and the Communications Revolution*, Demos, London 1993, p 2.

20 Home Office, *Broadcasting in the '90s: Competition, Choice and Quality*, HMSO, London 1988 (Cmnd 517), paras 6.9 and 6.15.
21 Quoted in Robert McChesney, *Telecommunications: Mass Media and Democracy: The Battle for Control of US Broadcasting. 1928-1935*, Oxford University Press, New York 1993.
22 Georgina Henry, 'ITV Current Affairs Shows "Must Deliver" ', *Guardian*, 6 May 1992, p 3.
23 Adam Smith Intitute, *Omega Report: Communications Policy*, Adam Smith Institute, London 1984, p 41.
24 *Ibid.*, p 4.
25 Robin Scott, 'Public Brodcasting: The Changing Media Scene', *Intermedia*, Volume 8, Number 6, 1980, p 17.
26 John C. W. Reith, *Broadcast Over Britain*, Hodder and Stoughton, London 1924, p 218.
27 BBC, *The BBC's Evidence to the Hunt Committee*, BBC, London 1982, p 1.
28 National Heritage Committee, *The Future of the BBC Volume 1: Report and Minutes of Proceedings*, House of Commons Session 1993-4, HMSO, London 1993, para 78.
29 *Ibid.*, para 105.
30 Hargreaves, *op.cit.*
31 Home Office, *op.cit.*, para 592.
32 *Ibid.*
33 *Ibid.*, para 563.
34 Department of National Heritage, *The Future of the BBC: A Consultation Document*, HMSO, London 1992 (Cmnd 2098), para 6.25.
35 BBC, *op.cit.*, 1992, p 86-7.
36 *Ibid.*, p 67.
37 *Ibid.*, p 39.
38 National Heritage Committee, *op.cit.*, para 26.
39 BBC, *Responding to the Green Paper*, BBC, London 1993, para 5.9.
40 *Ibid.*, para 102.
41 *Ibid.*, para 104.
42 *Ibid.*, para 107.
43 *The Economist*, 1994, p 20.
44 National Heritage Committee, *op.cit.*, p 17.
45 BBC, *op.cit.*, 1992, p 21.
46 P. Gilroy, *The Black Atlantic: Modernity and Double Consciousness*, London, Verso 1993.
47 BBC, *op.cit.*, 1992, p 22.
48 Home Office, *Broadcasting in the '90s: Competition, Choice and Quality*, HMSO, London 1986 (Cmnd 517), para 327.
49 Jay G. Blumler, 'Television in the United States: Funding Sources and Programming Consequences' in Jay G. Blumler and T. Nossiter (eds.), *Broadcasting Finance in Transition: A Comparative Handbook*, Oxford University Press, 1991, p 90.
50 McKinsey and Company Inc., *Public Broadcasters Around the World*, BBC, London 1993, p 13.
51 ISBA, *The Future of the BBC: The Case for Mixed Funding, Including Advertising on BBC Television and Radio*, The Incorporated Society of British Advertisers Ltd, 1993, p 5.
52 See National Economic Research Associates, 'Subscription' in Tim Congdon

et.al., Paying for Broadcasting: The Handbook, Routledge, London 1992, pp 92-164.

[53] David Boulton, *The Third Age of Broadcasting*, Institute for Public Policy Research, 1991, p 6.

[54] See Andrew Graham and Gavyn Davies, 'The Public Funding of Broadcasting' in Congdon *et.al, op.cit.*, p 207.

[55] *Ibid.*, p 203.

[56] McKinsey, *op.cit.*, p19.

[57] Graham and Davies, *op.cit.*, p213.

[58] National Heritage Committee, *op.cit.*, para 54.

Working in Television: Five Interviews

Peter Keighron and Carol Walker

So what is to be done about British television in the 1990s; or rather, what are socialists to do about it? How are they to live through the many problems and challenges outlined in the previous chapters?

The following interviews, conducted between the summer of 1992 and spring of 1994, are intended to offer some snapshots of what it means to be on the left in broadcasting today. The interviewees do not represent 'the left' in television in any formal sense; they speak as individuals, often politically isolated individuals. If this chapter, and the book as a whole, can make a small contribution towards breaking down that isolation, then it will have served its purpose.

Stuart Cosgrove and Don Coutts

Producer Stuart Cosgrove and director Don Coutts formed the Glasgow-based production company *Big Star In A Wee Picture* in the 1980s. Stuart Cosgrove came to television from a background in teaching theatre and journalism; he was editor of the New Musical Express for a time. Don Coutts started out in the film industry before joining the BBC's Community Programme Unit. As well as producing films for television, including *Half Way to Paradise* (1988), *Big Star* have also produced a number of music videos. In March 1994, Stuart Cosgrove was appointed commissioning editor for Independent Film and Video at Channel 4. *Big Star In A Wee Picture* will close down at the end of 1994 when Don Coutts will launch a new company called *Move On Up*.

Q: What difference does being based in Scotland make to the way you work?

Coutts: *Big Star in a Wee Picture* although it's a joke name it's a real name in that it's the Scottish equivalent of a big fish in a wee pond. In Glasgow we probably know all the 'politicals' or the mediators or the cultural writers. It is very, very small, very small.

Cosgrove: I'm not trying to gain any more brownie points, but, in a sense, independent companies based in London don't have to be loyal to anything other than their own economics. I think that we have to be loyal to something that's to do with the kind of national culture that we've inserted ourselves into, because Glasgow is, TV-wise, much more deprived than London is.

I like it, it brings back into politics a degree of emotionalism which intellectually I was always taught in the 1970s, when I was drowning in Brecht, that I always had to refract things through rational discourse. And then when I started to think about it I thought, well actually feminism doesn't do that, gay rights don't do that. They're not always engaged in rational discourse, they're engaged in things like 'structures of feeling' – I am a woman, I am different, and there's a way where, as a Scot, I'd sort of reserve the political right to say: no, I feel differently about an issue. There's something that makes me emotional, and in a way emotions can be 'charged' politically and I don't agree that I always have to reflect them through some sort of rational discourse.

Q: Is there such a thing as a formally identifiable left programming in television?

Coutts: I only recognise (left programming) in the individual pieces that are from a rather scattered community. I don't ever see a collective current. I certainly don't think there's a movement.

Cosgrove: I think there's a series of active traditions though. One consistent tradition is what you could call 'rough justice' broadcasting – the World in Action programme on who bombed Birmingham, the Guildford things – all of those things which have been active in the pursuit of wrongful arrests, campaigning against injustice. I would see that as being a traditional thing of left

185

broadcasting, although I recognise that that could be purely liberal reportage as well.

Coutts: If you're talking about a collective movement it either has to be in something like the [BBC's] Community Programme Unit, or something like Channel 4's Independent Film and Video Department where you gather together a mass of left programme making. But that actually fails if it's not programmed or packaged properly.

Cosgrove: I suppose I'd want to ask: What is the left? By the left do we mean the post-68 generation of people that grew up within that set of debates about socialism, feminism and multiculturalism. Is that the left? Or is the left people that have grown up around notions of ethics of humanism and socialism? In which case certain episodes of Everyman and Heart of the Matter, for instance, could be seen as left programming.

Coutts: One of the problems is that we're all separate and our separateness allows us to be prey to the marketplace, prey to bankruptcy, prey to not working, and then you end up doing fucking anything that keeps you alive. Whatever we say the rules of the market place apply much more than they did ten to fifteen years ago and that market place is not about a political ideology it's about providing certain things for certain audiences and, however we feel about it, that audience [for left programming] is shrinking.

Q: Where do you see the next generation of left programme makers coming from?

There's a lot of liberal programme makers, born in the late 1930s, early 1940s and 1950s, who are growing older and I'm not convinced that there's a new intake in the same way, perhaps because these people are children of Thatcher rather than of 1968. I don't know where programme makers come from now. The lefties and the liberal lefties are probably in their 30s, 40s, 50s coming up to their 60s. Is that, within official broadcasting, being 're-stocked' at the bottom? It's not people coming from the same tradition...

Q: What do you mean by 'tradition' exactly?

Cosgrove: The people that shaped public service broadcasting as a tradition were often people who had been in the war and had come through the wartime where their relationship to society wasn't formed entirely in the universities or Oxbridge. I think that probably made them more anti-fascist in an experiental sense, and it also made them much greater defenders of principles of democracy (even though some of them were complete shits).

We have to get away from the idea that the left are people like us who have been exposed to a *City Limits* agenda, because that's a very specific notion of the left.

There's a mood that I feel is wrong on the left. There's a sense in which we're kind of smug and knowing. You see it in journalism and television. It's one of the things that I hate most about myself, in terms of the generation of things of the left that I feel I represent, this way where you kind of absorb and almost drown yourself in a love of kitsch and playing around with irony – the whole postmodernist sensibility where you kind of say, 'aren't we so sophisticated that we can laugh'. So you justify all sorts of things on the basis that it's kitsch: 'hey it's taking the piss!'

Q: What about other working class traditions, traditions of workers' organization and solidarity. How do they effect your role as independent producers?

Coutts: In the last four or five years the role of the trade unions has changed utterly. Even in the 1980s they had some strength and power. Nobody even mentions it now. We always insist, unofficially, that people should be trade union members, but officially your're not even allowed to do that.

Q: How do those wider political issues effect you as producers?

Cosgrove: Take restrictive practices. This is the debate that we have all the time. I don't know what is the ideologically most justifiable: A camera operator, a trade-unionist, a BECTU member, because he is skilled and because the union has been powerful in the past, as a freelancer he manages to negotiate £190 per day. So if they work five days he can earn up to £600-£700 in a week. Now is it more justifiable that you stick rigidly to that negotiated sum of money when a 21 year-old woman who's coming two years out of college – and you don't have a woman camera-operator in the whole of your country – comes and says, 'I'm really, really desperate for a break and I'll do it for £200 for the whole week.' Now what do you do as a progressive company. Do you say you will go with that set of progressive values against union rates? Or will we protect the power of that male employee?

Coutts: What you end up doing is nibbling at both ends. Taking on a trainee and dropping the rates. Certainly I know I employ work practices that I wouldn't have done five years ago. We go out sometimes without a PA; five years ago I would have said 'never over my dead body do I go out without a PA'.

Cosgrove: One of the big problems is that ideologically the trade unions' history was founded on a particular notion, an ideology of gaining better material wealth for its members that was its principal reason. And there came a time, in the 1970s and 1980s, when that no longer became a sustainable way of negotiating within the economy itself. For me the really sad thing was that for our union, the ACTT, and for quite a lot of the trade unions, it could have realigned itself around things like training and education, but it would have had to happen in the 1950s not in the 1980s really.

Cosgrove: In the unions in the 1970s, when new technology came in, people would say 'In order to handle this new technology, we want ...' And it was always a financial reward, an extra 50 pence an hour or double time, whatever. Maybe what they should have been saying is if the BBC want to convert to digital suites costing £6 million we want Sony to build us a crèche. Had they traded on issues that were not [about] financial gain but were actually institutional in terms of the protection of other sets of arguments around education, multiculturalism, training all of those things, I think the trade unions would have organized their status institutionally in the industry in a different way. Because the point at which they've got one strength is that they can powerfully negotiate around money, the point at which they're split they're split forever.

Coutts: But part of the problem is that you're dealing with management, mostly in ITV, who were making vast amounts of money, and I think the problem is that the Trade Union movement didn't see far enough ahead to see that that was going to change. They're still making money but it's not in the same vast globules that they were.

Q: How do you square your personal politics with your role as independent producers, small businessmen?

Coutts: *Big Star* is actually a quintessential capitalist company. Our company is completely hierarchical. We run it, we make decisions, we have the profit, utterly. Because of past experiences we decided that's what we'll do.

I'm a member of the democratic left, so there's one half that's that and in the other half you're making decisions about terminating somebody's employment. It's interesting but quite painful. But it also makes you quite ruthless as well.

Q: You mentioned, Don, that you thought the CPU was one of the few identifiable centres of left programming. Why did you leave that for the independent sector?

Coutts: I left the BBC because I'd been at the CPU for five years and I used to wear dungarees and have long hair and they set up a new title for me which was a 'Producer's Mate'. Basically I'd become a stereotype. I couldn't operate anymore because whatever I said it was 'oh it's the lefty hippy in the corner', and once you become a stereotype you cease to have any power. In a sense I just had to go.

I also thought that if I formed an independent company I'd be able to make more radical programming. The joke is that I've never been able to make more radical programming since then. If you look back over it [the CPU] it's been the most radical programming in the world but I thought that the Community Programming was ghettoised and that if I went to Channel 4 we'd be able to make really radical programming that would go out at 9 pm on a Friday and the world would be changed. (**Cosgrove**: the only thing that changed was Channel 4). And I also got a higher salary.

Q: Who do you represent, as programme makers? Who do you make programmes for?

Coutts: We hope that our interests represent interests that other people have, I don't think we're making programmes specifically for ourselves, but the programmes we make are very much about us, his idea and me not liking it, arguing, it's very much two people. We've always said that when we fall out or decide not to work together then it stops.

Phillippa Giles

Phillippa Giles joined the BBC eleven years ago as a secretary. She worked as a script editor on serializations of classics before becoming a freelance producer in the Drama Department. In 1989 she produced a three-part adaptation of Jeanette Winterson's book *Oranges Are Not the Only Fruit*, and in 1990 she produced a series of new 20 minute plays under the banner of *Debut on Two*. 1994's screening of *A Dark Adapted Eye* completed a trilogy of Barbara Vine adaptations. 1994 saw the release of her first feature film, *Great Moments in Aviation*, which re-united Beeban Kidron, the director of *Oranges Are not the Only Fruit*, with writer Jeanette Winterson. Phillippa Giles is now an Executive Producer.

Q: How easy was it for you to move through the ranks of the BBC?

I think that its quite hard to get where I've got to. There is a glass ceiling, and I'm still finding that now. The thing that's such a great frustration as a drama producer is that you can't always get your ideas on screen. The decisions made about which ideas go ahead are not in my hands. So, even though it looks as though I'm in a powerful position, I've got no power unless I can say the things that

I want to say. They are all my ideas but the more provocative ones don't get through.

Q: How did *Oranges Are Not the Only Fruit* come about?

Winterson's book had come out several years earlier and won prizes. I took the project to the Head of Drama and we commissioned a pilot episode of the first part and it went from there. There is a problem with the form of the book. Its not an easy adaptation; it's very stylized and I think this may have put a lot of people off. Also it's probably the first time such a strong lesbian story has been told on television. People often think that that because they haven't seen it, then it can't be done. *Oranges* was my proposal. I believe that we're not very good at showing the full range of groups in British society, and that includes colour and race as well. It is very important to put people up there on the screen saying slightly different things so that there's not just a small slab of middle-class, middle-aged society on the screen.

Q: Why did you choose to go into television drama rather than film?

I think television is a crucial art form, it actually does speak to the whole of Britain. There's nothing more powerful than that. If you're in drama what you want to do is communicate. Look at the British films last year, there was only about twelve of them and they haven't really done that well, except probably *Riff-Raff*, which is the only one that actually spoke to a wider audience rather than being very arty.

Q: What is the most ideal form in which to get a subversive message across?

I don't think that the message has to be subversive. But the message has got to be, 'Hey, listen it's not always going to be the same'. You need to get people's attention to get them to think that there's more things to get to know about than just what you read about in The

Sun. I would say 'soaps', but I want to push back the boundaries of the style as much as the content, and with a lot of the format soaps you can't suddenly take it out of its bounds of naturalism. Maybe with soaps you can get a bit of this *Play For Today* thing in, because you have a long running strand and you can bring in all these things in terms of the writing. But when you've got a three-parter like *A Fatal Inversion*, it is subject to other people who look at the script and everybody knows what's going to go out. Whereas with a soap, maybe you can get away with somethings.

Q: Why do you think that you could only do what you're doing at the BBC?

I could probably have done *Oranges* at Channel 4, but the BBC still has the largest raft of production. Where Channel 4 to do about three or four major series a year, we do fifteen, so there's just more opportunity, is what I mean.

Q: What sort of audience response did you get to *Oranges*, and how has that response been picked up by people higher up in the BBC?

In terms of the gay content, there was a lot of response and there continues to be. It goes to so many film festivals round the world, and everybody wants it, it's just phenomenal really. The response is very strong and personal. People say that *Oranges* must have opened so many doors, and in one respect it has, because the next project I'm working on with Jeanette Winterson has gone through very easily. But it hasn't meant that I've been able to open doors for other people, except perhaps for Jeanette. I think that the very fact that I did the Barbara Vine next just shows that it hasn't. Although I'm very proud to have done the Barbara Vine, there are lots of other projects of mine which have not gone through. My favourite one is a post-feminist idea. It's a polemic about pornography for women, that involves the whole debate and doesn't take a view, it discusses the whole thing. Though it is quite provocative and that hasn't got through yet, they can't say no and they won't say yes.

What is important to do is to contrast that with the fact that I have things like that ready to go, but what's happened is that I've made the Barbara Vine. That does tell a story.

Q: What about your relationship as producer with women writers?

I work a lot with women, I tend to make that my thing. It's not that I won't work with men. It's just that I think women need the help more, and so I see myself as someone who can facilitate that, whereas other people won't. With the Barbara Vine I definitely chose only to work with women writers, trying to help them do more mainstream stuff. The BBC do have quota for female employees but the jobs they tend to be doing are not the jobs which actually choose what goes on the air. I believe that there is a commitment within the BBC, and that they do want to encourage women, but it's still on their terms and not ours or mutual terms, and that's where I have a problem, because what I was going to say about women's writing was this thing about finding new forms. I do think that women have a slightly different voice and a slightly different way of telling stories, which is not actually being used at the moment. And so what I'd like to do is be able to try and give those a bit of space and I don't think they've got any air time at all. Sometimes these sorts of ideas are difficult to communicate to my bosses, who are all male, because you can't articulate them very well. There's often something very visceral about the work and it often doesn't go into two-line selling documents very well.

Q: Is there more of a pressure on you as a woman producer?

I think that we're all in that position at the moment because of this short term contract, freelance arrangement. I think that when there would be more pressure on me as a woman, would be with a project like the pornography one. Then certainly, I know that if I failed with that, then there'd be nothing else. But you've got to be prepared to take that risk; what if they said yes?

Q: Would you consider yourself as a radical producer or a left producer?

Probably radical in the sense that I want to say things that are not being said at the moment. I am a member of the Labour Party, although I wouldn't like to say that I'm politically aligned in as much as I wouldn't ever do anything that I couldn't relate to, but it doesn't mean that I have to be prescriptive. But things which I think are good ideas, I would think are radical, but not somebody else's. It's very personal. I think you have to be very subjective as a producer because if you don't believe in what you're doing you just can't go through the motions.

Q: What do you think is left of public service broadcasting that we can keep?

It has been eroded, but I think there are still these little nooks and crannies. Because I'm here I have all these people and support round me. Because I'm here I have quite a concerted policy about colour-blind casting and things like that. I can make sense of continuity. Whereas if I was always out there working for different people it might be more difficult to push things like that. There's something about the corporateness of the BBC which allows you to do things where not everything is discovered until it's too late. You can slip certain things through and then they realise. I think also at a local level, (i.e. my Head of Department and to some extent the Head of Drama) there is still a sense that they are not there because of the money. They couldn't be and so they do want to safeguard certain things. There is still a sense of support. I am not on my own, I am supported by people.

Ken Loach

Ken Loach joined the BBC in the 1960s. He established his reputation as a director with sensitive and committed political dramas like *Cathy Come Home* (1966) and *Kes* (1970). His work since has spanned television dramas, series and documentaries, as well as feature films for theatrical release. In the early 1980s, his television documentary on trade unions and their response to Thatcherism, *A Question of Leadership*, was banned by the IBA. In the last few years his work for the cinema has met with popular and critical acclaim, both in Britain and abroad. His film *Riff Raff* (1991) received the Prix Italia as well as the Berlin Film Festival's European Film of the Year Award. His 1993 feature *Raining Stones* received the French Critics' Circle Prize for Best Foreign Film and the Jury Prize at Cannes, as did his 1990 film about Northern Ireland, *Hidden Agenda*. He is currently based at Parallax Pictures and his most recent work is a film about the Spanish Civil War for the BBC, written by Jim Allen.

Q: What sort of political potential did you see in broadcasting when you joined the BBC in the 1960s?

I went in [to the BBC/television] as a head-in-the-clouds would-be artist. But things very quickly changed because it was clearly a very exciting place to be working in, with good writers like John McGrath and Troy Kennedy Martin (who I worked with on *Z-Cars*). They were challenging a medium that I didn't understand the basics of – never mind how to change it. Also, in *Z-Cars* you were trying to make drama out of the stuff of ordinary people's lives. And out of that I was asked to be a part of the team that did the single plays.

That was really the politicizing event, not only because [of] the people who worked there, like Tony Garnett and Jimmy McTaggart; but through them – particularly the writers, they put their politics and their experiences into what we were doing. It's through them that I began to start to look around and see what was going on in the world.

Q: How would you describe the dominant political position of people working at the BBC?

There weren't many people from the left in the BBC at all. There were only two or three people there who could even remotely be called that. Most of the people there now, and as far as I can remember, have been good honest professionals who have done the work that's been put in front of them, doing the best work they can, making the best judgments they can. There were one or two producers and directors, and the group of writers they brought in, but the overall picture, if you walked round the fifth floor of the BBC, by and large was a very non-political organisation. We weren't even represented by the ACTT, we had no union, we didn't even win union recognition of the main unions.

Q: Why do you think the BBC drama you were involved in had such an impact?

Sidney Newman, Jimmy McTaggart and Tony Garnett managed to get regular air-time once a week for new drama which would deal with contemporary issues at a time when there were only two effective television channels, so that the audience was effectively half the nation. It wasn't like it is now. So you had access to a big audience and you had it regularly so that, week after week after week, you could build up something that tried to be challenging, contemporary and present a different point of view to the accepted point of view put in the news.

Plainly, what does have an impact is [seeing something] week after week, like the old *Wednesday Play*. We were on the air week after week, and people tuned in with the intention of viewing something, and therefore you can effect how they see the world. You could do it regularly, and you had a big audience. Those were the two things, both of which I think have now disappeared.

Q: How did BBC management view what was happening?

The reaction from the BBC was split. It was always a challenging relationship because it was ambivalent. On the one hand they liked the fact that we were getting good audiences and winning some public interest, but they were also very nervous, as they always have been, about their relationship with politicians and beyond them.

Cathy Come Home, for example, was by and large approved because even Tory politicians got on the bandwagon and said: this is helping to solve the problems of the homeless. And it was only the right-wing headbangers like Mary Whitehouse who would complain.

Q: Do you see any continuity, either in form or content, between the work you did in the 1960s and 1970s and current television drama.

I don't see any link between 1960s, 1970s BBC drama and current drama. I don't see it in the acting, shooting, editing and I don't really see very much in the politics. What tends to happen is that accountants will take a decision and then producers and directors will try to find some sort of aesthetic rationale for it and talk about 'real television' and all that, which I think is nonsense.

Q: You came from a background in the theatre, why do you think television is a more effective medium for socialists to work in?

The response of the audience, just by scale of numbers, [to] television is just plainly and infinitely more important [than theatre]. Even if you're talking to one million people the quality of the relationship may be slightly less, but the overall impact is much more important. Also something that goes out on television has a status that something in theatre doesn't have, simply because it's the medium of the news, it's the medium of the national event, of when war is declared. It is the important medium, so if something is on television it has a status which the theatre doesn't have. You expect the theatre to be full of misplaced radicals banging away about something. The scale of the communication and the authority that the box in the corner has is the most important thing.

Q: In the wider context, what do you think of television as a medium, both as it is and the potential it has?

Television is about fooling people, perhaps not consciously, I think television is a key element in the way people's consciousness is manipulated. Television reduces the audiences response, it makes it individual, it's inward-looking. The problem with starting from scratch, in a socialist society, would be trying to move towards a different use of the technology of television, to use the technology to make ourselves an outward rather than inward-looking society, using it in such a way that it wasn't about all the material going into the nuclear family or into your individual flat or house, but that we tried to develop a habit of seeing things in more communal, collective situations whether it's clubs or pubs, community or social centres, whatever. It's just healthier if you see things in groups. You get a healthier response, you talk about it, it's a way of removing the passivity of the response.

Q: Where do you see the possibility of change coming from and where, as a socialist, do you see hope for such change?

It's a political question really. What are the elements that are progressive, where is the strength and how can things move on. When you know the answer to that, then you can see where the stories are that will reflect that and will give you some hope. The optimism is that sooner or later people do fight back. Sooner or later people will always fight back, sometimes, well usually, in a very *un*politicised way. But they will fight back in the end so, even if it's just a cry of anger, it's finding a way to express that, because without that nothing will move on.

In *Riff Raff*, for instance, the kind of experience and observation of the writer is that people do turn up every morning with smiles on their faces and do give back as good as they get, perhaps in devious ways. People aren't just passive victims, they do dish it out as well, and it's finding a way of channelling that potential to dish it out in more constructive ways than burning down a building. We hope to leave the audience with that challenge rather than to have someone make a speech about it, which would be unrealistic.

Q: You've done very little work in documentary; in what way do you think drama can be a more effective form than documentary?

In fiction you get much more involved in the story. I think the ones that I get involved in really cut through the glass wall that separates fiction from fact. With *Cathy Come Home*, that's what got people on the raw a bit, because the news people felt their territory was being invaded. That was the intention, of course.

There has to be a way of breaking-getting through. I think it's different in the cinema where that becomes rather a mannerism, which is obtrusive. You don't need that. But being presented with this seamless image on the television, then you've got to find some way of punching a fist through the screen. I think it's a different challenge.

How do you achieve that without being crass?

It's about what is going to work for a specific idea, what's appropriate to that content. It's the old cliché, the content has got to dictate the form, it really has. There was a long tail of Brechtian heresy. The man himself did quite outstanding work in the theatre and was something absolutely to revere, but not in the way [of] some of his disciples, [who] have turned his ideas into mannerisms. You've got to be aware of what the audience is going to be interested in, and how they're going to follow it, and what they're going to make of the person addressing the camera; and it's got to relate to the real flesh and blood of the people working on it.

Q: How useful did you find those debates on Brecht and realism that dominated so much of 1970s film and television studies?

There was a lot of very sterile debate which absorbed some – though not much, because it was really rather insignificant – of the energy of the left. So that instead of pursuing the ideas that lay behind, for example, *Days of Hope* – which was about how do you get a leadership to organize and build on the strengths of whatever resistance there is at the time – instead of dealing with that, they went on to talk about period costume drama.

But we took those films around quite a lot, and if you showed it to an audience of trade-unionists they would talk about their own leadership and how they could organise at branch level, which was a

199

much more concrete and sensible way to discuss the film. That's the kind of discussion you want, rather than discussing the semiotics of it, which is a bit of an indulgence, I think.

Q: How do you view the left's response and engagement in broadcasting?

I think the left doesn't talk analytically enough about what broadcasting is, a basic analysis of it, what the function of the institutions are. The left is an ideological discussion by and large … There cannot be a consensus in the nature of opposition politics or you'd end up with a party like the Conservative Party, where everybody subscribes to the same general point of view. The left can never be like that, it must always be about competing answers and different points of view because society produces all kinds of different opposition groups – labour, feminist, ecological, etc., etc. – and even within those there will be competing answers, so it's bound to be fragmented. It needs a major event, like the miner's strike, to which people can say: we will all march together under a single slogan. But short of that, it's difficult to see how it cannot be fragmented.

Q: Where do you see the left beginning to fight back in broadcasting?

It needs to be the union because that's the only place where you've got any strength, ACTT [now BECTU] never got out of the problem of defending the permanent jobs and attacking casualization, which has meant not being able to defend the interests of freelancers. They've never found a policy that unites the interests of freelancers and the permanently employed; they've always defended the interests of one over the interests of the other. It needs an overall view of the industry which finds a proper scheme of employment which everyone can fit into.

The union is where broadcasters should organize themselves. It's a coherent entity, it has its strengths. Otherwise the left is just a collection of disparate individuals who have no real strength when it comes down to it. It's the guys who have got their hands on the cables, on the switches. That's where we've got strength when it comes down to it; the programme makers are easily dispensed with.

The left has got to oppose undercutting of union agreements. I've done one or two interviews where the guy who operates the camera is also the man who sets the lights, the man who sets the microphone and then goes out and racks the pictures. That's one person doing everything, so the quality is bad, which management don't care about. And this is independent companies. As an individual I've reported it to the unions but we've got to do it collectively. We've got to say, this is not acceptable and anyone who operates it loses their union card. We've got to re-establish trade-unionism at grass roots level because they've destroyed it.

Q: Where do you see hope for the left in broadcasting?

You've only got to read Reith's diaries and you know you're really dealing with the state, and you can't expect them to give up this power. I suppose it's a question of whether the fight is worth fighting. Then you think, well it isn't worth fighting, but then you meet people who have not got a pot to piss in and they fight back, so you think well, Christ, we have to. If people on a council estate can go on a rent strike, we in our soft world in Soho at least need to fight back as well. You need to fight back and keep making demands on the system, even though you know the system can't answer them. It's the old notion of transitional demands. You've got to demand things which are plainly fair, which the system can't supply. You keep exposing it at whatever level.

Nadine Marsh-Edwards

After studying mass communication and sociology at Goldsmiths' College in London and a year as an assistant film editor, Nadine Marsh-Edwards became a founding member of *Sankofa Film and Video* in 1983. Mainly funded by Channel 4, under the Workshop Agreement, *Sankofa* made a number of challenging works, including

Passion of Remembrance (1986), *Dreaming Rivers* (1988), *Perfect Image* (1988) and *Looking for Langston* (1989). Workshop funding stopped in 1990 by which time Marsh-Edwards had already started working as producer on her first feature film, *Young Soul Rebels* (1990) (directed by Isaac Julien). In 1993 she produced *Bhaji On The Beach*, and executive produced *Home Away From Home*. She is currently developing a drama series for the BBC.

Q: How did you make the move from media student to media practitioner?

I had been having discussions with Isaac Julien who was a student at St Martins. We thought it would be a good idea to try and work with each other and other young black people by setting up a company where black film-makers could work together and have more control over what we produced. We were basically just very, very young and new and wanted to try things. We didn't fully know what we were letting ourselves in for, but knew that we wanted to make films and we wanted to have images of ourselves up on a screen that were different to what we could see at that time.

Q: How important was Channel 4 and the Independent Film & Video department to *Sankofa*'s development?

It seemed at the time that they were genuinely interested in trying to build an infrastructure for film that was different. They were interested in the prospect of there being new types of film-makers and programme-makers, and provided the money and space for us to be able to do that ...

They were very definitely our entry points, and we were determined to make the best use of it we could for as long as it lasted. We just didn't realize how quickly it was going to be over.

Q: Unlike much of the alternative and workshop sector *Sankofa* soon began to concentrate on drama rather than documentary. Why?

Black people have been making films for some time here. They have mainly been documentaries. And black people have been the subject of documentaries, mainly in a very negative light – associated with bad housing, can't get a job, mixed relationships, etc. They're all areas which need to be investigated because people need to know what the reality of different people's lives are, but we felt that this was also doing us a disservice because here were young black people trying to obtain money. But we were supposedly products of this very negative lifestyle, so how could we persuade people to believe in us if they thought that's all we were made up of – negativity, paranoia, lack of opportunity, all those labels that are foisted onto black people all the time.

We wanted to show other parts of our lives, the parts which are the same as other people. When it comes down to basics you have to make a living, you have to pay the rent, you have a laugh, you get married, you don't get married, you're gay, you're not gay; all those things which we know we are. The images we never ever saw on TV or film. At that point, all we saw ourselves portrayed as was literally, the shopkeeper, the prostitute and the drug pusher. And we wanted to change that, add to the debate and make a difference.

We thought that the best way to show people these other lives was to do it through drama because it normally means you get a bigger audience and it's a way to entice people into a world that you want to show. That was the strategy at the time, and I think it still is a good strategy for pulling people into a subject matter that they might find too political or difficult and not want to watch.

Q: How did the decline of the workshops begin to affect you?

We suddenly kept being told about a 'mixed economy' and we had to learn a new 'Thatcher-speak' language. Funding for our infrastructure became less and less by the late 1980s. First the GLC funding stopped and then Channel 4 funding stopped around 1990.

Fortunately by then we'd made a few films and were known and so we basically started to contact different departments within Channel 4. But because we'd always gone to Alan Fountain's department it was like starting again. Channel 4 had changed, it seemed as though it didn't really want things that were too different. Luckily I had already started work on *Young Soul Rebels*, and we had started to work with other filmmakers outside the group to make sure there was money coming in. So gradually this idea of a mixed economy (grant aid and earned income) kind of filtered through and began to make sense to us and we've operated like that ever since. The main difference is we don't get wages. We haven't had wages for years, you only get paid when you work on a project with adequate funding. The rest of the money that we earn from film hire, etc. goes towards office overheads and project development.

Q: Why did the black workshops emerge when they did and why did they not spawn a new generation of workshops?

The emergence of us, *Black Audio, Ceddo* and *Retake*, happened at a very particular time, a very particular point in our history. There was flash and we were all there, we'd all been waiting for the moment to arise that we could take advantage of, and we did. We did a lot of talks at colleges, schools, community centres, all over the country, wrote a lot of articles and just basically made ourselves known and visible. Our voice was very loud. We made an intervention into political and aesthetic arenas where people like us hadn't been before.

We were able to do that because we knew their language, because we'd been taught that language, and we were probably the first generation of black people here who could do that. Because we did come up through the art-based world, we could have those arguments quite successfully, and argue for a space to be created for people like us to do the work we felt we had to.

After that moment, Thatcher's children arrived. So the idea of working together collaboratively was not something that was on the tip of everybody's tongue: it was no longer fashionable. People became very individualistic. Fortunately now there are a lot more black people working in television and film than there were but it is very 'me' orientated. We were taught by people of the 1968 generation so obviously a lot of that is in us and will remain in one way or another.

Q: To what extent are you trying to address a black audience?

Currently I work on films that are informed by and shaped within a black experience so obviously I want black people to enjoy our films, but I'm not really sure what a 'black audience' is as such. I watch TV and go to the cinema all the time. What percentage of black people do you think I see that I can identify with? If it's one per cent that's a lot. But it doesn't stop me going, it doesn't stop me wanting to watch the film. I'm still interested in what's going on. I still want to be entertained. I still want to be made to think. So I apply all of those rules to any film that I want to make. If black people go to see those films that I am involved with then I'm happy, but I'm equally happy if a mixed audience goes to see it because I'm making films about the world I live in. I live in London and that is a mixed world.

Q: Have the prospects for black people wanting to work in film and television changed significantly in the ten years or so since you've been working in the industry?

It has changed, at least now the concept of wanting to work in the industry has become a reality whereas when we were starting it was like saying you wanted to be a brain surgeon without having done your 'O' Levels. When we started, for us to have got an all-black crew for a documentary would have been really, really, really hard, maybe impossible for the standard of broadcast television. But now we can pick and choose, we can decide which black technicians we want to work with. Unfortunately that is not yet true for a drama shoot.

Q: And what about the funding and commissioning, have black people moved into those areas to the same extent?

Everybody's very quick to give you an equal opportunities form to fill in for your company but then when you walk through their door you don't see any black people. There's a lot of talk about equal opportunities but I don't personally see that much actually being done by the institutions. At least now they consider black stories to be something that can be of interest to a general audience, but I think that jump from black stories being interesting to black people being in control of making those stories is still not happening often enough.

Q: How do you feel about the 'responsibility' that any film by black producers and directors in Britain seems to carry?

It can be a nightmare because of course everybody looks so eagerly towards the film opening and going to see it. They want to see the film they imagine and if that film doesn't live up to what they want to see they consider it to be a bad film. The problem exists because we have no choice. You can't choose between *Bhaji On The Beach* this week or *Salaam Bombay* next week because there's five years difference between the films being made. Your choice is so limited that the audience expectations are so great.

Q: Does a commercial success, like *Bhaji On The Beach*, open a lot of doors or is funding still as difficult?

Hopefully it will mean that the people who put money into this film in the first place, the people who had faith in it, and us as filmmakers, will be prepared to take risks again in the future on us and other film-makers. We had to convince them that it was a story that *everyone* would want to go and see even though it had a black subject matter. Normally when you talk to most film and TV financiers, as soon as you say 'black subject matter' that means no money, *unless* it's got a star like Denzil Washington in it or it's about drug runners. In the light of this film finance reality, there we were wanting to make a film about a group of Asian women going to the seaside – that's a pretty hard sell. So hopefully what *Bhaji*'s success says is: look, there is the space for different stories to be told and that these stories can be universal and appreciated by everyone. Hopefully, eventually, Channel 4 and others will be prepared to take another chance because it might pay off. If they don't, more films like *Bhaji* may never be made and that would be a loss for all of us.

John McGrath

John McGrath is an independent producer with Edinburgh-based *Freeway Films*. Though his roots, and much of his current work, are in theatre (in the 1970s he ran the *7:84 Theatre Company*), McGrath has continued to write and produce drama for television. In the 1960s he wrote for the BBC's ground-breaking *Z-Cars* series and in 1976 he produced *The Cheviot, The Stag and the Black, Black Oil*. He has continued to produce work for both BBC and Channel 4 for the last decade. In 1989 he became a non-executive director of Channel 4.

Q: What particular problems does working in television drama, rather than theatre, present?

Television does deliver your work to an audience but it's so heavily mediated. In most cases it's mediated through executives and a system that is there to either increase ratings or please advertisers or both. But there's more than that, there's a whole culture of television through which your work has to be mediated and that culture of television is dominated by two things. One is the kind of experimental, the iconography of modernism, the bold end of television drama, which is really post-Royal Court ideas of theatre, and the other end of it is looking for mass-audience appeal, which is usually soap. So you have that kind of split. Now to do the kind of work I was doing in theatre is very difficult given that those are the sort of polarities of television. It is difficult to find a corner in there through which you can work, which is why I spend a lot of my life in theatre.

But working in television is worth it because it does deliver a very large audience who are the kind of people I try to reach in the theatre. When I started to work on *Z-Cars* I suddenly realised that this audience watching *Z-Cars* was the audience I was interested in.

Q: But isn't the television audience, however large, always more distanced than the theatre audience?

On *The Cheviot, the Stag and the Black, Black Oil* there was a huge feedback in terms of letters, all the schools in the Highlands taped it and are still playing it, and it's on-going in terms of still being shown in regional theatres, festivals, discussions...

Q: Is it a problem for a socialist writer to reflect working-class issues and interests in the present period?

The problem of the writer [writing] about working-class life is certainly no greater than the problems of the people trying to live those lives. They manage to have quite a lot of resources, in terms of entertainment, comedy and song; and strength. Strength of character, political strength, strength of will. And I think that if you're allowed to write properly about working-class life you have that whole range of ways that people themselves have found to keep themselves going to give positives to what you're writing.

Q: How do you make politically effective television in the 1990s?

My opinion is that theatre, novels, television, whatever, are only effective if they are part of something that is already going on, some movement within society towards change. When *Cathy Come Home* came out in the 1960s there were very strong, vocal groupings of all kinds demanding that some attention be paid to this problem, and when Jeremy Sanford wrote the play it was effective because [it] said what a lot of people were working for and trying to say. I feel that way about theatre too. Theatre is most effective when it is actually saying what a lot of people have got to say.

I think that now people are a lot more confused and befuddled by the figures and arguments that come out. The whole of politics appears to be PR. And so people are finding it much more difficult to galvanise campaigns around issues because the government's PR is excellent.

I had direct experience of it at the Arts Council. 'The Glory of the Garden' [Arts Council Report] was one of the most triumphant PR exercises that the Arts Council has ever undertaken. Four years before, Roy Shaw had simply and brutally cut forty-two companies and the Arts Council was decried all over the place. Now Rees Mogg wanted to do exactly the same thing and so he employed these PR people who simply dreamt up the positive way to present this. They dreamt up this whole philosophy of regionalism and taking these companies out to the regions. Absolute shite. Absolute lies. But it was triumphant. And under those circumstances it is very difficult for a mass campaign to take off about anything to do with that area. Similarly with housing, they produce figures and PR and massage the figures. People are confused.

That's why, in a way, broadcasting is very important because probably the most vital role of broadcasting is to provide information now: clear uncluttered information and then people can begin to work things out. That's the public service, telling people what is actually happening is a public service.

Q: How can the left best intervene in the debate over the future of the BBC?

The BBC is, theoretically, about public service broadcasting and, although it's muddied the waters about what that concept actually means, what the left should be doing in terms of the BBC is defining what public service broadcasting is actually about. Is it about ratings? Is it absolutely essential for the BBC to maintain its current output? What is the meaning of a public service, as opposed to being a servant of the government, which is what it is at the moment?

Those contradictions have got to be pointed out. If the BBC were truly a public service organization it would require greater independence, greater financial as well as political and social independence, and it would require a much stronger and more secure fiscal base for its activities.

Q: Does the BBC have its own answers to these questions?

I think the BBC has behaved in a very stupid way over the last 15 years in expanding its capacities. I think it behaved very imprudently. Instead of concentrating on programmes, it concentrated on buildings and huge staffing requirements. It's paid lip-service to cutting down the number of staff but it never has, and now it's got to and it's in real trouble. And, in the middle of all this, it's lost sight of what public service broadcasting can be. It really has.

And so, ideologically, I would say what the most helpful thing from the left would be to force a redefinition of public service broadcasting, and to try and make sure that the BBC fulfilled that remit. In the same way that Channel 4 has a remit, the BBC needs some definitions sorting out; a remit which is quite specific, which is written down and referred to constantly by executives, commissioning editors and programme makers.

There's got to be a very carefully planned, orchestrated and very vigorous campaign of, I would say, 'assistance' to the BBC in its thinking.

The other thing that I think we should be trying to do is to define what we mean by 'quality' in television, what we mean by standards in television. There was that whole debate about the quality threshold of commercial operators, which was a joke – it was always referred to by them as a 'beauty contest' – and there the language was totally dominated by the advertisers' needs. At all the conferences that I went to on quality television, the people with the most say, the people who defined what it was, were the advertisers. And what quality meant to them was that it delivered a specific audience. It didn't have to be a large audience, but it had to be a targeted audience.

Now that's not my definition of quality, it's not the left's definition of quality, but it was the definition of quality that lay behind the thinking of the Broadcasting Act. We've got to challenge that and as far as I'm aware nobody is really challenging that in an effective way.

Q: What about Channel 4?

Channel 4 is mediated through this television culture and the important thing with Channel 4 is to keep that culture open and sharp, available and accessible. To keep the Channel's culture open. And not to foreclose it either, on the one hand, by driving them into a defensive posture where they're saying: 'Oh but we did put out programmes about this and that', and then they recite you programme numbers; or by complacency: saying 'thank God Channel 4's there and isn't it wonderful' – because it isn't good enough; and it never will be good enough because as soon as it's good enough somebody will stop it.

Q: What are the forces that threaten to delimit the Channel in the 1990s?

If Channel 4 is producing an image to the world of rather settled self-contained compartments which are actually trying to dictate what they want to fit in the slots then the slot culture, the slot mentality, will drive people away and they'll say there's no point in sending that to Channel 4 because there isn't a slot for it.

The smaller independents now are being dominated by the larger ones who frankly are only interested in filling slots, they're only interested in finding out what Channel 4 wants and having a little meeting and thinking of something that will fill that slot and having a very efficient team who will write the kind of proposal that will fit exactly into that slot and will get made, and then they'll take their 10-12 per cent production fee – that's the way those companies operate. It's not how I saw Channel 4 at the beginning.

Q: You've talked before, in relation to theatre, of the need to

build 'The Resistance'. Where do you see the basis for such a movement within broadcasting?

All I can say is that it's present in a smallish and randomly scattered group of producers and executives in broadcasting. People like Wearing or Barry Hanson, who are able to use their reputation to have programmes aired which are not toeing the line or compromising.

In terms of this struggle I think the only place people can anchor themselves, though it's a rather threadbare rope, is to the Labour Party. If you're serious about getting something done you work with the Labour Party and try and influence the way they behave. I think a lot of people have influenced the way they behave in opposition, it's a question of affecting the way they behave in parliament that's a problem. One remembers Harold Wilson's terrible campaign against the BBC and his tendency, once in power, to crush opposition. But it would be an unnecessary fatalism to say that all Labour leaders would do the same thing, nevertheless you have to be fairly cautious about total identification with Labour in this area.

Q: Where do you see socialist ideas and initiatives on broadcasting coming from?

In a peculiar way, the radicalism of the right has made the posture of the left more one of a kind of nostalgia and conservatism than it really ought to be. Any radical, philosophical and political rethink of the role of broadcasting in society, along the line of an Enzenburger or a Raymond Williams, has not appeared, so far, on any political platform and I wouldn't say that the Labour Party would be capable of such a rethink. But then it's up to people to push, that's what politics is about, pressure.

Notes on Contributors

Jane Arthurs is Senior Lecturer in Cultural Studies at the University of the West of England in Bristol. Before taking up this post, she taught video production and media studies in Warrington and London. Her previous publications have been on gender and technology in the television industry, and on popular feminism in film.

John Corner teaches in the School of Politics and Communication Studies at Liverpool University. His books include the edited collections *Documentary and the Mass Media* (1986), *Popular Television in Britain* (1991) and *Nuclear Reactions* (1990) which he co-authored. *The Public Address of Television* is forthcoming. He is an editor of the journal *Media, Culture and Society*.

Thérèse Daniels is Lecturer in Social Sciences at South Bank University. She was formerly Researcher on the British Film Institute's 'Black and White in Colour' project. She is editor with Jane Gerson of *The Colour Black: Black Images in British Television* (1989), and author of *Black and White in Colour* (accompanying notes to the BBC documentary series).

Sylvia Harvey is Reader in Broadcasting Policy at Sheffield Hallam University. She is the author of *May '68 and Film Culture* (1978) and co-editor with John Corner of *Enterprise and Heritage: Cross Currents of National Culture* (1991) and co-editor, with Kevin Robins, of *The Regions, The Nations and the BBC* (1993). She has published widely in books and journals on the subject of documentary film, British independent cinema and contemporary British television. She is currently working on issues of impartiality and regulation in broadcasting.

Stuart Hood has worked in broadcasting for most of his professional life. He was head of BBC Television News and then Controller of

Programmes, BBC TV. He has worked as a freelance producer, scriptwriter and documentary film-maker for the BBC, ITV and Channel 4. He has written widely on the media.

Peter Keighron is a freelance media journalist.

Graham Murdock is Reader in the Sociology of Culture at Loughborough University and a Professor of Communication at the University of Bergen. He has written widely on the political economy of the communications industries, mass media and politics and the impact of new communications technologies. He is a joint author of *Demonstrations and Communication* (1970) and *Televising 'Terrorism'* (1983) and joint editor of *Communicating Politics* (1986). He is currently completing a book on broadcasting and citizenship.

Karen Lury Lectures in Film and Television in the Department of Theatre, Film and Television Studies at the University of Glasgow. She has completed research on 'Quality Television'. Her current research is on representations of youth and television aesthetics.

Colin Sparks works at the Centre for Communication and Information Studies at the University of Westminster. An editor of *Media Culture and Society*, he has written widely on the media, both in that journal and elsewhere. He is a member of the Socialist Workers' Party.

Mike Wayne teaches Film and Television Studies at the West London Institute of Higher Education, Birkbeck College and at Middlesex and North London Universities. His book *Theorizing Video Practice* is forthcoming.

Brian Winston is Professor and Director of the Centre for Journalism Studies at Cardiff, the University of Wales. He was the first director of the Glasgow Media Group, which produced *Bad News and More Bad News* and he has an Emmy for documentary scriptwriting.

Carol Walker is a Lecturer in Media studies at the University of Luton.